The Great Northern Railway (Ireland)

by
Edward M. Patterson

THE OAKWOOD PRESS

© E.M. Patterson, 1962 & Oakwood Press

First Reprint 1986
New Edition 2003

British Library Cataloguing in Publication Data
A Record for this book is available from the British Library
ISBN 0 85361 602 7

Typeset by Oakwood Graphics.
Repro by Ford Graphics, Ringwood, Hants.
Printed by Cambrian Printers, Aberystwyth, Ceredigion.

A view looking north along the down platform at Dundalk. *Duffner*

Title page: Great Northern 'P' class 4-4-0 No. 73 *Primrose* stands at Dublin (Amiens Street) with the Railway Congress train on 10th July, 1895. *R. Welch*

Front cover: 'S' class 4-4-0 No. 171 *Slieve Gullion* is seen leaving Portadown with a special for Belfast in July 1963. This locomotive had entered CIE stock in 1958 and passed to the UTA in June 1963. Withdrawal came in December 1965, but happily this fine locomotive has been preserved by the Railway Preservation Society of Ireland.
I. Pryce/Colour-Rail/IR569

Published by The Oakwood Press (Usk), P.O. Box 13, Usk, Mon., NP15 1YS.
E-mail: oakwood-press@dial.pipex.com
Website: www.oakwood-press.dial.pipex.com

Contents

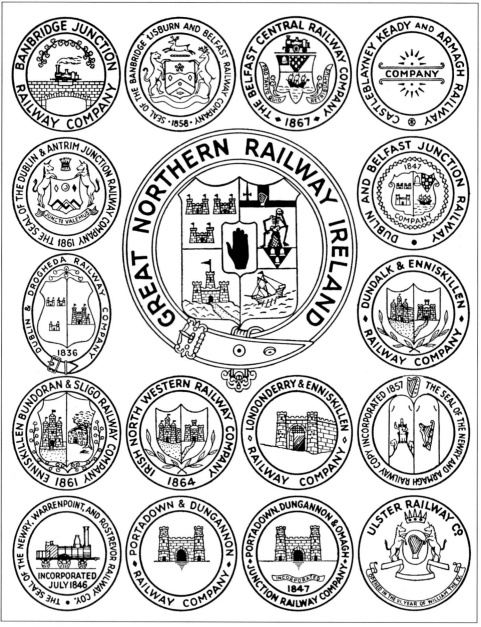

Seals of the companies forming the Great Northern Railway of Ireland. The Northern Railway, 1875-1876, used the same device as the later GNR.

Publisher's Note

In this edition of *The Great Northern Railway (Ireland)* Dr Patterson's text remains largely unaltered, except where more recent research has revealed new data. Appendix One (List of Stations and Halts) has been significantly revised and updated. No attempt has been made to include a history of the former GNR(I) lines under UTA/NIR/CIE/IE auspices.

The publisher would like to thank Charles Friel of the Railway Preservation Society of Ireland, and the custodian of the late author's Irish negative collection, for his invaluable assistance. Thank you also to Irish Railway Record Society members John Langford and Robin Linsley who carefully studied Dr Patterson's original text; their updates and comments have also been invaluable. Finally, thank you to Mrs Anna Singer, the author's daughter, for her help and co-operation in seeing this new edition to fruition.

Abbreviations

BCR	Belfast Central Railway
BCDR	Belfast & County Down Railway
BL&BR	Banbridge, Lisburn & Belfast Railway
BNCR	Belfast & Northern Counties Railway
CDRJC	County Donegal Railways Joint Committee
CIE	Coras Iompair Eireann
CK&A	Castleblayney, Keady & Armagh Railway
CVR	Clogher Valley Railway
D&BJR	Dublin & Belfast Junction Railway
D&D	Dublin & Drogheda Railway
D&E	Dundalk & Enniskillen Railway
D&KR	Dublin & Kingstown Railway
D&MR	Dublin & Meath Railway
DN&G	Dundalk, Newry & Greenore Railway
DR	Donegal Railway
DSER	Dublin & South Eastern Railway
DW&W	Dublin, Wicklow & Wexford Railway
FV	Finn Valley Railway
GAA	Gaelic Athletic Association
GNRB	Great Northern Railway Board
GNR(I)	Great Northern Railway (Ireland)
GS&WR	Great Southern & Western Railway
IE	Iarnrod Eireann
INWR	Irish North Western Railway
KK&A	Kingscourt, Keady & Armagh Railway
L&CR	Londonderry & Coleraine Railway
L&E	Londonderry & Enniskillen Railway
L&LS	Londonderry & Lough Swilly Railway
LMS	London, Midland & Scottish Railway
LNWR	London & North Western Railway
MGWR	Midland Great Western Railway
N&E	Newry & Enniskillen Railway
NCC	Northern Counties Committee
	(of the Midland Railway, later London, Midland & Scottish Railway)
NIR	Northern Ireland Railways
NIRTB	Northern Ireland Road Transport Board
NW&R	Newry, Warrenpoint & Rostrevor Railway
PD&OJR	Portadown, Dungannon & Omagh Junction Railway
RPSI	Railway Preservation Society of Ireland
SLNC	Sligo, Leitrim & Northern Counties Railway
UR	Ulster Railway
UTA	Ulster Transport Authority

Passengers purchase their tickets at the booking office at Great Victoria Street station, Belfast on 18th July, 1958. Prominently displayed above them is a diagrammatic map of the Great Northern system. If you look carefully you can see where the Lisburn-Banbridge-Newcastle and Scarva-Banbridge lines, which had both closed to passengers on 1st May, 1955, and the Dungannon-Cookstown line, which closed on 15th January, 1956, have been painted out. Surprisingly the line from Newry to Greenore is still shown, this had closed on 31st December, 1951.   *Author*

Chapter One

Introduction

The Great Northern Railway of Ireland, GNR(I), maintained an independent existence for 77 years, much of that time prosperously established as the second largest and certainly the most enterprising of the Irish railway systems. Springing basically from the need to link Dublin and Belfast by rail, the Great Northern was the result of amalgamation of numerous smaller companies.

The system began in the mid-1830s when the Ulster and the Dublin & Drogheda (D&D) railway companies were formed. Ireland's population had by then risen to more than eight million, and it was increasing. Dublin was the capital and the only considerable city, but Belfast had embarked on industrialisation and was growing at a phenomenal rate. Between the two places the best means of communication was by coach, a tedious 100 mile journey over rough roads. It took longer indeed to travel between Dublin and Belfast than it did to cross from either in a small vessel to the port of Liverpool.

Perhaps because no gathering of company promoters could be assembled who would agree on such a far-sighted railway policy, the Dublin-Belfast link had to be forged piecemeal. The Ulster Railway (UR) got to Portadown from Belfast by 1842, and from Portadown it headed towards Armagh and Monaghan. At the Dublin end, after a late start, Drogheda seemed a good enough goal, and it was reached in 1844. A third company, fittingly named the Dublin & Belfast Junction Railway (D&BJR), made plans to bridge the gap from Drogheda to Portadown and accomplished this in 1853.

Rail access to Londonderry was similarly done in stages, the Londonderry & Enniskillen Railway and the Portadown, Dungannon & Omagh Junction Railway (PD&OJR) participating. Between these routes, the Ulster had reached Clones, which was already on the course of the Dundalk & Enniskillen Railway (D&E). Secondary and branch lines were supplementing these main routes. Navan and Oldcastle lay on a branch from the D&D; Bundoran on the west coast and Warrenpoint on the east were in rail contact from 1866.

Amalgamation of the four main line companies of the area took place in 1875-6, forming first the Northern and then the Great Northern Railway. Entry into the territories of the Belfast & Northern Counties Railway at Cookstown, and the Belfast & County Down at Castlewellan, came later.

Optimism prevailed during the progenitors' first 10 years, but the disaster of the Potato Famine in the late 1840s initiated wholesale emigration from Ireland. A tradition developed, and in the course of a century the population shrank by half. So it was that the Great Northern, in common with the other Irish railways, instead of being overwhelmed with traffic coming from the growth of large towns, was presented with the opposite difficulty of paying its way in a country which progressively became more and more deserted.

In spite of the effects of a diminishing and redistributing population, the Great Northern was at its most prosperous in the 30 years or so preceding World War I. The political and technical changes which followed that conflict

N
LONDONDERRY
LETTERKENNY
ST. JOHNSTON
CARRIGANS
PORTHALL
STRABANE
STRANORLAR
GLENTIES
SION MILLS
VICTORIA BRIDGE
NEWTOWNSTEWART
MOUNTJOY
DONEGAL
KILLYBEGS
OMAGH
PETTIGO
FINTONA JUNC.
BERAGH
KESH
TRILLICK
FINTONA
BALLYSHANNON
CASTLECALDWELL
DROMORE RD.
BUNDORAN
BELLEEK
IRVINESTOWN
BUNDORAN JUNC.
SIXMILECROSS
BALLINAMALLARD
ENNISKILLEN
LISBELLAW
MAGUIRES BRIDGE
SMITHBOROUGH
LISNASKEA
NEWTOWNBUTLER
CLONES
NEWBLISS
REDHILLS
BELTURBET
BALLYHAISE
LORETO
CAVAN
REPUBLIC OF IRELAND
OLDCASTLE
Great Northern Railway
G.N.R. Running Powers.
D.N. & G.R.
Lines owned or worked by C.D.R.J.C.
Border.
0
25 MILES

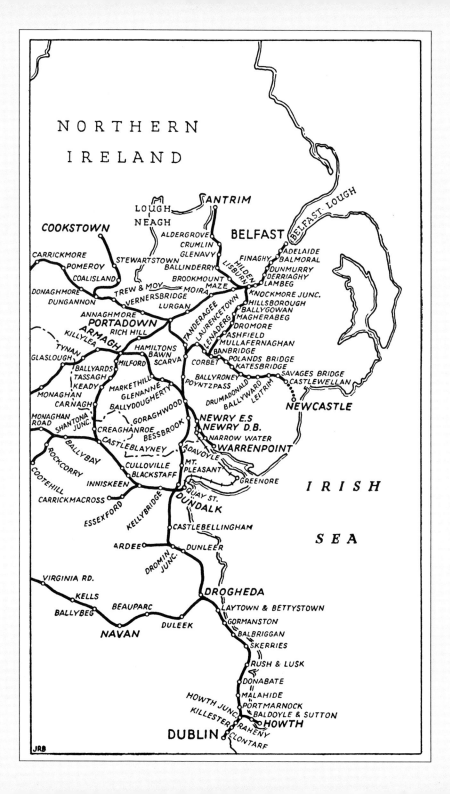

produced a rapid change in fortunes: the political division of Ireland, civil war, tariff restrictions, and above all the development of road transport, all reacted against the Great Northern. Falling receipts and soaring operating costs brought the company to its knees shortly after the end of World War II. Five years of shared nationalisation followed, during which much of the system suffered closure. In 1958 what was left was divided and administered thereafter by the Ulster Transport Authority (UTA) and by Coras Iompair Eireann (CIE).

In this history of the Great Northern Railway we first examine the system in its individualistic beginnings, four decades before the union of 1875-6. Once embarked upon its career, the Great Northern was probably the most interesting of the major Irish lines by reason of its varied inheritance. Even as recently as 1957, it possessed the unique distinction of simultaneously employing steam, diesel, electric, and horse traction on the 5 ft 3 in. gauge.

Two members of railway staff take a break in this atmospheric photograph of the interior of Belfast Great Victoria Street station, between platforms 4 and 5, viewed from the buffer stops. Boyne bridge, visible in the background, carries Durham Street over the railway.

Author

Chapter Two

The Ulster Railway

Ulster was the most thickly populated of the four Irish provinces in the 1830s. In it the county of Armagh, with around 500 people to the square mile, was the most densely peopled of any Irish county. But the population distribution was changing rapidly, for 35 miles north-east of Armagh city was the town of Belfast, rising rapidly as its merchants expanded cotton and linen manufactures and transatlantic trading. Belfast grew from a town of 25,000 persons at the beginning of the 19th century to a city 12 times that size a 100 years later.

Early in Belfast's growth a gathering of its merchants discussed on a November day in 1835 a proposal to build a railway from Belfast to Armagh. For its day the scheme was perhaps more realistic than that which had been mooted 10 years earlier, when the Leinster & Ulster Railway Co. proposed to link Dublin with Belfast but failed to get Parliamentary sanction for the plan.

By 1835, however, the Dublin & Kingstown Railway (D&KR) was in its first year of existence and as Ireland's first railway was a pointer to the enterprising Ulstermen. The Belfast to Armagh scheme found ready support for its subscription list, a Bill was submitted for Parliamentary consideration, and the necessary Act was passed on 19th May, 1836, incorporating the Ulster Railway Co. The Act authorised a joint stock capital of £600,000, with a further £200,000 to be raised by loan. Keen interest was displayed in the shares by Liverpool and Manchester buyers, as well as by local persons.

The newly-constituted Board of Directors of the UR spent the months in making a number of minor revisions to their plan, and in putting the work out to tender, before construction began on 3rd March, 1837. Railway engineering in Ireland was in its infancy, a lengthy spell of wet weather intervened, and the work of construction went more slowly than had been planned. Much of the excavation was through soapy clay, and care was necessary to avoid and to repair small landslips in the sides of the cuttings. The red-brick suburbs of the present day along Lisburn Road did not exist, and the pick-and-shovel gangs found themselves employed along a quiet slope that rose towards the Malone Road, then the main road to the south. To the other side stretched the marshlands called the Bog Meadows. The making of the line did not involve any major engineering problems, and if the progress was slow, the work was sound. Two years were occupied in reaching the town of Lisburn, a distance of 7½ miles. The line was single-track, and one intermediate station was provided at Dunmurry.

From the start the Directors had been concerned with the decision on the best gauge at which to lay their track. This was still a matter for the individual railway, no legislation yet existed, and the UR Board members did not feel themselves bound to follow the example of the Dublin & Kingstown Railway and to adopt a 4 ft 8½ in. gauge.

In 1836 a Royal Commission had been appointed 'to consider and recommend a General System of Railways for Ireland', and as their terms of

An early view of the exterior of Great Victoria Street station.   *Lawrence*

A 1960s view of the canopy which was added to the station frontage at Great Victoria Street.
Notice it still bears the legend 'Great Northern Railway'.   *C.P. Friel Collection*

reference extended to the matter of gauge, the UR Directors asked them for a decision in advance of the issue of their formal report. The commission's guidance was given and was accepted. So the Ulster Railway laid its rails 6 ft 2 in. apart, therein copying Brunel's Great Western line both in a broad gauge and in screwing the rails down to longitudinal timbers.

The longitudinal timber sleepers were of American pine with a 12 in. by 6 in. cross-section. Underneath them, every 10 or 15 feet, were placed cross-sleepers; these measured 10 ft by 12 in. by 4 in. at rail joints, and 10 ft by 8 in. by 4 in. intermediately. The rails were of Dowlais iron, bridge type, and weighed 53 lb. per yard; they were fixed to the longitudinal sleepers by 8 in. by 3 in. screws, set 16 in. apart. A contemporary description tells us that the cost of laying the permanent way, including timber, screws, bolts, labour, and cartage, was 20s. per yard. Wages paid to tradesmen engaged on the work ranged from the mason's 24s. and the bricklayer's 21s. to the carpenter's 18s. a week.

The Belfast terminus consisted of a block of offices built of Ardrossan stone, with behind it a shed for passengers. The latter measured 240 ft in length by 100 ft in width and contained two platforms 26 ft wide, each raised 15 in. above rail level. There were three lines of rail in the station itself, each of which was furnished with a turntable 16 ft. in diameter to enable the engines to 'run around'.

In January 1838, the Board of Directors had sent John Godwin, their engineer, across to England to interview makers and to contract for the supply of three locomotives. When the first of these was unshipped at Belfast it formed a public spectacle, 'was drawn up from the quay by ten horses and was attended by immense crowds of spectators, who incessantly cheered its progress through the streets'. Coaching stock was also on order, and the Belfast press enthusiastically reported that 'four splendid carriages (one of them of the first class, and a really magnificent article) as well as a very powerful locomotive, now attract crowds of visitors to the terminus at Glengall Place'. With their appetite for travel thus suitably whetted, the townspeople eagerly read the announcement that 'THE PUBLIC are respectfully informed that the First Section of this line, from Belfast to Lisburn, will be OPENED for the transit of passengers, on MONDAY, the 12th of August instant'. There were to be seven trains daily each way, and the fare '1s. in the First Class Carriage, 6d. in the Second Class, Children Half Price . . . Each train will stop at Dunmurry for *One Minute,* going and returning, to receive or set down passengers'. It must have been a little sobering for some of the voyagers to read that there was 'No Reduction for the Intermediate Stage'. The line began to operate on the appointed day in 1839, when no less than 3,000 people enjoyed the novelty offered to them and were undismayed when one of the engines suffered a minor derailment.

Although the start of railway working in Ulster was generally welcomed, the Ulster Railway had to withstand caustic criticism from more than one quarter. The Belfast Presbytery, on hearing that it was planned to run trains on Sundays, expounded forcibly on the inevitable increase of vice. One clergyman is reported indeed to have declared to his flock that he would 'rather join a company for theft and murder than the Ulster Railway Co., since its business is sending souls to the devil at the rate of 6d. apiece'. He went on to make the

GNR 'U' class 4-4-0s No. 201 *Meath* (*left*) with the 1.30 pm to Warrenpoint and No. 203 *Armagh* with the 1.50 pm to Dungannon await departure at Great Victoria Street on 21st July, 1958.
Author

A general view looking south-east across Lisburn station about 1880 when the footbridge was added. The two prominent structures on the skyline are Lisburn Cathedral (Church of Ireland) (*left*) and the Market House (*right*).   *Lawrence*

startling claim that 'every sound of the Railway whistle is answered by a shout in Hell'. The counter-argument that sin would be likely to abate, since the public-houses were situated on the public roads and not on the railway, appears to have gained little support, and some hard things were said about the neglect of the sanctimonious to denounce the use of road travel on the Sabbath.

Strong opposition came as well from certain of the landed gentry, and notable absentees from the first lists of supporters were the Lords Donegall, Downshire, and Ranfurly. Serious allegations were made that smoke from the engines would kill birds and would terrify cattle into withholding their milk. Horses would become extinct, and sparks from the fires would set homes and factories alight.

The Ulster's Directors wisely refrained from entering into the violent cross-currents of local controversy. They kept strictly to business and operated their Lisburn line with modest success. By mid-1840 their establishment totalled 55 persons:

Engineer	2 Fitters
Superintendent	21 Police, wages 10s. per week
Secretary	4 Porters
3 Booking Clerks	1 Guard
1 Driver, wages 50s. per week	2 Watchmen
2 Firemen, wages 24s. per week	10 Waymen, wages 10s. per week.
6 Coke and water fillers and cleaners, wages 10s. 6d. per week	

The next task of the company, as defined by their Act of Parliament, was the extension of the line to Portadown, but progress with the gathering of the necessary capital was disappointingly slow. Originally independent of state aid, the Board formally applied to the Board of Works for financial assistance, and this body recommended that the Treasury advance them £40,000. The sum of £16,000 was offered, to be indignantly rejected by the company and then accepted on its increase to £20,000. With this backing, and with what invested capital was available, extension progressed in stages with William Dargan as contractor. Shareholders got some encouragement in the form of a 1½ per cent dividend in 1840. By 18th November, 1841 trains ran as far as Lurgan, and on 31st January, 1842 a temporary railhead was established at Seagoe. The final mile from there into Portadown proved particularly difficult since soft ground near the River Bann made foundations insecure. The station premises had to be heavily underpinned before the first train worked in from Seagoe on 12th September, 1842.

By this date, the powers granted by the 1836 Act for the Portadown-Armagh section had lapsed. The company were content to rest for a spell, and to recompense their shareholders in healthily increasing half-yearly dividends: a 3.8 per cent average in 1843, with 5.05 per cent in 1844 and 5.56 per cent in 1845.

The original decision of the UR to run only first and second class carriages seems peculiar, in view of the large wage-earning population then moving to Belfast. The management soon revised their ideas and in March 1840 advertised: 'On and after April 6th a class of carriages at ninepence being established, the fares will be - 1st class one shilling, 2nd class ninepence, 3rd class sixpence.'

A view along the platforms at Lisburn from the front of a 10.30 am up 'Enterprise' on 21st July, 1958. The 9.40 am (Saturdays only) from Antrim is seen approaching in the distance.   *Author*

W.H. Mills' Lisburn station up platform showing the building and canopy in 1985.
Charles Friel

GNR 'P' class 4-4-0 No. 54 passes through Knockmore Junction with a passenger train bound for Antrim. The single line staff has just been taken from the signalman (*right*). The main line to Portadown continues straight on while that veering to the right is to Banbridge.

The station frontage at Lurgan, another W.H. Mills station, in the 1960s.   *C.P. Friel Collection*

The coaches were the usual four-wheelers: the firsts had four compartments each with eight upholstered seats, while the seconds had four compartments each with 12 wooden seats. The gross weight of the firsts was 4½ tons. The seconds were more lightly built and were open at the sides, though the ends were closed and a roof was provided. Both classes had roof seats for the guards or police. In addition the rolling stock included a number of goods wagons, and it was among the contents of these that the third-class passengers were introduced to the rigours of springtime travel.

By November 1841, third-class travellers had increased to such an extent that it was found necessary to give them a wagon to themselves, in which the occupants presumably chose to stand or to sit, as space or the weather permitted. The Ulster Directors described this innovation as 'A third class open carriage, giving as much accommodation as is given in a similar class of carriages in English railways'. They had sides 4 ft 9 in. in height, surmounted by a 6 in. iron railing.

It was on an up train on 26th February, 1842 that one W. Green, a passenger in the third class, perhaps weary of standing, saw a vacant seat on the roof of an adjacent second and clambered up to it. The guard, George Irwin, who was sitting on the roof of a carriage further along the train, noticed Green and warned him to return to his own carriage. Green paid no attention at first, but after the guard had climbed along the carriage roofs to where he was, argument persuaded him to descend. Irwin, standing as he saw Green safely down, failed to notice a bridge ahead towards which the train was running at 25 miles an hour. He was struck on the head, his skull was fractured, and he fell into the open third. By the time the train reached Lisburn Irwin was dead. Green was arrested on arrival at Belfast.

The reaction of the directorate, later in the same year, seems to have been one of alarm at the growing demands of the third-class passengers. So, to popularise the superior classes, the thirds and the goods wagons were run together as a separate train. This procedure was in vogue until 1848, by which time Parliament had seen to it that rough seats were put into the open thirds. Goods traffic had by then increased to such a degree that the included passengers had become an embarrassment, and the open thirds were again attached to the passenger trains.

At the September 1848 meeting of the UR Board one Director, seeking to retain the third class on a separate train, remarked that 'many of those people who formerly always travelled first class now dropped down to the second class, while the dirty coats went further down to the third class among the unwashed'. His proposal was not adopted, and in the next year there was provided the first of the roofed thirds. The open thirds continued in use for another seven years, then on 17th January, 1856 Patrick Flanagan fell from an open carriage near Lisburn and was badly injured; this accident, and the mounting tide of public opinion, resulted in the withdrawal of the remaining open thirds later in the year.

Though the Ulster Railway had made praiseworthy efforts to conform to a generally agreed gauge from the start, the matter became the subject of debate again in 1843, by which time the Dublin & Drogheda was laying its track. The latter company had made its road bed wide enough to take the 6 ft 2 in. gauge, but cross-channel developments were by now tending to favour a narrower format. John MacNeill, the D&D's Engineer, proposed a gauge of 5 ft 2 in. and this was agreed at Board level. The Ulster, seeing that chaotic conditions would develop if such random evolution was permitted, asked the Board of Trade to intervene and to force the D&D to adopt the Ulster's gauge. The Board of Trade, and the Irish Board of Works, both refused to adopt compulsion, for which they had no legal powers anyway. Meanwhile MacNeill of the D&D had added oil to the flames by suggesting that the solution lay instead in the Ulster narrowing its gauge to 5 ft 2 in. In an effort to ease the deadlock, the Board of Trade ordered their Inspector-General of Railways, Major-General Pasley, R.E., to report and to recommend. In forming his opinion Pasley sought the views of a number of railway engineers. The answers which he received do not appear to have included Brunel's Great Western 7 ft 0¼ in., and in general they gave 5 ft as the narrowest and 5 ft 6 in. as the widest advisable. Neither of these were yet in vogue in Ireland, and so, acting impartially, Pasley split the difference. In due course compulsory legislation went through, and 'An Act for Regulating the Gauge of Railways' became law on 18th August, 1846, covering both Great Britain and Ireland, and fixing 5 ft 3 in. as the gauge for future railway construction in Ireland.

This Act did not force the Ulster to change its existing track, and although the Directors were indignant at the outcome of the argument, they were not unaware of the potential difficulties that would face them if they retained their Belfast-Portadown section at a gauge of 6 ft 2 in. Already the Armagh Extension Act had been passed, and the company had been forewarned by Parliament's insistence on the addition of clauses enforcing the 5 ft 3 in. gauge for this new portion. Some recompense was given by providing that a part of the cost of conversion would be shared by the proprietors of the four contiguous lines. The total cost of conversion was £19,246, and compensation amounted to £13,742. It took much effort in the courts before the Ulster collected its dues; the D&D held back until 1851, when it contributed £3,319 4s. 7d., and grudgingly added a further £48 the next year. The Newry & Enniskillen (N&E) resisted making its payment of £3,997 until 1856.

The change of gauge was at once started. The line up to then had been single, apart from a 16 chain passing loop at Moira, and each station had but one platform. Bridges were fortunately double width. Conversion began by laying an up line to the new gauge and opening it on 4th January, 1847 for all the goods traffic. Passenger traffic meanwhile was worked on the old broad-gauge line, which was served by the existing platforms. From January to May the two gauges ran side by side. During this period crossovers were put in at the stations, and broad longitudinal timbers were used to carry a mixed gauge at the platforms. Passenger traffic in new rolling stock was then diverted to the up line, along with the goods, while the original line was relaid. On its completion, the two lines were put into normal use as down and up lines, these descriptions referring to the terminus at Belfast.

In 1845 steps were taken to obtain a new Act, as a preliminary to recommencing the drive to Armagh. Leaving Portadown station on this extension, the River Bann crossing gave some difficulty while sound bridge

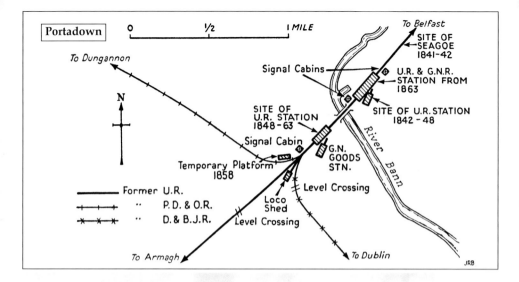

The north end of Portadown station with 'VS' class 4-4-0 No. 206 *Liffey* departing from platform 3 with the 7.12 am to Belfast on 15th June, 1957, while a railwayman removes a lamp on the signals. *A. Donaldson*

The southern approach to Portadown station from the bridge over the River Bann, 17th April, 1955. *H.C. Casserley*

foundations were sought. A 5-span timber bridge was erected and lasted for 25 years before it was replaced by a heavier version in stone and iron. On the remainder of the way much boggy and wet land was encountered in the lower levels. The line was opened to Armagh on 1st March, 1848.

At the same time as it began to work its Armagh extension, the Ulster opened a new station at Portadown. It was west of the River Bann, at Woodhouse Street and on the site of the present goods yard. Its old station east of the river was abandoned. Certain shareholders voiced their doubts regarding the need for a new station, but the Board were confident that the changed site would be more convenient to the town and would be better placed to serve other companies who were proposing to form junctions nearby. These were the Dublin & Belfast Junction and the Portadown & Dungannon companies, which joined the Ulster's line in 1852 and 1858 respectively.

As traffic developed, the Ulster's second Portadown station was found to be rather small. The site did not favour expansion, and although much underbuilding was necessary, a return was made across the river to the site of the first station. The third station was opened on 1st July, 1863. After a life of over 100 years, Portadown's third station was considered to large - it was no longer an important junction - and was replaced by a new utilitarian structure west of the river (roughly on the site of the second station) and this was opened on 5th October, 1970.

With its original scheme complete, the company waited some years before taking the line beyond Armagh. On 15th June, 1855 an Act authorised extension to Monaghan town, and in February of the following year the famous William Dargan began work for an agreed price of £100,000, exclusive of station buildings. The 16½ miles were opened on 25th May, 1858.

Twelve miles past Monaghan stood Clones, reached *en route* by the Dundalk & Enniskillen Railway on 2nd February, 1859, and beyond it again the county town of Cavan. The Ulster's Directors envisaged a useful addition to their traffic from these two places. By an Act of 1st August, 1856 they extended from Monaghan to Clones. That was, however, the limit of their uninterrupted progress, and in the financing of the Clones & Cavan Extension Railway Co. they had to come to terms with their neighbours. The Act, dated 1st August, 1859, allowed the Ulster to contribute £30,000; £20,000 each came from the D&D and the D&BJ companies; the Dundalk & Enniskillen found the remainder and built and operated the line. It was opened on 7th April, 1862, just three months before the D&E was renamed the Irish North Western Railway (INWR). The Monaghan to Clones section was still in progress, and this was opened on 2nd March, 1863; Clones then became a railway crossroads and an alternative through route between Belfast and Dublin was established, via the Midland Great Western and Mullingar.

During the completion of the Ulster's primary scheme, the connection in the Dublin direction had been made with the D&BJ Railway in January 1852, though it was not until the Boyne viaduct was complete in the next year that through running from Dublin became possible. Across the Sperrin Mountains the Londonderry & Enniskillen Railway (L&E) had reached Omagh from Londonderry by September 1852. Already action was being taken to close the

The approach to Armagh station viewed from a train from Portadown on 27th September, 1957.

Tynan station looking towards Armagh. Tynan was the junction for the Clogher Valley Railway. CVR railcar No. 1 has arrived on the extreme left.

A view along the platform at Monaghan looking towards Clones, 19th July, 1958. *Author*

Clones station on 19th December, 1959, looking towards Dundalk. *Brian Hilton*

Dungannon station looking east.

Omagh Markets Junction, 5th August, 1958.   *Author*

Portadown-Omagh gap and give rail access to Londonderry from Belfast. The first proposal was embodied in an Act of 1847 for a 13½ mile line from Portadown to Dungannon, with £154,775 of share capital and £51,585 of loans. The scheme hung fire for a number of years, and re-enactment was necessary in 1853. With the Ulster helping financially, the Portadown & Dungannon Railway Company started work in 1855, and the contract was given to the English firm of Fox, Henderson & Co.

At the Portadown & Dungannon's meeting in August 1856, good progress was; reported, but two months later the contracting firm failed and work ceased. William Dargan was then asked to finish the line. By November, the Directors sought authority to extend their line to Omagh and to lease it to the Ulster Railway. The line to Dungannon was opened on 5th April, 1858 to a station in Gortmerron townland, a mile east of the present station. At the Board of Trade inspection, official dissatisfaction was expressed at the lack of proper signalling at Portadown Junction. Trains were prohibited from using it, and so that traffic could begin, a temporary platform was built 40 yards west of the junction from which passengers walked to the Ulster's station at Woodhouse Street. The platform was only used for a few months, while adequate signalling was being installed.

In August 1858, Royal Assent was given to the Bill incorporating the Portadown, Dungannon & Omagh Junction Railway Company. The extra 27 miles of line were built with £100,000 of share capital and £33,000 of loans. The rooted objection of Lord Northland, the owner of Northland Demesne, to the smoke and fumes of trains forced the company to drive a single-bore tunnel through a hill on his estate, south-east of Dungannon town.

While satisfactory receipts began to come in from the open portion of the PD&OJR, construction progressed across the windswept moorland between Pomeroy and Carrickmore. A branch line was considered, sanctioned by an Act of 12th June, 1861, linking Dungannon with Aughnacloy, but it was never built. In September 1861 the PD&OJR's line was completed to a junction with the L&E at Omagh. It was leased to the Ulster for 999 years, at around 55 per cent of the profits, until under an Act of 1875 the PD&OJR and the Ulster were amalgamated on 1st January, 1876.

Less successful than the PD&OJR was the Dublin, Belfast & Coleraine Railway Company, which received its Act of Incorporation on 3rd August, 1846. The Chairman was the Rt Hon. George R. Dawson of Castledawson, and the Engineer-in-Chief Sir John MacNeill. This company proposed to form a junction with the Ulster Railway at Armagh. It was to run as an extension of the Newry & Enniskillen Railway, from Armagh up the west side of Lough Neagh to Coleraine and Portrush Harbour, with branches to Randalstown and Ballymoney. No construction was undertaken, and as the company's powers for the compulsory purchase of land expired in August 1851 the proposal was abandoned.

Three other lines, all small concerns, came under the Ulster's wing. The first came into being by an Act of 14th June, 1858, which authorised the incorporation of the Banbridge, Lisburn & Belfast Railway (BL&BR), 15 miles 17 chains of single track, with a capital of £150,000. The line left the UR at Knockmore, a mile from Lisburn. By a further Act, dated 30th June, 1862, arrangements were made for the BL&BR to be worked by the Ulster Railway Company.

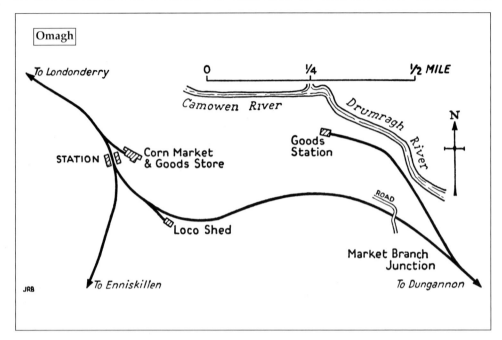

Omagh South cabin lay in the fork of the lines to Dungannon and Portadown (*left*) and Enniskillen and Clones (*right*). This view was taken on 12th August, 1957, the line to Enniskillen and Clones was to close later that year on 1st October.   *A.E. Bennett*

Omagh station viewed from the north in 1933.

'SG' class 0-6-0 No. 176 (here as UTA No. 44) takes water at Omagh on 28th July, 1964. The line curving away to the left was to Enniskillen (closed in 1957) and is in use as a siding.   *Author*

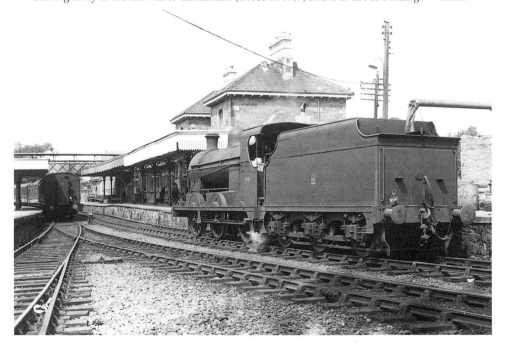

A view looking south towards the station of the lattice girder bridge at Crumlin on the GNR line
to Antrim, 29th December, 1958.   *Author*

The Great Northern's passenger accommodation in Antrim was a bay platform at NCC station.
Here we are looking across the GNR's tracks to the NCC station. Left to right are the GNR's
engine shed (unusually a through shed) with the main station building beyond. The platform
was extended and the NCC signal cabin moved during World War II. The light engine sitting by
the balloon tank is NCC 'U2' class 4-4-0 No. 77. The GNR's goods yard was to the left of the
photograph.   *L&GRP*

GNR 'UG' class 0-6-0 No. 146 arrives at Banbridge station with a train from Lisburn, 25th April, 1951 and crosses the branch from Scarva. *T.J. Edgington*

Eight years later, on 13th November, 1871, Knockmore became a double junction when the 18½ mile line of the Dublin & Antrim Junction Railway was opened. It had been sanctioned on 11th July, 1861; like the BL&BR it was leased and worked by the Ulster Railway.

Authorisation was obtained on 28th June, 1861 for the Banbridge Extension Railway, 12 miles of track connecting Banbridge and Ballyroney. Capital investment was fixed at £90,000 with £30,000 in loans, and working arrangements were entered into with the Ulster, D&BJ, BL&BR and Banbridge Junction railways. The fortunes of this concern soon became far from happy and by 1865 the Extension Company was bankrupt and the works lay incomplete and derelict. It was not until after the formation of the GNR(I) that the Ballyroney section was completed. A projected branch to Rathfriland was never built; it was to have connected with a Downpatrick to Newry line which similarly never progressed beyond the planning stage.

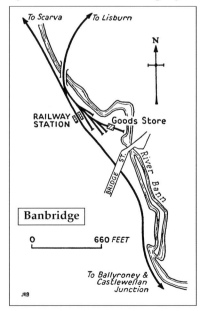

The early autocratic attitude which the Ulster's management adopted towards the third class' travelling comfort was slow to alter. Not until 1864 were return tickets sold to them. Such broadening enterprise was presaged a year earlier when the Ulster made the pioneer introduction in Ireland of gas lighting in the carriages. The idea was greeted with enthusiasm by the public, who had been used to the flickering light of a colza wick. It cannot have been perpetuated, however, for neither the GNR(I) used it, nor did their other constituent companies.

Ballyroney station, looking south, in 1956, one year after the closure of the Banbridge to Castlewellan line.   *Stations UK*

The care exercised by the Ulster's management in steering their concern through waters liable to storms is seen in the following notice which was printed and circulated to their station masters shortly before the Orange processions on 12th July, 1870:

ULSTER RAILWAY
MANAGER'S OFFICE, BELFAST
9th July, 1870

To the Stationmaster . . .

I have to request that on MONDAY next you will call together the Staff at your Station, and caution them all not to attend any Meeting *on the Twelfth* nor to take part in any demonstration or public proceeding on that day; not to come into any unpleasant contact with the public, and to avoid making use of party expressions, or anything to indicate any party feeling; and if any of the public make use of party expressions to them, they are to make no reply.

And they are particularly to avoid drink, or anything that is likely to get them into trouble, but to do their duty peaceably on that day as on other days, and to keep themselves orderly and quiet.

THOMAS SHAW

The management of the Ulster Railway was sound, and its original planning was well conceived. Their conduct of the undertaking yielded a robust dividend to the shareholders during all of the company's career. The annual dividend to ordinary shareholders, determined after interest on debentures and dividends on preference stocks had been met, was usually around 5 per cent. For 16 years out of 25 it was above that figure, and in 1873 it rose to 7½ per cent.

Chapter Three

The Dublin & Drogheda Railway

The first move in the formation of the Dublin & Drogheda Railway came from Thomas Brodigan, of Pilton House near Drogheda. In the early part of 1835 this gentleman published a letter in which he advocated the building of a line from Dublin to Drogheda. In the following August he enlarged upon his theme to a Dublin audience under the chairmanship of George A. Hamilton of Balbriggan. The meeting considered a choice of routes northbound from Dublin, and it was resolved to ask William Cubitt, the well-known engineer, to form his opinion before further action was taken. Two months later Cubitt reported on his survey and favoured the coastal route. Dublin had then a population of around 220,000, by far the largest town in Ireland, and the administrative capital.

The coastal route had many opponents; ignoring Cubitt's considered opinion, they forthwith formed a splinter group in vigorous opposition to the majority and proposed a Dublin-Navan-Armagh line. Conciliation efforts by the Drogheda party were rejected, and the Dublin & Drogheda Bill was countered at the Parliamentary committee stage. To further their efforts, each side gave a rather biased interpretation of a traffic census which they each had held on the roads through their respective territories. For persons without local knowledge it must indeed have been difficult to decide upon the validity of the opposing statements: the population of the coastal strip was claimed by the one to be as dense as in a town, by the other merely confined to a few villages and fishermen's huts. One witness speaking on behalf of the coastal route referred to the country along the proposed inland line as to 'a view of beggary on every side, thatched cabins and nothing but misery'.

The proposed siting of the Dublin termini showed striking variation in taste and sense. The coastal proponents thought to start from opposite the General Post Office in Sackville Street (now O'Connell Street). The inland party chose, less appropriately, at first 'the waste ground near the Basin at Blessington Street', but modified this to an equally inconvenient site in Prussia Street, between the later stations of Broadstone (MGWR) and Kingsbridge (GS&WR).

The taking of evidence by the Parliamentary committee developed into a hard and lengthy struggle, which began on 2nd May, 1836 and did not end until 29th June. Out of its hearings, the committee favoured the coastal route. It now seemed likely that, by the time the House of Lords had dealt with the Bill, it would fail to get passed during the session. To secure some recompense, the opposition offered to expedite matters by withdrawing further objection provided that their expenses were met. To secure this co-operation £1,710 out of an agreed total of £7,810 was paid over. Nevertheless, certain members of the opposition saw fit to reopen argument during the passage of the Bill through the Lords. Sanction was only given after the company undertook not to oppose in the next session any northern trunk rail route that might be recommended by a Royal Commission to be appointed, and which would be promoted by the inland party and its northern associates. So was the last hurdle wearily

'PP' class 4-4-0 No. 74 stands at Dublin Amiens Street station with a Balbriggan local on 14th
August, 1951.   *H.B. Priestley*

Dublin Amiens Street Shed with 'T1' class 4-4-2T No. 185 and 'QL' class 4-4-0 No. 127 present in
1931.   *L&GRP*

surmounted and the Dublin & Drogheda Railway Act passed on 13th August, 1836, while its promoters were faced with a bill of close on £30,000 for legal expenses.

The fight had embittered some potential supporters, and as a result the gathering in of money was slow. It was not until early 1838 that the D&D Directors announced to the shareholders that at last they were about to start work, and the section from the Royal Canal to Portmarnock was advertised for tender. On 18th June W.R. Weeks obtained contracts totalling £49,830 over 6½ miles of railway, and he soon had 400 men employed.

Compared with the Ulster's early days, the start of the D&D was indeed stormy. Weeks had only got work well started near Kilbarrack when on 13th July, 1838 the second report of the Royal Commission was made public. To the horror of the D&D Board, it recommended a northern trunk line out of Dublin via Navan and Armagh. Urgently the Directors put their case to the Government in London, but they were unable to obtain a clear picture of how it was proposed to implement the commission's recommendations. Possible losses had to be cut, and constructional work halted.

Principally through the energetic efforts of George A. Hamilton, the Chairman of the Board, it became evident over the next 18 months that the Government would not undertake the building of the Navan route. So far as the D&D was concerned, valuable time and money had been lost, and already the Ulster Railway had begun to work part of its line. Further financial support was needed, and the backing came, largely through the efforts of an influential section of the shareholders in the Manchester area. A further Act of Parliament was necessary, too, and urged by Daniel O'Connell, it went through in 1840.

The company appointed John MacNeill, the first Professor of Engineering at Trinity College, Dublin, to be its Engineer-in-Chief. Messrs Jeffs were given the contract for the abandoned section between the Royal Canal and Portmarnock, which included the Killester cutting and the Clontarf embankment. Much of the line north of this was made by William Dargan and by his colleague William McCormick. Construction began again at Hollybrook on 12th October, 1840.

Experience had shown the need to make certain small changes in the original plan. Amiens Street was chosen as the terminus, and the section from there to Sackville Street was not built. Across Clontarf Bay the line was routed more to the west, farther from certain objectors at Dollymount. At Skerries a slight seaward diversion was made and a tunnel avoided.

Before the line was opened to the public, the company organised a number of trial runs for the benefit of its more influential friends. On 6th January, 1844 a short completed portion of line near Malahide was used to convey Lord and Lady Eliot, Lord and Lady Talbot, and others up and down. On Monday, 18th March, a more ambitious trip to Drogheda started from the unfinished canal bridge, the engine *Nora Creina* and seven coaches conveying no less than 565 persons, including the Lord Lieutenant of Ireland. On their triumphal, if crowded, procession up the coast they were saluted by the coastguards' guns at Baldoyle, Malahide, Skerries, and Balbriggan. On arrival at Drogheda the guests were suitably refreshed in preparation for the return journey. The press reported that 'Dr MacNeill, the Engineer-in-Chief, gave a sumptuous cold collation in the evening at his residence, Rutland Square, of which the greater part of the company partook. A brilliant ball closed the enjoyment of the evening'. Two more successful trials were run on 12th and 15th April. Then on 23rd May, as a tribute to his legal skill, Daniel O'Connell, accompanied by a further selection of guests and complete with a military band, was taken along the length of the line.

The climax to these excursions came on 24th May, 1844, when Earl de Grey, the Lord Lieutenant, descended into a great excavation on the east side of Amiens Street and laid the foundation stone of the terminus. First things first: the company had completed its line of railway before building its terminus. The ceremony was followed by a banquet, set in one of the great arches beneath the railway. When the gathering had paid suitable tribute to the caterer's efforts, they all ascended to the track to see the first train go off, at three o'clock. That accomplished, and the D&DR formally opened, the Lord Lieutenant conferred the honour of knighthood on the Engineer-in-Chief as he knelt beside his track.

In this first summer the company offered the public three types of train - the mails, the quick, and the mixed. The first of these called only at Malahide and Balbriggan and ran between stations at 30 mph. The mixed trains called at all stations and handled all the goods; with shunting they had an overall speed of only 18½ mph. The quick trains were intermediate in their performance. The mails and quick took only first and second class passengers; the third class had to be content to go in the mixed trains.

Of the two termini, only that at Amiens Street was a permanent structure from the first. At the Drogheda end, a temporary wooden building was in use for nine years, awaiting the completion of the great Boyne viaduct. The Dublin terminus, designed by William Deane Butler, also housed the company's offices and was substantially built of Wicklow granite at a cost of £7,000. It was not completed until 1846; until then the company's affairs were run from offices at 22 Marlborough Street. From the footpath at Amiens Street a flight of steps, 22 ft high, presented a formidable barrier to luggage porters on their way to the platform. Thirty years later a long sloping roadway was built, to give vehicular access from Store Street to platform level.

Due to the high level of the rails leaving Dublin, the line was carried over no less than 75 arches between the terminus and the Royal Canal. The canal, 144 ft wide, was crossed by a single-span lattice girder bridge made in wrought iron by Grendons of Drogheda. The single span was exceptionally long for its day, but it enabled the company to avoid an exorbitant charge for making an intermediate pier in the canal. By 1862, the canal had become the property of the Midland Great Western Railway (MGWR), which was more sympathetic and gave permission for two piers to be placed to give the bridge added support. The strengthened canal bridge continued to carry increasing loads until its complete rebuilding 50 years later.

A short way north, the Tolka River was bridged by an iron girder structure and the Dollymount road by a double-arched stone bridge, built on the skew. Half-way to Drogheda, Balbriggan Harbour was crossed by 11 arches.

Besides these engineering works, others were required where the line encountered broad river estuaries on its way north. The first of these was between the Tolka River and Clontarf, since filled in on the landward side. The others were at Malahide and at Rogerstown. At all three sites the line was carried on massive stone-faced embankments and the rivers themselves were spanned by timber viaducts. In his first report to shareholders after the opening, Sir John MacNeill wrote:

> The whole of the Works on the Line, including the Embankments, the Cuttings, the Masonry the Timber Viaducts, the Bridges and the Embankments, and Stone Pitching over the different Estuaries, have withstood the severe test of last winter in the most satisfactory manner. Not the slightest injury was sustained by the unprecedented high tide and storm of the 9th of October last, except a small portion of the Eastern side of the Embankment at Rogerstown Estuary, which was washed down by the spray and surge of the tide which rose above the Pitching or stone facing which protects the side of the Embankment; this slight injury, however, was repaired in a few hours without causing any delay or inconvenience to the Traffic.

In spite of MacNeill's enthusiasm, trouble was soon experienced at the Malahide viaduct. The moving sands caused the wooden structure to subside, and the track had to be levelled by wedging, at a cost of £474, in 1851-2. In 1860 massive stone piers were set in the tideway and the viaduct was completely rebuilt.

The permanent way was solidly built throughout, and grey limestone from the cuttings formed a well-drained basement to the ballast. Bridge rails were used, but in contrast to the Ulster's practice, they were fixed to cross-sleepers. Between Dublin and Skerries the original bridge rails were replaced around 1876 by Harty's bridge rails, weighing 82½ lb. to the yard. Flanged rails did not come until after the formation of the GNR(I).

Even before the main line was open, a branch was planned to Howth. The Directors hoped that the branch might resurrect Howth Harbour as a packet station and eclipse Kingstown, then served by the D&KR on the other side of Dublin Bay. Although Howth never regained its former importance as a seaport, we have evidence of the D&D's intention to encourage the Howth tourist industry: the 1859 timetable stated that holders of first and second class returns were entitled to a cold bath in the company's bathing boxes, during the bathing season. The branch has always flourished and still provides an excellent service for commuters living at Howth, Sutton, and Baldoyle.

McCormick obtained the £11,500 contract for the building of the Howth branch and began work in March 1846. By 30th July, 2¾ miles of single line were opened. By August, the Engineer-in-Chief reported: 'the remaining portion of the works . . . will be completed before November . . . The embankment across the Howth estuary is progressing rapidly and will be finished in six weeks, up to the Terminus at Howth Harbour'. In spite of Sir John's hopeful forecast, construction went slowly; McCormick handed over to Dargan, and the branch was not opened throughout until 30th May, 1847. Like the main line out to Malahide, the branch was double-track.

The second D&D branch was an offspring of the Dublin & Belfast Junction Railway, whose Act of Incorporation empowered it to make a branch from

'VS' class 4-4-0 No. 209 *Foyle* on the Tolka River bridge on 26th May, 1957 with a Belfast to Claremorris (for Knock) excursion. The structure in this view came into use on 12th January, 1956 after the original bridge over the Tolka was swept away by flooding on the night of 8th/9th December, 1954.   *A. Donaldson*

'T2' class 4-4-2T No. 115 restarts an up local train away from Howth Junction. The branch to Howth veers off to the right.   *A. Donaldson*

The branch terminus at Howth on 28th July, 1958. AEC multiple unit No. 619 stands in the platform. Notice the sign indicating the Hill of Howth Tramway (*see pages 97 and 98*).   *Author*

An engraving of Baldoyle station. This station had a very short lifespan, it opened in 1844 and was closed in 1846 when the Howth branch was opened.

After engraving in John d'Alton's History of Drogheda, 1844

Malahide station building, another W.H. Mills survivor, in September 1980.   *Charles Friel*

A view, looking north, of Balbriggan viaduct and the station beyond.   *Duffner*

Drogheda to Navan. It was to diverge a short way on the Dublin side of the original D&D station. Since it would have been severed from its parent line, the position was rationalised by a further Act by which the D&D bought the line from the D&BJ. At the same time the company obtained powers to extend the line to Kells and thereby open up the most fertile part of Co. Meath.

The Drogheda-Navan section was opened on 15th February, 1850 and the Navan-Kells section on 11th June, 1853. The branch was subsequently taken out to the little town of Oldcastle, to which traffic was first worked on 17th May, 1863.

The Oldcastle branch was crossed a short way west of Navan by a line that ran from Clonsilla Junction near Dublin to Kingscourt, and was unconnected with the D&DR. This branch was opened from Clonsilla to a junction near Navan on 29th August, 1862 by the Dublin & Meath Railway (D&MR). The northern part, built by the Navan & Kingscourt company, was first opened to an intermediate station at Kilmainham Wood on 1st November, 1872, and to Kingscourt on 1st November, 1875.

The D&MR Company had running powers over the D&D's line from Navan to Kells. This had come to it as the result of a proviso in the D&D's Act covering the extension to Kells. Since the D&D's route to Kells from Dublin was undoubtedly circuitous, it was provided that, should any direct line be subsequently made from Dublin to Navan, its owners should have running powers between Navan and Kells. The D&MR thus automatically fell heir to these running powers. One of these D&M trains, forgotten about by the D&D crossing keeper at Newgate Crossing a couple of days after the working arrangement began on 15th December, 1862, ran through the unlighted gates which were closed against it. The collision killed a horse, demolished the cart, and injured its driver and the driver of the engine.

The Dublin & Meath Company benefited from the running powers to Kells and was able to draw off a large proportion of the Dublin-bound traffic. The Dublin & Drogheda attempted to meet the competition by cutting fares and by introducing express trains.

The D&MR was leased to the Midland Great Western from 1st June, 1869, who discontinued running to Kells from 1st October, 1869. Some time later an agreement was made between the MGWR and the D&D to divide the passenger receipts between Navan and Kells in the proportions of the previous few years. The MGWR made a platform at Navan Junction.

From the start, the D&D carried three classes of passengers. The Railway Regulation Act of 1844 required that third class carriages be covered, and rendered a repetition of the spartan behaviour of the early Ulster patrons unnecessary. The third class, or 'Parliamentary', carriages of the D&D each held 60 passengers and protected them from the elements by 'sliding glass windows in the doors and sliding shutters in the sides'. From these beginnings, third class travel was thus encouraged, and at the half-yearly meeting of proprietors on 26th February, 1846, the Directors remarked: 'It is also extremely gratifying . . . to find that the additional comfort and accommodation they have provided in their Third Class Carriages, for the poorer classes during the winter months, has been marked with such an extraordinary increase in the number of passengers.'

An early engraving of Drogheda station and town.

Drogheda station, looking north, on 12th August, 1951. At the down platform is 'QG' class 0-6-0 No. 154 which has just arrived with a train from Oldcastle. The line from Oldcastle and Navan joined the main line just south of the station. No. 154 would have had to propel its train a short distance along the down line before reaching the platform. The engine and carriages for a local train to Dublin are stabled, on the right, in the siding behind the up siding.   *H.B. Priestley*

A view along the platform at Navan looking towards Kells on 30th July, 1958. *Author*

Kells station frontage on 25th July, 1960. *Author*

'LQG' class 0-6-0 No. 164 arrives at Kells with an up goods on 26th July, 1960.   *Author*

The station layout at the branch terminus at Oldcastle on 25th July, 1960.   *Author*

In the first six weeks of 1845, the number of third class passengers was 21,589, while in the corresponding period of 1846 the total had risen to 33,069.

These promising results were scarcely established before the disaster of the Irish Famine struck the country. This was due to blight which ruined the potato crop, the staple foodstuff of the peasantry. It was long before the days of chemical fungicides, and starvation faced many thousands. In March 1847, the Board commented:

> The last six months have been a period of severe trial . . . the loss of the Potato Crop has been attended with the most calamitous results; a considerable proportion of the population in the vicinity of your line . . . have been in consequence severe sufferers; they have had few or no crops to bring to market and have therefore been unable to contribute to the traffic of the line.

There was a marked loss in traffic receipts, especially in the third class, and to compensate for the revenue loss fare increases were made in first and second classes. The modest half-yearly dividends which had been distributed up to then were advisedly foregone for two years.

The trouble was added to when signs of dissension became apparent among the members of the Board of Directors. Thomas Brodigan, already referred to as one of the founders of the company, became aggrieved at his treatment by his fellow Directors. The trouble seems to have arisen as far back as early 1837, when Brodigan had made an unsuccessful application to the Chairman to be made manager, only to find that Peter Eckersley was appointed, probably largely through the influence of some of the Manchester shareholders. Brodigan made public criticism of the company's failure to recompense him adequately for his early efforts. He claimed £3,000 for his personal expenses sustained during the promotion of the D&D. He followed this up with a damaging series of accusations of mismanagement against the rest of the Board and against Eckersley. His claims were refused. Brodigan then brought his case to the Dundalk Assizes on 15th-16th July, 1847, where he was awarded £674. The Directors then publicly replied to his various accusations and were thereby able to clear the troubled air.

Critics again assailed the sorely-taxed Directors in the following year when, at the half-yearly meeting on 2nd-3rd March, 1848, the shareholders appointed a committee 'to investigate into the affairs of the company'. Within a short time the committee reported, certain criticisms were made, some of which the Directors repudiated but the need for strict economy was admitted. Eventually, however, the rigours of Famine, Brodigan and Economy passed behind, and in the 1850s a healthy dividend began to be paid to the shareholders. The chairmanship of the Board came in 1851 to James W. Murland, who held that position until the amalgamation of the D&D; he thereafter continued as Chairman of the Northern and the Great Northern companies until his death in 1890.

A very early view of the Boyne viaduct before rebuilding *c*.1880. The locomotives on this train are probably the Dublin & Drogheda Railway Nos. 10 (of 1862) and 21 (of 1864), both 0-4-2 Beyer, Peacock engines - possibly they are still carrying D&DR livery.   *Lawrence*

The Boyne viaduct viewed from Drogheda North signal box on 30th July, 1958.   *Author*

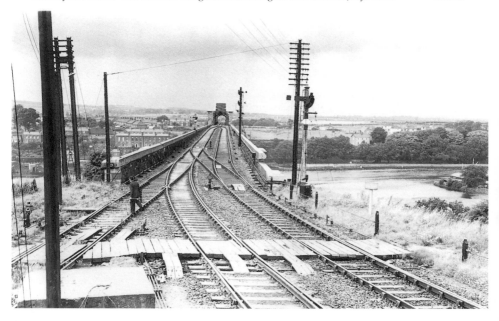

Chapter Four

The Dublin & Belfast Junction Railway

The first meeting of this company's promoters took place on 6th April, 1844 in the D&D's offices, under the chairmanship of Lord Charlemont. Two days later the Prospectus was issued. Parliamentary sanction was given on 21st July, 1845, empowering the Dublin & Belfast Junction Railway Company to build a line from Drogheda to Portadown, by way of Dundalk and Newry, a distance of 63 miles, with a 16¾ mile branch from Drogheda to Navan. The line was to share termini with the Ulster at Portadown and with the D&D at Drogheda. As we have already seen, it was soon arranged that the ownership of the Navan branch would be transferred to the D&D, which was better placed to operate it. On the main line work began from the high ground north of the River Boyne, and a temporary station, 200 yards north of Newfoundwell viaduct, did duty until the opening of the Boyne viaduct. The main line was opened to Dundalk on 15th February, 1849.

In the interim period, construction went slowly, as the contractor's work fell behind schedule for a variety of reasons. At the Board meeting on 12th March, 1847, it was reported that 3,231 men and 210 horses were working on the main line and on the Navan branch, but this was insufficient. In consequence the Directors had to meet incessant criticism by their own shareholders and by their neighbour companies, both of whom impatiently awaited the financial returns which were to accrue on the completion of the Junction company's works. The prospect of even partial completion to Dundalk was welcomed by the D&D, since it would join them with the Dundalk & Enniskillen's line, then under construction. Indeed, the Dundalk-Castleblayney section of the D&E was opened concurrently with the Drogheda-Dundalk portion of the D&BJR in 1849. It then became possible to get from Dublin to Belfast in eight hours, using the lines of four railway companies and road transport between Castleblayney and Armagh.

Intake of capital had been disappointing, and the efforts of construction had brought the funds of the Junction company to such a low ebb that application for a £120,000 Government loan became necessary before extension could be attempted north of Dundalk. The next section to be opened, on 31st July, 1850, took passengers 10½ miles beyond Dundalk to a temporary station at the Wellington Inn of which no trace remains. The gap between the junction and the Ulster lines was now down to around 24 miles, and in place of the Castleblayney-Armagh route, Belfast passengers went by road to Portadown for a time. Meanwhile William Dargan's men were working on a relatively level stretch, much of it through marshland, south from Portadown by Tanderagee and Scarva, and he reached Mullaghglass near Goraghwood on 6th January, 1852. The intervening six mile gap to the Wellington Inn involved an ascent through the hills on the west of the deep Newry valley, with deep cuttings in granite near the summit. On the way, a deep valley near Bessbrook village was bridged by the great Craigmore viaduct, a graceful series of 18 arches, each 60 ft in span and from 70 ft to 140 ft in height, these last being the highest in Ireland. The Wellington Inn was reached from the north on 10th June, 1852, and thereupon continuous rail travel became possible from Belfast to Newfoundwell. Between there and the D&D's northern terminus the traveller went as he saw fit, through the streets of Drogheda and over the road bridge.

The need for a railway bridge across the River Boyne was urgent, and the 1848 loan had specified that it was to be built without delay. Planning and design had already started, for as early as 1846 Sir John MacNeill, consulting engineer to the Junction company, had put forward plans for a lattice girder structure, though no further action had matured. In 1849, James Barton had been appointed Engineer to the D&BJR, and in June of that year he sent circular letters to several ironworks asking for designs for the Boyne viaduct. Considering the replies, MacNeill advised the Directors that either a lattice girder bridge of his own design, or a tubular bridge submitted by Fairbairn, would be suitable. Barton, when asked to comment in detail on MacNeill's plans, found that they were incomplete, and he transferred one of his assistants to MacNeill's Dublin office. The revised design was ready in November 1850, and with the Fairbairn design it was advertised for tender. Meanwhile the ever-careful Barton had painstakingly re-examined the lattice girder designs, found them faulty in certain respects and generally too weak, and had advised against their adoption as then planned. Further calculations were urgently made by Barton and his assistants Schaw and Powell, while Professor Hart of Trinity College assisted in checking. The drawings were completed by the end of May. MacNeill then re-examined them and appended his signature as consultant. On 3rd June, MacNeill showed the drawings to the members of the Board, who were no doubt most anxious for work to proceed and promptly adopted them. Tenders were called for, and on 21st June, 1851 the contract was given to William Evans of Cambridge at a price of £68,000.

The girder portion of the bridge over the Boyne consisted of a central span of 226 ft, flanked by two spans of 141 ft. Masonry approach viaducts were to lead in over the valley slopes with 12 arches to the south and three to the north.

Before work had long begun it was found that the alluvial clays in the valley were not going to provide a good foundation, and that earlier trial borings had been interpreted over-optimistically. It took a year to bring up the piers of the approach spans to ground level. The four heavy piers to carry the girders were more difficult still, and in two cases the cofferdams had to go down 32 ft. The most northerly pier in the tideway, No. 14 from the south end, needed an even deeper cofferdam to get a footing, and it was not until October 1853 that this was obtained, 43 ft below low water. The effort and delay had broken the contractor, and he had declared himself bankrupt. Barton, backed by his Directors, bravely determined to finish the incomplete works, and it was under his guidance that the base was found for Pier 14.

The months were slipping by, profits were being lost by the unavoidable delays, and in an effort to hasten the completion of the recalcitrant pier, the wages of the stonemasons were raised to 7s. a day, then a fantastic figure for Ireland. By February 1854, MacNeill reported that at last Pier 14 was 17 ft above the Boyne Water, and that he was putting in hand the purchase of iron for the girders. The work progressed, but war with the Russians had the unfortunate effect of raising the price of iron, while the severe Crimean winter of 1854-5 retarded work on the exposed girders. Most fittingly, Barton and his assistant Stoney attended to the ceremony of driving the last rivet, and the job was done. The necessary inspection by the Board of Trade followed and was done with customary care; perhaps the most spectacular part of it was the deflection testing when two trains each of 550 tons were brought together on to the two tracks crossing the girders. Formal approval was given, and traffic began to use the bridge on 5th April, 1855.

Though the best part of four years had passed since plans had gone out for tender, and the estimated building time had been over-run by more than two years, rail traffic had already begun to cross the Boyne. The transport needs of the great Dublin International Exhibition had reinforced the public demands in the early part of 1853, and the unfortunate Evans and the Junction company had co-operated in the adaptation of the great wooden scaffolding. By reinforcing and modifying it, a single track was able to be laid across the 80 ft span at an extra cost of £2,000. A critical Board of Trade inspection enforced a 4 mph speed limit and a train weight below 100 tons.

To cover the extra costs, the Junction company promptly made a surcharge of 8d. on their passenger fares. Strongly-voiced objections were at once made by the public while the D&D and Ulster companies regarded the addition as a violation of the standing agreement on rates and fares. The D&D effectively emphasised its feelings by lifting some rails at its side of the junction and the surcharge was soon removed.

The wooden scaffold bridge, if it enabled through running, never enjoyed much public confidence or popularity. Additional fender piles had to be driven to prevent possible damage from ships, and a 'break of journey' concession was allowed to nervous passengers so that they could circumnavigate the erection by road. Nevertheless, in its short life the temporary bridge carried around 6,000 trains, totalling 400,000 tons in weight.

Once the viaduct was completed, the Junction company was able to devote attention to the track. Now that through Dublin-Belfast running was possible, the line was carrying an increasingly frequent service of trains and the inconvenience of single-line working was making itself felt. Already doubling had been carried out over about three miles of line on the Wellington Bank from the time of opening. Most of the rest of the track was doubled between 1858 and 1860, but between Goraghwood and Portadown the work was not completed until 1862.

An extra-mural activity of the D&BJR was the leasing and working of the Banbridge Junction Railway. This concern started its activities soon after the D&BJ's track had been laid south from Portadown towards Goraghwood. The bustling market town of Banbridge lay some five miles to the east. So it was that on 8th November, 1852 the inaugural meeting was held at the Downshire Arms Hotel in Banbridge under Robert McClelland's chairmanship. The company was incorporated on 20th August, 1853 under the encyclopaedic title of the Banbridge, Newry, Dublin & Belfast Junction Railway, and was allowed a capital of £60,000 to make 6¾ miles of single track, joining the main line at

GNR 'V' class 3-cylinder compound 4-4-0 No. 84 *Falcon* passes Dundalk works with a passenger train on 15th May, 1950. The wagon shop is on the left, the tallest structure is the loco erecting shop and that on the extreme right is the paint shop.   *H.C. Casserley*

Class 'JT' 2-4-2T No. 94, formerly *Howth*, on the 12.55 pm to Greenore train at the Square Crossing, Dundalk on 27th March, 1951.   *Author*

Dundalk Central signal box. In the background can be seen the DBJR's Dundalk Junction station and the INWR platform which closed in 1893 and were replaced by the present Dundalk station, 18th July, 1958.   *Author*

A general view of Dundalk station looking south in May 1945.   *Duffner*

A view looking north at Dundalk in the 1930s from the Carrickmacross Road bridge. The left side of the island platform is for Greenore trains and the right for Enniskillen. The carriage sheds can be seen in the distance on the left.   *Stations UK*

A 1950s view of 'LQG' class 0-6-0 No. 159 which has arrived at Dundalk with a lengthy goods train from Portadown.   *N.C. Simmons*

'T2' class 4-4-2T No. 69 arrives at Goraghwood with a train from Newry on 16th August, 1956. A Dublin-Belfast train is on the right. *H.B. Priestley*

GNR 'V' class 4-4-0 No. 85 *Merlin* arrives at Goraghwood with a southbound express on 16th August, 1956. The Newry-Armagh line lies beyond the platform on the right. *H.B. Priestley*

A southbound goods train passes Scarva. The former Banbridge bay platform is on the right.
A. Donaldson

Scarva station looking north.   *Real Photographs*

Scarva and running to Banbridge. The line was opened on 23rd March, 1859, and by an Act of 25th May, 1860 it was leased to the D&BJ at a rental of £2,000 per annum.

The Junction company also interested themselves to the extent of £20,000 in the Clones & Cavan Extension Railway, which, though not near any of their own track, might be expected to contribute traffic to it over the D&E.

From its beginnings to its amalgamation, the activities of the D&BJ company were comparatively uneventful. At the time of construction of the Boyne viaduct, the company seems to have regarded it as more important that the shareholders should get their dividend than the county its rates. The story of the seizure of a train in 1853 is told by G.R. Mahon:

> July 5th also happened to be the first day of the County Louth Assizes and saw the Dublin & Belfast Junction Railway in trouble as a result. An incident which occurred at the Newfoundwell station at Drogheda was described by the *Louth Advertiser* as 'a most extraordinary way of executing the powers of the law'. Apparently the Collector of the County Cess could not get payment of rates due by the railway company and, as he was due to show proof of every effort to collect them, or prove they were irrecoverable by the first day of the Assizes, he determined on drastic measures. He and a number of assistants descended on the station shortly before the departure of the morning train to the north and, producing a warrant, proceeded to take possession of the train. Unfortunately for themselves, six Grand Jurors proposed travelling on the train and were in a great hurry to get to Dundalk in time for the opening of the Assizes as otherwise they could not be sworn in. The six harassed gentlemen remonstrated with the collector, but without avail. He resolutely refused to allow the arrested train to proceed until his demands were acceded to, as eventually they were. Apparently they must have got to Dundalk in time, for one account stated that the lost time was pulled up by increased speed and that the released engine 'snorted along the line which had just been freed'.

The dividends on the ordinary stock reflect the course of events: they reached 5 per cent in 1853-5, but thereafter dropped slightly and in general fluctuated between 4 and 4½ per cent, with 1864 and 1869 poor years at 3¾ and 3⅞ per cent. Of the three major concerns that became the GNR(I), it consistently paid the lowest dividend and no doubt its shareholders were not averse from the prospect of union with the D&D, which formed the initial stage of the genesis of the Great Northern.

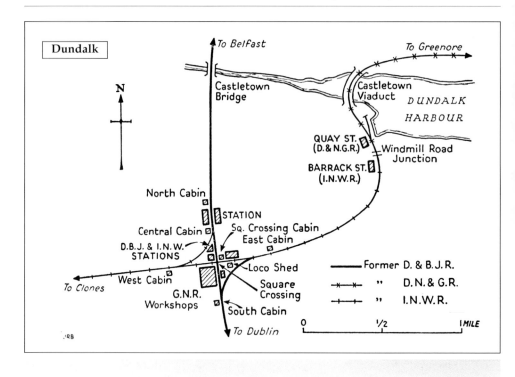

Castleblayney station looking west.   *Locomotive Publishing Co.*

Chapter Five

The Irish North Western Railway

This railway began as the Dundalk & Enniskillen Railway, but it took over the working of three neighbouring concerns which gave it access to the western and northern coasts, and in consequence it was renamed the Irish North Western Railway, or more familiarly, 'The Irish North'.

The earliest stirrings of the Irish North, if unsuccessful, were coeval with the growth of the Ulster Railway. An Act of 1837 sanctioned the Dundalk & Western Railway, a scheme which was to link Dundalk and Ballybay, between Castleblayney and Clones. After a ceremonial and well attended turning of the first sod at Dundalk in May 1839, the scheme languished and was abandoned.

The incorporation on 21st July, 1845 of its successor, the Dundalk & Enniskillen company, was contemporaneous with that of the Dublin & Belfast Junction. In spite of its title, the D&E was to build only as far as Clones, 40 miles from Dundalk, and was to share the responsibilities and expense of the remaining 32 miles to Enniskillen with the nascent Newry & Enniskillen Railway Company. In fact, the N&E, remotely and badly run from London, got neither to Clones nor to Enniskillen, and the powers to build this section were transferred to the D&E.

Construction began on 15th October, 1845 from the Dundalk end, but it went slowly, and the section to Castleblayney was not opened until 15th February, 1849. The eastern terminus was at Barrack Street, from where the line swept round the edge of the town in a great curve, crossing the D&BJ line on the level at the well known 'Square Crossing'. From the opening until the end of 1850, the line was worked under contract by William Dargan. The track was laid with the then fashionable 15 ft iron high bridge rails.

To the west of Castleblayney the country was rougher, with many outcrops of rock and stretches of peat bog. The extension towards Clones was carried out piecemeal as money came in, with further Acts to extend the powers. The next six miles to Ballybay were not opened until 17th July, 1854. About this time the Board considered branching from Ballybay to Armagh to tap the Ulster's traffic, but wiser counsels prevailed and construction was pushed on towards Newbliss, reached in July 1855. Parliamentary powers were then obtained to make a branch from a junction at Shantonagh, near Ballybay, through Cootehill to Cavan, where the Midland Great Western was shortly to drive its line.

Evidence of the difficulties of securing adequate foundation for the line where it passed over bogland was seen in early January 1856, when 30 yards of track subsided a couple of miles west of Castleblayney. The company's consulting engineer, Sir John MacNeill, had 'the matter rectified by one of his ingenious processes' while passengers tramped the muddy gap to join another train beyond. The company blamed the contractors, Moore Bros, for faulty work, and after months of disputes further construction was handed over to Messrs McCormick, Green & Smith.

The railway was opened to Clones and Lisnaskea on 7th July, 1858, to Lisbellaw on 16th August, 1858, and to Enniskillen on 15th February, 1859.

GNR 'U' class 4-4-0 No. 202 *Louth* passes Shantonagh Junction signal cabin with a GAA special bound for Monaghan on 3rd June, 1956.   *A. Donaldson*

Shantonagh Junction in July 1958, after the lifting of the Cootehill branch. The branch had been closed in 1955.   *Author*

The first timetable of the services on the complete line shows the D&E running four trains each way on weekdays. They left Dundalk at 5.00 and 10.55 am and 3.25 and 7.15 pm and Enniskillen at 5.00 and 11.40 am and 12.15 and 3.55 pm. Apart from these, there were mail workings between Dundalk and Castleblayney carrying only first and second class, which connected with mail coaches. Castleblayney must have been a busy place at night in those days, with the down mail arriving at 12.25 am and unloading mail and sleepy passengers into the Enniskillen and Omagh coaches. Road traffic from these two county towns would then come in to join the up mail train, which left at 2.10 am and had passengers into Drogheda two hours later and into Dublin by 5.25 am. Return tickets were valid only on the day of issue, unless for stations over 50 miles apart, or if issued on a Saturday or Sunday, then until the Monday. Children under 12 were carried at half fare, and each adult could take one child under three years of age free, *provided that it was a member of the passenger's family*. How this was to be determined in doubtful instances was not stated in the timetable.

The branch line was opened to Cootehill on 18th October, 1860; thereupon the remaining section to Cavan was abandoned. Already the powerful Ulster Railway saw the road open to Clones, via Monaghan, and it had been the main sponsor of the Clones & Cavan Extension Railway, which received its Parliamentary sanction on 1st August, 1859. So it came about that the Ulster Railway was indirectly responsible for conferring upon the station in the quiet village of Cootehill the dignity of a terminus. The D&E bowed to the inevitable and put what spare energies it had into its share of the Clones-Cavan line.

On 1st January, 1860 the D&E took a lease in perpetuity of the Londonderry & Enniskillen Railway (*see Chapter Six*). Six years of nightmarish working had convinced all concerned with the L&E that they would do better to leave their line to be run by the nearest experts and merely to draw an adequate rent. This extension of its powers was a courageous act on the part of the D&E, for it had never been any too successful at making its own line pay. It did, however, see in its added responsibilities a rationalisation of the coast-to-coast workings, and thus emboldened it changed its name to the Irish North Western Railway by an Act of 7th July, 1862. At the same time it was authorised to raise almost £300,000 to put its house in order and 'to complete the Belturbet line and other unfinished works'.

The Clones to Cavan line, worked by the Irish North, had been opened on 7th April, 1862, and the Belturbet branch referred to in the July Act was planned to diverge from it at Ballyhaise. The financial position of the Irish North worsened, and the Belturbet branch was not completed until Great Northern days.

Railway activity at Clones became busier when on 2nd March, 1863 the Ulster Railway opened its Monaghan-Clones section, thereby providing a new inland route from Belfast to Dublin, via Cavan and the MGWR.

On 11th July, 1861 there was incorporated the Enniskillen & Bundoran Railway Co., with powers to build a 36 mile line from Lowtherstown to Bundoran. On 30th June, 1862 it was empowered to extend 23 miles to Sligo, as the Enniskillen, Bundoran & Sligo Railway, and to join the MGWR at its western terminus. The INWR was authorised to hold much of the capital, and from the opening, on 13th June, 1866, it worked the line for its owners. The Sligo extension was never built, and Bundoran remained a terminus at the centre of a small but thriving tourist district.

'SG2' class 0-6-0 No. 182 takes water at Clones on 14th September, 1956. Meanwhile 'P' class 4-4-0 No. 26 is involved with fitted vans.   *Charles Friel Collection*

'UG' class 0-6-0 No. 79 outside the roundhouse at Clones on 7th June, 1957.

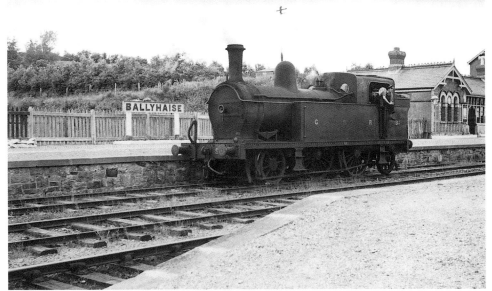

'JT' class 2-4-2T No. 91 is the Belturbet branch engine on 7th June, 1957, seen at Ballyhaise.

'PP' class 4-4-0 No. 106 has just arrived at Cavan with a train from Clones on 18th April, 1955.
H.C. Casserley

'JT' class 2-4-2T No. 91 runs round its train at Belturbet. A Cavan & Leitrim train is in the bay on the left.   *Revd John Parker*

Belturbet station, looking west towards the GNR buffer stop (and Ballinamore) from under the canopy on 23rd March, 1959. A coffin lies on the station platform. A Cavan & Leitrim train is visible in the distance in the bay platform.   *Author*

'U' class 4-4-0 No. 204 *Antrim* has just arrived at Bundoran Junction with a train from Bundoran on 29th June, 1957.

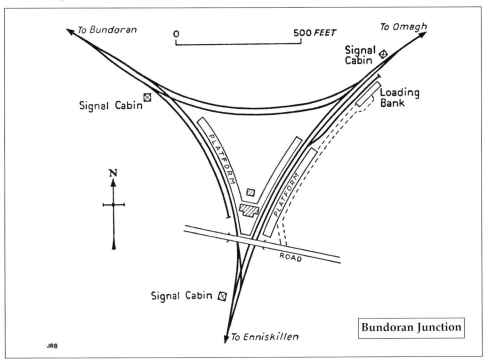

Even though it had no pretensions at reaching either Dublin or Belfast, from time to time the Irish North became aware of the activities of the protagonists of the old inland route between the two cities. The course of the Irish North lay across that route, and the northern extension of the Dublin & Meath Railway, the Navan & Kingscourt, was capable of thrusting north from its terminus. In 1866, then, the Navan & Kingscourt Railway lodged a bill for a Castleblayney extension, with powers to join the Irish North Western and to have running powers over part of its line. This thin end of the Dublin wedge was never built, and the Castleblayney, Kingscourt & Armagh line, opened in 1909-10, and the proposed Mullingar & Kells Railway four years later were feeble remnants of the original plan.

The Irish North was stated to be 'in a state of pecuniary embarrassment' in 1864, and an Act was obtained for the reorganisation of capital and the extinguishing of arrears of dividends. The management under Henry Plews was efficient enough, but the line suffered from its thinly populated and non-industrial hinterland. Londonderry at its northern extremity was linked from 1855 to Belfast via the Londonderry & Coleraine Railway and the lines south of Coleraine, and this competitive line drew much of the traffic that might have benefited the INWR.

Apart from Bundoran, the area served by the line had little to offer to the growing business of tourism. In spite of the efforts of Plews, ably aided by Clifford in the Barrack Street locomotive department after 1870, the fortunes of the line declined, and no dividend was paid after 1862. There was a loss in working during the second half of 1874 of nearly £1,000. Even though they received scanty compensation, the proprietors must have greeted with relief the merger of the company into the Northern Railway of Ireland on New Year's Day, 1876.

'U' class 4-4-0 No. 203 *Armagh* has arrived under the roof at Bundoran on 29th June, 1957.

Chapter Six

The Londonderry & Enniskillen Railway

London influence was dominant among the promoters and Board of this line, which obtained its Act of Incorporation in July 1845. The line was to link the two towns named by way of Strabane and Omagh, and it went through Parliament with practically no opposition from landowners.

The line was first surveyed by George Stephenson in 1837, but by the time that plans for obtaining the Act were in progress, Sir John MacNeill had added the company to his list of consultancies. The Directors soon decided that MacNeill's surveys were hastily made. MacNeill resigned and sued the Directors when they saw fit to disagree with his recommended route between Strabane and Omagh. In his place Robert Stephenson was appointed, who submitted a revised and less expensive route. Stephenson dryly comments, in his report to the Board dated 18th August, 1845:

> We are informed that the Surveys were made in haste, and that Sir John MacNeill, in the midst of his then pressing engagements, did not himself have time personally to go over the Line: this is much confirmed in many parts of the Line; and we, therefore, have no hesitation in suggesting alterations . . .

The contractor Leishman started work between Londonderry and Strabane in October 1845, and that section was opened to traffic on 19th April, 1847. The northern terminus had been the subject of some difference of opinion during planning; initially it was opened at Gallows Strand, on the west bank of the River Foyle some way south of the bridge linking the two halves of Londonderry. The site was not convenient, and an extension was made to the Foyle bridge and opened in April 1850.

Receipts from the first year of operation were most discouraging, and in alarm the Board tried in 1848 to get sanction to abandon the Omagh-Enniskillen portion. Their defeatist attitude was however thwarted by the Marquis of Abercorn, whose land was to be traversed for nearly 10 miles by the line.

Further construction went slowly after this bleak start. William McCormick built the entire line in stages from Strabane to Enniskillen. It was opened to Newtownstewart on 9th May, 1852, to Omagh on 13th September, 1852, and to Fintona on 15th June, 1853.

From a junction ¾ mile from Fintona the remainder of the line was extended southwards, to Dromore Road on 16th January, 1854 and into Enniskillen on 19th August, 1854. With their only branch thus formed between Fintona Junction and Fintona, the company got Board of Trade permission to work this part of their system by horse traction. This tranquil and adequate arrangement continued until the line was closed 104 years later. Steam locomotives were admitted to the branch for goods trains.

The original permanent way on the Londonderry-Strabane section was laid with 75 lb. double-headed iron rails, held in chairs on transverse sleepers. After this fairly orthodox beginning, the Directors seem to have been led astray, for

Londonderry Foyle Road station on 10th September, 1936 viewed from the Craigavon bridge looking north. The River Foyle is on the extreme right. The wagons in the foreground are standing on the Londonderry Port & Harbour Commissioners' line.   *H.B. Priestley*

Londonderry engine shed on 12th July, 1931 with the River Foyle beyond. Unusually the shed doors are closed. Alongside the shed stands 'PG' class 0-6-0 No. 103, also visible is ex-Ulster Railway 'C' class 0-6-0 No. 137.   *L&GRP*

Strabane station looking in the up direction in 1937 with the GNR goods yard on the extreme left. The narrow gauge station is on the right.   *L&GRP*

View looking north with 'QG' class 0-6-0 No. 155 is seen next to Strabane North signal cabin. Note the narrow gauge track and rolling stock of the CDRJC in the foreground. The CDRJC/GNR interchange shed is in the distance on the left.   *John Langford*

A view from the Camel's Hump of parallel viaducts cross the River Mourne to the south of Strabane station. In the foreground is the narrow gauge viaduct with a County Donegal Railways railcar and train approaching from Stranorlar. The Londonderry & Enniskillen Railway viaduct can be seen in the background.

Newtownstewart station in 1965 looking north.   *Stations UK*

they decided to lay from Strabane to Enniskillen 60 lb. double-headed 20 ft rails held in large cast-iron chairs which rested directly on the ballast without sleepers. Peter Barlow, a member of the Board, had invented the chairs. They were in two portions, bolted together, thereby avoiding the use of keys. In place of fishplates at the joints, extra large chairs were used; they weighed 2 cwt. each and were connected to iron tiebars to hold the rails to gauge. Wrought-iron tiebars were also used at intermediate positions between rail joints, one per rail in hard ground, two or three where the foundations were soft. The whole arrangement was rigid and inflexible, and it was soon found that the joint chairs were liable to fracture when stressed by frost.

There were four classes of passenger accommodation, probably all in four-wheelers. Six carriages were supplied by Perry of Bristol and were assembled at the Lisahally works of the neighbouring and friendly railway, the Londonderry & Coleraine. Open thirds came from Bromhead and Hemming. In August 1853 a local newspaper said of a new coach shipped from Liverpool:

> It contains three compartments capable of holding 12 passengers, the centre in each being fitted up for first-class passengers, and the other two for second class. On the roof are also arranged six rows of seats each holding six passengers, the ascent to which is attained by upright iron ladders placed against the sides of the carriage. The carriage will thus carry 72 passengers; it is also fitted with a capacious luggage box at each end.*

In spite of never being prosperous, the L&E was quite enterprising. The company built market houses at Newtownstewart, Omagh, and Fintona and thereby drew the produce of the farming hinterland to the lineside. It was also a large shareholder in the Lough Erne Steam Navigation Co., who ran a paddleboat *Countess of Milan* from Enniskillen to Belleek and to Belturbet on alternate days. Excursions were often run to Enniskillen to connect with this steamer, and on these occasions the surfeit of passengers were accommodated in one or two barges, towed behind the *Countess*, while entertainment was provided by a band.

By early 1855 the company's finances were in a deplorable state. On 23rd July an Act was obtained authorising the company to lease the line for 21 years to McCormick, who was by now a debenture holder and a creditor. Other creditors became pressing, and about this time the Londonderry Sheriff was advertising the sale of goods and chattels of the L&E to meet their demands. The grim situation was eased by an Act of 21st July, 1856, permitting the issue of further debenture and preference stocks.

The hand-to-mouth existence of the L&E was altered in early 1859, when the D&E entered Enniskillen and connected the L&E with the rest of the Irish railways. It speedily became apparent to the Londonderry's Board that the line from Dundalk to Derry had better be run as one concern. Neither railway was prosperous, but the D&E was the larger and the better equipped. The necessary Act was obtained, and the D&E was empowered to lease the L&E's line for 99 years from 1st January, 1860. Thereafter the Board of the L&E, sitting remotely at 4 Coleman St Buildings, London, was content to receive the rent from the operators (the Irish North Western Railway from July 1862) and to distribute the profits. The rental was at first £26,000 pa, with a gradual increase after three years

* This may have been the original Fintona tram car (1854-83).

The station approach at Omagh on 28th July, 1964. *Author*

'PP' class 4-4-0 No. 25 at Fintona Junction on 28th April, 1951 with an Omagh to Enniskillen train. *T.J. Edgington*

'Dick', her driver and passengers pose for the photographer on the Fintona tram, 22nd April, 1948. On the top deck is a youthful Richard M. Casserley   *H.C. Casserley*

Dick and the tram arrive at Fintona terminus on 19th August, 1951. The goods platform is on the left. Note the Belfast Bakeries containers on the right.   *H.B. Priestley*

Enniskillen station viewed from the south in 1933. Note the bay platform for the Sligo, Leitrim & Northern Counties Railway.

'PP' class 4-4-0 No. 42 at Enniskillen engine shed on 29th June, 1950.   *T.J. Edgington*

based on 20 per cent on all gross receipts from the two railways above £95,000 a year until the rent reached £33,000 a year. This was enough to pay preference and guaranteed dividends, and an ordinary share dividend of 5 per cent.

On the amalgamation of the INWR with other lines in 1875 to form the Northern Railway of Ireland, the L&E lease was taken over. The L&ER remained a separate company into the GNR(I) era, until it was bought out in 1883.

A noteworthy feature of the early days of the company was the rapid succession of managers and locomotive superintendents. There were seven of the latter in a 10-year span, among them J.S. Domville who later occupied the same position on the Belfast & County Down line. Their lack of permanency was reflected in the locomotive stock, an unsatisfactory and inadequate collection.

Enniskillen engine shed yard and the south end of the station on 23rd December, 1955, with 'PP' class 4-4-0 No. 12 in the foreground and 'LQG' class 0-6-0 No. 161 beyond.

Author

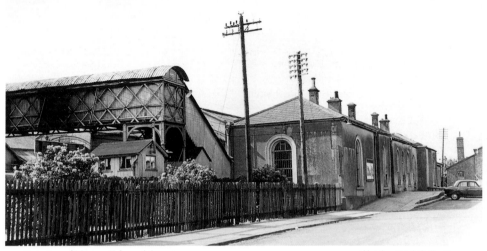

Exterior of Newry Edward Street.　　　　　　　　　　　*Charles Friel Collection*

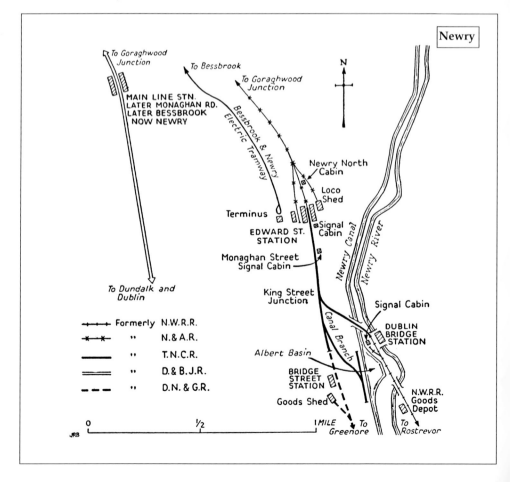

Chapter Seven

The Newry Railways

Over a century before the railways came to Newry, that town had assumed some importance as a port. Situated at the seaward end of a deep valley and but a short way from the sheltered, fjord-like Carlingford Lough, the town lay between the foothills of the Mourne Mountains and the granite slopes rising to Slieve Gullion. By 1726, Newry had assumed such importance as a centre of trade that the Customs House was removed there from Carlingford town. In 1730 Parliament authorised the construction of a canal from Carlingford Lough to Lough Neagh; this was finished in 1742 under the Newry Navigation Co. and barges began to ply into the interior of Ulster. A century later, the area was ripe for railway development. Within a short time the attention of cross-channel investors was attracted, and in rapid succession two Acts went through to cover the making of railways both up and down the valley. So did the Newry & Enniskillen and the Newry, Warrenpoint & Rostrevor (NW&R) railways come into being.

First of these companies, the Newry & Enniskillen, received its Act of Incorporation on 31st July, 1845 and planned to link the towns of its title via Armagh and Clones, a total distance of 71¾ miles. The scheme was, on the face of it, sound, but it suffered a first jolt when Parliament insisted that the Clones-Enniskillen part should be made first and expenses shared with the Dundalk & Enniskillen whose Act had been passed at the same time.

The early promise of the N&ER soon faded. The area around Newry was peopled by small farmers who suffered greatly in the Potato Famine. Capital accumulated slowly, and it was not until 17th August, 1846 that the first sod was ceremonially cut at Newry. Though the company employed John Godwin, of Queen's College, Belfast, as their consulting engineer, management was based on London, and remoteness fostered inefficiency. Money was wasted in various ways, and although there were no major engineering obstacles, construction proceeded appallingly slowly.

The completion of a 3½ mile stretch to Goraghwood took until August 1853. Its opening had been authorised on 7th January, 1854, but a shortage of rolling stock caused the postponement of services until 1st March, 1854. At last the first train was drawn out of Newry, headed by a Sharp, Stewart 2-2-0WT engine that had come second-hand from the Londonderry & Coleraine. The company's total rolling stock consisted of two engines and three carriages, one of each class.

No goods vehicles had been provided for, and arrangements were made with the D&BJR to work goods traffic into Newry with its own vehicles, from the junction between the two lines at Goraghwood. In the months following the opening, bitter complaints were made by the N&E against the D&BJ's unfair handling of goods services: instead of working them over the N&E the Junction company used its own station at Mullaghglass. This station was then renamed Newry (Armagh Road). The Railway & Canal Traffic Act of 1854 made such obstruction illegal and should have eased the situation. Enmity continued,

Newry Edward Street looking south, 18th April, 1953.   *H.C. Casserley*

DN&G 0-6-0ST No. 2 *Greenore* arrives at Newry Edward Street on 4th June, 1932 with stock for
a train to Greenore. The engine shed is obscured behind the water tank.   *H.C. Casserley*

however, and in 1855 the D&BJ replaced Mullaghglass by another station, called Newry (Main Line), slightly nearer the town and thus even better calculated to attract both goods and passenger traffic.

The delayed opening and the poor receipts of the Newry-Goraghwood fragment combined to deny the shareholders any dividend. Capital amounting to £135,000 had been swallowed up already. The two meetings of shareholders in February and August 1855 were angry ones. At the first, a Mr Anderton asked for the appointment of a committee of investigation to enquire into the company's affairs. Alarmed at this, the chairman, W.F. Spackman of London, managed to postpone judgment by proposing Anderton as auditor. The report which emerged criticised Spackman for illegally making payment to himself for work done on an extension to the Albert Basin in Newry. The excuse that the work had been done personally to save the company £20,000 produced a temporary respite for Spackman. Further criticism, however, emerged from the investigations, and Spackman was forced to resign. On 9th October, the new Chairman, C.A. Lattimore, informed shareholders that certain dubious transactions in the company's shares had been worked by the former Chairman and by his son, W.F. Spackman, Jun., who too conveniently had been engaged as Secretary. It appeared too that much of the unharmonious relationship existing between the N&E and the D&BJR were the direct result of Spackman's behaviour. In an urgent effort to improve matters, Lattimore and the new Secretary, T. Weatherhead, came across from London to meet the D&BJ's management. At this time the liabilities of the N&E totalled £10,874, while their assets were only £3,919.

An improvement in neighbour relationships was reported at the next half-yearly meeting on 28th February, 1856. Meanwhile feverish but unsuccessful efforts were being made to avoid payment awarded to the Ulster Railway after their change of gauge. Competition from the Junction company's new station on the hillside west of Newry was being keenly felt, and it became necessary to bring down fares. The unfortunate shareholders were finally given the astringent information that there could be no foreseeable future for the line as it stood, and that to make it pay it would have to be extended past Goraghwood and on to Armagh. Needless to say the original idea of reaching Enniskillen had long ago been abandoned.

The truth of Lattimore's statement was hammered home a year later, when the net revenue for the second half of 1856 was shown to be £3. As the only possible cure for its troubles the hapless company promoted a Bill, seeking renewal of authority to extend the line to Armagh, to make a link in Newry with the NW&RR, to abandon the Armagh-Enniskillen section, and to alter the name of the company to the Newry & Armagh (N&A). In spite of stiff opposition from the well-established UR and D&BJR, the N&A Act went through on 17th August, 1857. It is interesting to note that safeguards were included against the line passing too close to Armagh Observatory.

The only difficulty lay in the raising of £160,000 of capital. To arouse local support and interest, the Secretary's office was moved from London to Newry. Further rationalisation came by an Act dated 1st August, 1859, whereby the N&A were authorised to make use of part of the Ulster's existing station at Armagh, paying a rental for this facility.

Markethill station on the Newry & Armagh line.   *Charles Friel Collection*

The station at Markethill closed in 1955. By the time of this view (1960) the trackbed had quickly become overgrown.   *Author*

On the extension to Armagh the line passed through some hilly country, and two tunnels were necessary. One of these, at Lissummon, was the longest on any Irish line, 1,759 yards in single bore.

The line was opened to a temporary station in Armagh on 25th August, 1864, and in the following February it was completed to a junction with the Ulster. For the use of the station, the N&A was liable to charges which even today seem rather severe; evidently the Ulster was determined to exact all it could from the unwelcome visitors:

Working of signals	£100 per annum
Services connected with passenger station	£180 per annum
Services connected with goods station	Minerals 2d. per ton
	Other goods 7d. per ton
Use of Ulster Railway main line	£221 10s. per annum
Rent of passenger and goods stations	£233 6s. 8d. per annum

Ten years after completion the amalgamation of the larger companies to form the GNR(I) was imminent. In April 1876 this was accomplished, and the N&A found itself in contact with the same company at each of its termini. The benefits to other lines of absorption did not pass unnoticed. After three more years of precarious existence, during which it ordered an engine from Sharp, Stewart & Co. and was unable to pay for it, the inevitable loss of independence took place. On 30th June, 1879 the Newry & Armagh Railway was acquired by the GNR(I) on payment of £60,000 in cash and the issue of £165,000 of 4 per cent debenture stock.

The little Newry, Warrenpoint & Rostrevor Railway was less ambitious in its beginning. It was originally planned as an 8½ mile line linking the towns named in its title. Its promoters were mainly English, though once started they enlisted local support, and the affairs of the company were administered from headquarters which were initially in London, and from March 1850 in Liverpool. The Act of incorporation was obtained on 27th July, 1846.

As on the N&E, John Godwin was appointed engineer, and after his survey and recommendations had been considered, tenders were received from four contractors. That of £53,000 from William Dargan was accepted. The projected course of the line was level, and although sound foundations were necessary because of its proximity to waterlogged ground, construction presented no engineering problems.

Intake of capital was disappointingly slow, and this determined both the rate of progress and the degree of completeness of furnishings. Delays over land purchase prevented Dargan from starting work until the autumn of 1847, and the line was not finished until the spring of 1849. During that period Dargan had to press the Board for prompt payment on more than one occasion. Thus, in March 1848, he proposed to finish the work by the end of July, subject to being paid at the rate of £7,000 per month. This the Board was unable to do, and on 21st May, 1849, when Dargan attended a meeting of the Board, he informed the Directors that they owed him between £12,000 and £14,000. It says much for his magnanimity and for his confidence in the undertaking that at the same meeting he agreed to accept instead £10,000 in debentures.

Warrenpoint station viewed from the north on 20th July, 1933.   *L&GRP*

Ex-GNR 'PP' class 4-4-0 No. 74 (here renumbered 42) waits to leave Warrenpoint station on 9th June, 1961.   *W.S. Sellar*

The permanent way consisted of bridge rails, bought from the Rhymney Iron Co. and laid on longitudinal Memel pine sleepers. Both these commodities were ordered unnecessarily early. The timber arrived in August 1847 and the first shipment of rails in January 1848. The presence of the timber seems to have been an embarrassment to the Directors, for no sooner had it arrived than they tried to sell it to the Belfast & County Down Railway Co., and that failing, to Dargan himself.

Equally hasty was the ordering of the locomotives; in a burst of exuberance the Board had ordered no less than five from Bury, Curtis & Kennedy on 18th December, 1846. By June 1847, with the line not even begun, Godwin asked the firm to defer delivery. By March 1848, two of the engines were ready for shipment from Liverpool, and it was obvious that though they would not be needed, the company would have to prepare to receive them. After discussion, the makers agreed in April to hold them back for three months for a rent of 8s. 3d. a week, provided that the company paid for one engine and tender immediately and for the other within two months. Bury, Curtis & Kennedy got their payment.

By June 1848 it had become obvious both that the earlier hopes of a double line of track would have to be deferred for lack of money, and that five engines would not be necessary. Mr Chadwick, a Director, was authorised to ask Bury, Curtis & Kennedy to cancel the original agreement in respect of two of the engines. His negotiations were lengthy, for it was not until February 1849 that agreement was finally reached, the company paying Bury a penalty of £700. Although the third engine came in May 1849, payment for it was deferred and Bury's demands for cash were parried until 1854.

At the start of working, in May 1849, the working stock consisted of the three tender engines and three first and five second class carriages. The carriages were made by Wright & Co. of Liverpool. There was as yet no provision for third class passengers or for goods, and it is clear from the minutes that the Board regarded these as of secondary importance, to be dealt with locally at some unspecified date. The Board seem to have been taken aback in October 1848 by a quotation of £350 each for two turntables; Godwin was told, after discussion with the Railway Commissioners, to omit these on economy grounds, and as a result the engines had to run tender-first in one direction.

The finances of the company also dictated policy with regard to the stations; it was proposed to build these by direct labour. On 12th October, 1848, the Board ordered Godwin to provide for a permanent engine house at Newry and temporary passenger stations and goods accommodation there and at Warrenpoint. There is no mention of any sort of construction at Narrow-Water, which later became the only intermediate halt.

In spite of these shortcomings and mistakes, which reflect the inexperience of the Liverpool directorate, the opening of the line on 28th May, 1849 had all the customary triumphal accompaniments. A banquet was held at Warrenpoint, and the band of the 9th Hussars provided a musical background. Hopes were expressed that Warrenpoint would achieve importance as a seaport and that a heavy traffic of summer visitors would develop.

Once the line was open and working, a close watch was kept on the income. The revenue account up to the end of July 1849 showed a credit balance of only £55 13s. 2d. 'Extreme depression in trade' was blamed, and it was decided that

'P' class 4-4-0 No. 89, the former Single, waits to depart from Warrenpoint on 4th June, 1932.
H.C. Casserley

A busy scene as excursionists disembark from their train at Warrenpoint.   *David Lawrence*

better profits would be made if the working was leased. William Dargan was approached in mid-July, and a five-year agreement was concluded with him in October. He agreed to pay the company £50 per week, to divide equally gross receipts in excess of £80 per week, to buy the company's rolling stock at its cost price of £12,000, and to erect permanent station accommodation. As a result, the company was assured of sufficient income to meet debenture payments, for which it required £2,000 per year.

The arrangement with Dargan worked smoothly, and both parties seem to have profited. Towards the end of the five years it became clear, however, that Dargan was not interested in continuing the agreement, and the company advertised for tenders to work the line. In the end they decided to recommence operations on their own. Godwin arbitrated on the value of the rolling stock, and at £6,249 10s. it was taken over by the company. The stations which Dargan had built were valued at £1,583. William Maddison was appointed general superintendent at a salary of £3 per week, plus a bonus of 5 per cent of the surplus of net earnings over £2,600 per year.

Under Maddison's guidance, receipts were satisfactory. There seems to have been some growth of commuter traffic from Warrenpoint into Newry, for in May 1855 season tickets for first class passengers were introduced at £12 for 12 months. Second class seasons followed in August 1856 at £8. Maddison fell ill and became unable to attend to his duties, and he was given three months' notice in June 1858. His place was filled by John Dodds of Southport, who took office under much the same terms of salary as his predecessor.

In June 1852, nearly two years before the N&E began to operate between Edward Street station in Newry and Goraghwood, contact was made between the Boards of the two companies, and consideration was given to the best means of effecting a junction between the two systems. The NW&R, conscious of its isolation, realised that expansion of its traffic could only come if the line was linked to others. Godwin submitted plans and estimates of the junction line to Edward Street, but action on it was anything but precipitate. Neither of the interested companies had money to spend, and since the line had to cross the Newry Canal there were lengthy negotiations with the Newry Navigation Company, who had more to lose than to gain by any railway extension. The change of management and name of the N&E assisted matters, but it was not until 1857 that Parliamentary permission could be obtained to build the Town of Newry Connecting Railway. Messrs Greene & King built the ¾ mile link at a cost of £12,700, and it was opened on 2nd September, 1861.

For the next 20 years the NW&R worked its line unspectacularly but with a moderate degree of success. Warrenpoint never attained the importance of Newry as a port, and the opening of rail connection from Newry to Greenore in 1873 must have ended any hopes of cross-channel trading. Nevertheless the amalgamation of 1876 passed the NW&R by. Profits in the early 1880s were only averaging around £30 per week, and in October 1885 the company approached the Board of the GNR(I) with a view to merging. The complete undertaking was sold for £54,000, a sum that must have seemed small to many of the proprietors, for capital outlay had been nearly £160,000. The amalgamation was completed by the passage of the necessary Act on 4th June, 1886.

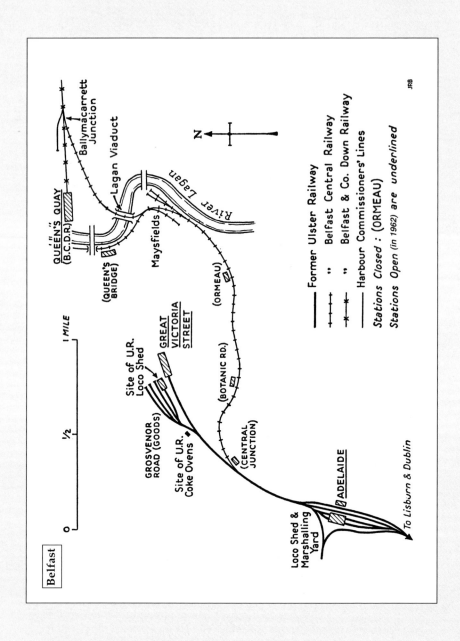

Belfast

0   ½   1 MILE

Loco Shed & Marshalling Yard

ADELAIDE

To Lisburn & Dublin

(CENTRAL JUNCTION)

(BOTANIC RD.)

Site of U.R. Coke Ovens

GROSVENOR ROAD (GOODS)

Site of U.R. Loco Shed

GREAT VICTORIA STREET

(ORMEAU)

Maysfields

River Lagan

(QUEEN'S BRIDGE)

QUEEN'S QUAY (B.C.D.R.)

Lagan Viaduct

Ballymacarrett Junction

N

JRB

—— Former Ulster Railway
—+++— " " Belfast Central Railway
—×××— " " Belfast & Co. Down Railway
—∗∗∗— Harbour Commissioners' Lines

Stations Closed : (ORMEAU)

Stations Open (in 1962) are underlined

Chapter Eight

The Belfast Central Railway

Initiated by a group of London gentlemen, the Belfast Central was incorporated by an Act of Parliament on 25th July, 1864. The intention was to connect the lines of the Ulster, the Belfast & Northern Counties, and the Belfast & County Down companies to a central station in the city. The site of the station was to be between High Street and Waring Street, with a frontage on Victoria Street. The scheme would have entailed the building of 5¾ miles of line. Capital was fixed at £300,000, with loans to £100,000.

Within a year Joseph Thornton had started construction. A second Act was obtained on 5th July, 1865, giving the company powers to make tramways on the quays on the east side of the River Lagan. In spite of this enterprise, however, money was slow to come in, and by 1866 Thornton had only built the part between the Ormeau Road and the Albert Bridge, too short to be of any practical use.

Negotiations for the projected central station site apparently fell through, for we next find the company, under an Act dated 31st July, 1868, getting authority to make the central station on a site occupied by the corporation's Pork Market. Extra capital was allowed and an extension of time to 1873. The original plan called for a single bridge across the river to the Belfast & County Down Railway, but by 1868 the scheme had expanded and a second bridge was proposed, allowing through running between the County Down and the Northern Counties lines. It is of interest that this triangular layout at the river crossing, though never built, was shown in a city map in a tourist *Guide to Belfast*, published in 1875 by A. & C. Black.

The elaboration of the company's plans did not stimulate the gathering of the necessary funds. The line was still unfinished and unworkable when the company became 'embarrassed in their affairs' and one financial crisis began to follow another. The company had defaulted on payment of a large loan from the Public Works Commissioners; it owed money for land taken over; and it had not paid Thornton for all his contract work. James Hutt, the Secretary, took an action against his employers to recover unpaid salary, and the Board of Directors resigned. New control resulted, and by a fourth Act of Parliament, dated 6th August, 1872, the works were forced forward. The new Board appointed Telford MacNeill, the son of Sir John MacNeill, as engineer.

The original plan had been severely pruned. No connection with the Northern Counties line was ever made except over dock lines; the central station was never built on either of its suggested sites; and the Lagan remained spanned by a single railway bridge. The Central's line started from its junction with the Ulster Railway, ⅖ mile out from the Great Victoria Street terminus; it circled below the Donegall and Lisburn Roads, Botanic Avenue, and Ormeau Road, to run by the west bank of the river before plunging below East Bridge Street some way west of the Albert Bridge. The facing points of the junction lay ahead, and the main line ran to a terminus on the west side of Oxford Street. To the right, the branch crossed the river and joined the County Down line. Neither the Belfast & County Down nor the Great Northern had supported the Central scheme, seeing nothing in it for themselves. So, as the line was eventually made, Central trains could only enter the neighbouring companies' termini by reversal, too time-consuming to be workable. The Central had to be satisfied with its own terminal stations, one at the junction with the Ulster at the Donegall Road bridge, the other at Oxford Street and named Queen's Bridge. Of the former, nothing now remains, but Queen's Bridge station remained as a rather mean, single-storey, stone building in use as railway offices until its demolition in 1960. Between the two there were two intermediate stations: Botanic Road (renamed Windsor) and Ormeau. Like much of the line, both were in cuttings below the level of the adjacent roadway.

The line was opened for traffic in 1875, no less than 10 years after the start of construction. Apart from its failure to unite the lines of the three major companies and provide a useful central station in the city, the fate of the Central was sealed by the start of street tramway operations. On 28th August, 1872, a service of single-deck horse-drawn tramcars, belonging to the Belfast Street Tramway Company, began to operate. Using 5 ft 3 in. gauge track, later narrowed to 4 ft 8½ in., they first worked from Castle Place to the Botanic Gardens. The tramway company prospered and gave the public what they had been waiting for. By 1878, its lines had extended to the Antrim and the Ormeau Roads, and in general a half-hourly service was run. The shuttle service on the circumscribed Central Railway had less to offer its customers.

In 1879, the Central Railway built its short tunnel from north of Queen's Bridge station, under the western end of the bridge itself and out on to Donegall Quay, where it joined the lines of the Belfast Harbour Commissioners. Then, before the impact of the trams was really felt, the company had its last fling. By an Act of 1880, plans were approved for extensions on the 3 ft gauge, mainly around the western periphery of the expanding city and crossing the Springfield, Shankhill, and Falls Roads. A third rail was to be laid on the standard gauge Central line. Then in the following year, authorisation was given for the 3 ft gauge lines of the High Holywood Railway and the Ballyclare, Ligoniel & Belfast Junction Railway, both of them supported by the Central and opposed by the BCDR and its neighbour the Belfast, Holywood & Bangor Railway, and also by the Great Northern. Capital was not forthcoming, and these narrow gauge city lines were never built. The plans were later formally abandoned.

The heaviest passenger traffic on the Belfast Central amounted to 17 or 18 trains each way. The journey time was 8 to 10 minutes. Fares were 2*d*. single, 4*d*. return first class, 1½*d*. and 2*d*. third class.

By 1884 it was clear to the disappointed and unremunerated shareholders that an independent future offered no promise. The Great Northern was approached, as the only likely purchaser, and in due course an Act was obtained dated 6th August, 1885, sanctioning transfer. The purchase price was £227,000, of which £100,000 went to repay the Public Works Commissioners' loan. Once under Great Northern control, passenger traffic was terminated on 30th November, 1885. Thereafter the line became a useful goods appendage to the Great Northern, with the County Down and the Northern Counties paying £1,600 and £500 a year respectively for the transfer facilities which it offered. Occasional passenger specials were worked between the County Down and Great Northern lines across the Lagan bridge, permitting through running from Bangor to Dublin.

The whole Belfast Central Railway section was, however, run down in UTA days, and was closed to all traffic between 1965 and 1976, when the line was totally refurbished and Belfast Central station and a station named Botanic opened. City Hospital followed in 1986, and in 1995 a new station was created, partly on the site of the old Great Victoria Street terminus, including a new curve on to the former Central Railway.

Belfast Queen's Bridge station, closed to passenger traffic in 1885 and seen here on 5th October, 1959. Queen's Bridge tunnel is visible in the distance. The buildings that dominate the skyline are in Oxford Street.   *Author*

Chapter Nine

Amalgamation

The process of amalgamation was thought of as early as 1847, when the Meath branch of the D&BJR was transferred to D&D ownership. The Act of Parliament necessary to effect that change gave the D&D Company in addition powers 'to amalgamate with the Belfast Junction, the Ulster, and the Dundalk & Enniskillen Companies whenever circumstances may render such a step desirable'. Freedom of action was highly prized among these young companies, and 28 years elapsed before any of them relinquished their independence.

Amalgamation was again discussed in 1868, when delegates from the various Boards of Directors in fact got some way towards resolution of the problems. The Ulster members, unwilling to see their prospering line linked to its weaker neighbours on the south and west, remained obdurate. The next move came in 1873, when application was made by the D&D for a regranting of their powers of amalgamation. This was given in due course. The proprietors of the D&D and the D&BJR resolved, at special meetings held on 27th February, 1875, to merge their two companies, and the decision became effective from 1st March, 1875. Thus was formed the short-lived Northern Railway Co. (Ireland). The stock and share capital of the less powerful Junction company was reduced by 22½ per cent in the process.

The first return of working stock of the Northern showed a total of 42 engines and 38 tenders. Coaching stock included 16 first, 15 second, 38 third class, and 22 first and second composites; in addition there were 22 luggage and mail vans, 2 Post Office sorting vans, 22 horse-boxes, and 22 carriage trucks. Merchandise stock consisted of 592 vehicles. During the first half of 1875 passenger and mixed trains ran 284,000 miles and goods trains 98,000 miles. The senior officials virtually maintained their status quo and managed Southern and Northern Divisions of the new company. A further stage was completed when the INWR joined the Northern Railway on 1st January, 1876. The capital of that shaky concern was heavily depreciated in the process. Ordinary shares were reduced from £30 to £5, and preference shares and stock by 50 per cent, but at least the proprietors could look forward to a steady dividend.

Though professedly aloof, the Ulster was now taking steps to join its forces with the others. As we have seen, the undertaking of the PD&OJR became absolutely vested in the Ulster Company on 1st January, 1876, in terms of an Act passed in the previous Parliamentary session. At its final half-yearly meeting, held at 1 pm on 29th February, 1876, the Ulster declared the usual robust dividend of 7½ per cent; at 2 pm there followed a special extraordinary general meeting at which approval was asked for, and obtained, to join with the Northern Railway Co. and to form as a result the Great Northern Railway Co. (Ireland). The amalgamation took effect on 1st April, 1876. The proprietors' capital did well out of the deal, for the Ulster's ordinary stock was assigned a premium of £24 10s. per cent.

At the same time as they joined forces, the Northern and Ulster companies were able to keep a wary eye on possible competition. The Imperial Credit Co. of London was attempting to promote the 'Northern Union Railways of Ireland' Bill, to make a line which would commence with a junction with the Belfast Central and proceed by Lisburn and Knockmore to Lawrencetown, between Banbridge and Scarva. The Northern and Ulster Boards successfully opposed the Bill on the grounds that the towns and districts concerned were already fully supplied with railway accommodation.

During the short life of the Northern, the Dublin North Wall extension was started, joining the line with the quayside station of North Wall owned by the London & North Western. The extension also joined the lines of the Great Southern & Western and the Midland Great Western.

The fusion of the companies into the Northern Railway (I) and the GNR(I) swelled the size of the board of Directors. The Northern board numbered first 16, then 18. With the incoming of the Ulster the total rose to an almost unmanageable 29. It took 10 years for this assembly to shrink down to a more manageable dozen.

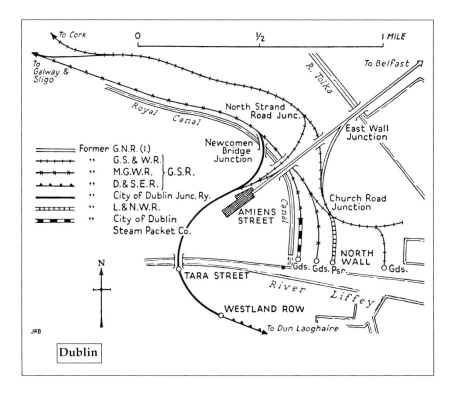

A view, looking north, of a rather forlorn Coalisland station on the Cookstown branch on 22nd July, 1962. The signal cabin is a modern replacement after a malicious attack.   *Author*

A view along the platform from the buffers at Cookstown on 29th December, 1955. In the platform we see an ex-steam railmotor and another bread container.   *Author*

Chapter Ten

The Great Northern Years

As might be expected from its origin, unification of control of the GNR(I) was inevitably slow. For 13 years there were three managers, each with separate jurisdiction, and the first General Manager was not appointed until 1890.

On the civil engineering side, the five senior members of the staff continued their separate tasks: Harty of the old D&D down in Dublin, Greenhill of the INWR and M'Cartan of the D&BJ in Dundalk, Atkinson of the Ulster in Belfast, and Glenny of the L&E at Enniskillen. Rationalisation came in 1877 when the austere William H. Mills was charged with the sole responsibility. The division of management in the locomotive department is referred to in Chapter Twelve. It came to an end with the retiral of John Eaton from his Ulster chieftainship in 1885. Even a unification of engine livery had to wait until he had gone.

Although the INWR had ceased to exist, the new company was immediately faced with the problem of how to treat traffic receipts from the Londonderry-Enniskillen section. This was still the property of the L&ER Co., and they were entitled to a rent, a part of which was contingent on the gross receipts of the INWR. To continue this contingent rent it would have been necessary to keep separate account of the earnings of the Irish North section of the GNR(I), and differences might have arisen as to diversion of traffic from it via the Portadown route. The Great Northern agreed to pay the L&E a rent of £32,500 for 1876, and to increase this by £100 a year until the maximum rent of £33,000 was reached. This arrangement continued until 1883, when the L&E promoted a Bill for amalgamation with the GNR(I).

In 1874, the Ulster and the PD&OJR companies had together promoted the Dungannon & Cookstown Railway Co. Construction proceeded during the period of amalgamation and was still incomplete when the Great Northern bought out the concern in 1877.

The three railways converging on Banbridge were also dealt with in 1877. The Ulster-leased Banbridge, Lisburn & Belfast Railway, and the D&BJ's Banbridge Junction Railway, came naturally under the aegis of the GNR(I) and ceased to exist as separate concerns. The Banbridge Junction must have disappointed its shareholders; it had cost £57,300 to build but was sold for only £3,350. The unfortunate Banbridge Extension Railway, which had lain unfinished for 12 years, was given a fresh lease of life. Due to delay in the completion of legal arrangements, work did not start on further construction until the second half of 1879. The expenditure of £41,000 saw the line finished, and traffic began to work to Ballyroney on 14th December, 1880. Completion of the scheme gave access into the heart of agricultural County Down, but so long as Ballyroney remained the terminus the line did not carry heavy traffic.

The working arrangement between the Dublin & Antrim Junction Railway and the Ulster was carried into Great Northern days, but it expired on 2nd November, 1878. As the Antrim Junction had failed to repay a loan from the Public Works Loan Commissioners, this body proposed to take possession of

Inniskeen, the junction for the Carrickmacross branch (*left*) on 31st July, 1958.   *Author*

Carrickmacross station.   *Real Photographs*

the undertaking. To keep the line open for public use, the GNR(I) took a temporary lease. The line was publicly auctioned on 24th January, 1879, and with only the Belfast & Northern Counties as a possible competitor, it was bought by the GNR(I) for £70,000. A further appendage had been tidied up. Later in the same year, the long awaited Dungannon-Cookstown section was completed, and it was opened for traffic on 28th July, 1879.

The Newry & Armagh entered the combine in 1879, and some six years later there followed the NW&R and the Belfast Central. Out to the west, the Enniskillen, Bundoran & Sligo Railway continued to be worked by the Great Northern for 15 years after the 1876 amalgamation. The proposed purchase of the Bundoran branch naturally appealed to the GNR(I) Board, when they were at last approached. Rather complicated legal difficulties over the ownership of the land delayed the transfer. It took until 1897 for the affair to be regularised, and the branch was then handed over to the GN for a payment of £87,877, a poor enough return to the shareholders, who had sunk £429,000 in their venture.

While the surrounding concerns were being gathered in, the Great Northern began to look around for sites for profitable branches. The company obtained an Act in 1881 which revived the long awaited Belturbet branch west of the Clones-Cavan line, and authorised as well a branch to Carrickmacross, a short way south of the Irish North line. The branches diverged at Ballyhaise and at Inniskeen. In both cases land purchase went through slowly and delayed the start of contract work for over two years. The Belturbet line was opened on 29th June, 1885, and that to Carrickmacross on 31st July, 1886.

In Co. Louth, an independent scheme to build a steam tramway from Dundalk to Ardee was opposed by the Great Northern in 1884. Seven years later the latter promoted a Bill for the construction of a branch joining Ardee with the main line at Dromin. The Act was passed on 27th June, 1892, and the short branch was opened for both passenger and goods traffic on 1st August, 1896.

The station frontage at Ardee on 28th July, 1960.   *Author*

At the southern end of the system, the City of Dublin Junction Railways were promoted by the Dublin, Wicklow & Wexford Railway (DW&W), to join its Westland Row terminus with the GNR(I) at Amiens Street. The Bill went through on 28th July, 1884. The direct, and inevitably expensive, route lay across the River Liffey, and joined GNR(I), Great Southern & Western Railway (GS&WR) and MGWR rails. The raising of capital was difficult, and assistance that was expected from the GS&W and the MGW failed to materialise. The cost was therefore largely borne by the DW&W, the GNR(I), and the City of Dublin Steam Packet Co. On its completion and opening on 1st May, 1891, through traffic became possible between Kingstown Pier and Belfast, and with good rail connections at both ends of the short sea crossing, more rapid transmission of English mails to the north of Ireland immediately resulted.

The tragedy of the Armagh disaster in June 1889 overshadowed the developments of the years that followed it. Apart from the heavy compensation, which the company met out of revenue, the legislation that ensued required the company, as it did all other British railways, to modernise their vehicle braking and to install block signalling and the interlocking of points and signals.

Apart from strengthening of their engineering and operating functions, changes took place in the rather diffuse management. The traffic manager involved in the Armagh accident, Thomas Cowan, was ordered to resign by the Board on 23rd November, 1889 and compensated financially by being salaried to the end of the following year. Further changes in personnel followed swiftly. Thomas Shaw, who had managed the Ulster Railway and had been manager of the Northern Division, resigned on an annuity. The Secretary, J.P. Culverwell, retired after 43 years' faithful service with the D&D, Northern, and GNR(I) companies and was generously superannuated. In his place was appointed Henry Plews, who had spent 23 years as manager of the North-Western Division at Enniskillen. It then became possible to cease working as three divisions and to appoint a General Manager. On 27th March, 1890, the Board received a letter from Thomas Robertson, superintendent of the line on the Highland Railway, accepting the general managership. From Scotland the management was further reinforced by John W. Philp, who left the North British to become goods manager. Then, after an association that had lasted 42 years, the sudden death of James W. Murland on 20th May, 1890 left the chairmanship vacant.

Murland's place was taken by James Gray, who had been deputy Chairman since 1878. In spite of these taxing problems and changes, the Board decided at their November 1890 meeting to order the cushioning of some third class carriages, hitherto bare board seats. Initially they attended to carriages used on the main line trains to Belfast and to Derry, as the minute put it 'at competitive points with other companies'.

By 12th August, 1891, Plews was able to report to the proprietors:

> The Block Telegraph wires have been erected on 329 miles of your line; Block Signal Instruments have also been fixed on 125 miles, which mileage is now completed and worked on the Block Telegraph System. The points and signals have already been interlocked at a large number of stations, and the whole of the Passenger Engines, and about three-fourths of the Carriage Stock, have already been fitted with the Automatic Vacuum Brake.

As an antidote to this satisfying statement, at the same meeting the Revd Mr Hunter of Knock, Belfast, moved the resolution 'that all Sunday traffic on this Railway be discontinued, save the running of one Passenger Train each way, at ordinary fares'. It was as well that the company had a strong management. Two years later the work of electrical block signalling was complete on the main line and branches.

To the west of Strabane the wide valley of the River Finn, reaching towards the Donegal mountains, had been linked by rail with the east through the Finn Valley Railway. This company opened the 13½ mile line from Strabane to Stranorlar on 7th September, 1863 on the 5 ft 3 in. gauge. At the Strabane end, it joined the L&E line, 30 chains south of Strabane station, which was shared.

From the start the Finn Valley was worked under lease by the Irish North. After 10 years, a fresh contract was made whereby the Irish North supplied engine power but the FV owned the carriages and wagons. This arrangement was continued into Great Northern days.

The extension of the Finn Valley's line to other parts of Donegal was inhibited by the poor receipts from the Stranorlar-Strabane part. The country was agricultural and far from thickly populated, and it seemed that a narrow gauge line would have more prospect of success. So on 21st July, 1879, with the two lines out of Ballymena, Co. Antrim, as models,* the West Donegal Railway Co. was empowered to make a 3 ft gauge line from Stranorlar to Donegal town. After the mountainous traverse of Barnesmore Gap, there was insufficient money to get the line beyond Druminin, reached on 25th April, 1882. It took state assistance to complete it to Donegal, four miles farther, by 16th September, 1889.

The Finn Valley, seeking a way out of its financial troubles, had become involved to the extent of £2,000 a year to the West Donegal, a charity that was to prove its undoing. The West Donegal was even less prosperous than the Finn Valley, and in an effort to improve matters, the two merged by an Act of 27th June, 1892 to form the Donegal Railway Company (DR). Stranorlar, in the middle of the system, had broad gauge out to the east and narrow to the west. It became more apparent than ever that the future of the DR lay in narrow gauge working. State aid from a paternal Government in London had furnished the narrow gauge lines from Donegal to Killybegs in 1893 and from Stranorlar up the upper Finn Valley to Glenties in 1895. Steps were taken to get rid of their broad gauge and to bring the Finn Valley section into line with the rest of the undertaking. On principle, the Great Northern opposed the change of gauge, since it would mean the end of its profitable working up to Stranorlar. The Donegal prepared the way for the change by making a separate station alongside the GNR(I) at Strabane, and regauged the whole of the old Finn Valley section during the weekend of Friday 13th July to Sunday 15th July, 1894. The modest carriage and wagon stock off the Finn Valley section was sold at a round figure to the Dublin, Wicklow & Wexford Railway; £1,000 was received for five carriages, a horse box, a carriage truck, 23 covered wagons, and four open wagons.

After 31 years, the association of the Donegal line with its broad gauge partner at Strabane was broken, but only 12 more years were to pass before the

---

* The Ballymena, Cushendall & Red Bay Railway and the Ballymena & Larne Railway, incorporated in 1872 and 1874.

tottering finances of the DR caused it to sell out and the Great Northern became a joint owner of the concern along with the Midland Railway (of England). The new owners agreed to extinguish Treasury and local liabilities, and from 1st May, 1906 the lines were controlled by the County Donegal Railways Joint Committee, with six Directors, three from each owning company.

Although the Great Northern must have hoped that its purchase of the Belfast Central would have ended competitive aspirations in the city, its fears were reawakened in 1892, when a London finance company lodged 'The Belfast City Central Station & Railways Bill'. This line, in so far as it would have affected the Great Northern, was to run from a junction about half a mile from Great Victoria Street across town to Smithfield, where a central station was to be built. The Great Northern's terminus would have been closed. Naturally enough, the Great Northern feared the scheme and took steps to oppose it; much to its relief, the Bill was rejected at the committee stage.

With the Midland Great Western Railway fringing the Great Northern to the south, it is hardly surprising that relations between the two were not always amicable. The MGWR was working the Dublin & Meath and Navan & Kingscourt's lines north to Kingscourt from 1875, and the terminus there remained a latent spearhead pointing to the soft underbelly of the Great Northern. Plews made a masterly understatement to the proprietors on 24th January, 1894: 'The Directors regard with feelings of regret the promotion by the Midland Great Western Company of this line', for the Midland had lodged a Bill to extend its line from Kingscourt to no less a target than Cookstown, by way of Armagh and Dungannon. Needless to say, the GN was prepared to oppose the passage of the Bill. It did not however get to that length, and after discussion the MGWR agreed to keep to its own territory, the GN doing likewise.

The peace of Kingscourt was short-lived. The Midland promised substantial financial backing to a concern styled the Kingscourt, Keady & Armagh Railway (KK&A), whose Bill went through Parliament in mid-1900 in spite of Great Northern opposition. The Great Northern had earlier expressed its intention to build an Armagh-Keady line and had seen its own Armagh-Castleblayney Bill rejected by Parliament in 1900. Presented now with an unpalatable *fait accompli*, they took the only course open to them and came to terms with the newly-formed KK&A company. After discussion it was agreed that the Kingscourt to Castleblayney section would not be built, thus preventing physical connection with the MGWR system. The company would be restyled the Castleblayney, Keady & Armagh (CK&A), the Great Northern would obtain a measure of control by subscribing £50,000 towards it, and it would work the line for 50 per cent of the gross receipts. The route was modified to conform to the Great Northern's wishes. The necessary further legislation was passed in the 1902 session of Parliament, and the last meeting of the KK&A Board was held in the Queen's Hotel, Chester, on 7th July.

On 27th October, 1902 the Directors of the CK&A held their first meeting in the Hotel Victoria, Northumberland Avenue, London. The association of the Great Northern with the CK&A was an expensive one; a second Act in 1903 increased the capital to be subscribed by the Great Northern by a further £300,000. Such was the price paid to secure independence from the Midland.

Keady station looking south. *Locomotive Publishing Co.*

Robert Worthington, described as the Dargan of the 1880s, obtained the CK&A contract and began work on the construction in 1903. After the usual optimistic start, under the supervision of the CK&A's Engineer, Sir Benjamin Baker, things went disappointingly slowly, and successive reports to the shareholders merely referred to 'steady' or 'fair' progress. The course of the line was to bring it over a summit 613 feet above sea level, which was probably the highest reached by a standard gauge line in Ireland; stretches of peat bog lay between rock cuttings; and on the northern slope towards Armagh were three major engineering works: the stone viaducts at Milford, Tassagh (11 arches), and Keady (7 arches). Worthington seems to have had a maximum of seven engines at work, but he fell so far behind schedule that in May 1908 the exasperated company took over his plant and works, including two engines *Molly* and *Kells*, and finished the construction themselves. The eight miles from Armagh to Keady were opened on 31st May, 1909. Shortly afterwards, *Molly* burst her boiler near Keady. The remaining 10¼ miles from Keady to Castleblayney were opened on 10th November, 1910. In the following year the nominal independence of the CK&A company came to an end with its vesting in the parent company. *Kells*, and another engine, *Mullingar*, which had also been Worthington's, became part of the GNR(I) engine stock in 1913.

In contrast to their fencing in the Armagh region, the GNR(I) and the MGWR were able to achieve a measure of collaboration in 1894 over the proposed purchase of the Sligo, Leitrim & Northern Counties Railway, an independent concern which owed money to the Board of Trade and was being offered for sale. The Sligo-Leitrim line was to be divided at Manorhamilton, where its works were situated. Negotiations failed, however, and the line remained independent until its closure in 1958.

0-6-0T Mullingar, GNR No. 204 (ex-R. Worthington, contractor) is seen crossing Keady viaduct.
Charles Friel Collection

Tassagh viaduct on 24th July, 1960.   *Author*

In February 1896, Robertson resigned from the general managership. The prosperity of the company was now at its peak, and a wise selection was undoubtedly made when Henry Plews was appointed to follow Robertson. Plews remained in that position until his retirement in November 1911, when he was co-opted a member of the Board of Directors.

The effect of the growing street tramway system in Belfast has been noticed in connection with the Belfast Central line. The last quarter of the 19th century saw the steady extension of the Belfast system, warily watched by the railway companies. Then in 1897 the Belfast Street Tramways, attempting to extend its lines out to Finaghy, came into conflict with the Great Northern. The railway company formally objected to the extension, and permission for it was refused by the Privy Council.

At the southern end of its line, the Great Northern was planning to improve access to the Hill of Howth by means of a tramway, thereby opening up the Hill for housing development and increasing the suburban traffic. Formal assent was given to the Bill on 6th August, 1897. The Hill of Howth tramway was laid to standard gauge, but owing to the severe gradients the use of steam-hauled trains was never considered, and traffic was run by electric tramcars. A power house was built at Sutton, its tall chimney forming a distinctive landmark. As might have been expected, there was some opposition and delay in connection with the purchase of the land, and the building of the line turned out to be considerably more expensive than the original estimate. The total cost was slightly over £100,000.

The tramway was opened from Sutton to the summit of the Hill on 17th June, 1901, and from the summit to Howth on 1st August, 1901. The total stock consisted of 10 tramcars and a service vehicle. Over the 5¼ mile loop, the annual tramcar mileage was generally between 80 and 90 thousand, but the variations outside this range are interesting. The maximum annual mileage was in 1930-2, when it was 124,000, and although the trade depression of 1933 is reflected in the sharp fall that year to 84,000, the following year saw a recovery, and from 1934 until 1941 the total remained above 110,000 miles. World War I produced a much greater fall in mileage than the 1939-45 conflict, and the minimum of 49,000 miles was recorded in 1919.

Viewed independently, the Howth tramway was a financial failure, and in the years before its closure anything between £10,000 and £14,000 were lost annually in its working. Whether or not the losses could be equated with its latent value as a feeder to the busy suburban train services to Sutton and Howth, it is difficult to judge.

As we have seen, workings on the Banbridge-Ballyroney branch began in 1880. After nearly 20 years, the logical extension of the line to the east coast of County Down caused the Great Northern and the Belfast & County Down companies simultaneously to put forward schemes. The Great Northern, as prime mover, planned to make a line to Newcastle, a tourist centre which had expanded largely as a result of the County Down company's efforts. In self-defence, the County Down retaliated, seeking to bridge the rail gap itself and to get running powers over the GN as far as Scarva, where the main line traffic would be tapped. It was decided to resolve the situation by sharing the building

Tramcars Nos. 3 and 4 stand outside the Hill of Howth Tramway shed at Sutton on 19th March, 1959.
R.M. Casserley

Tramcar No. 4 departs Sutton on 18th March, 1959. The GNR Howth branch can be seen on the right.
Brian Hilton

Castlewellan station *c.*1930, looking towards Banbridge. *Stations UK*

of the line, the two extensions meeting at Castlewellan. Running powers were granted to the Great Northern from there into Newcastle, which was just what it had hoped for; the running powers which the County Down obtained took it only to Ballyroney, a fair enough compensation on a mileage basis, but being useless from the aspect of traffic, they were never exercised.

Towards the end of the 19th century the Great Northern began to interest itself in the accommodation of tourists, in addition to their transportation. Since an improvement in the standard of hotel accommodation in selected resorts would contribute indirectly to traffic receipts, the company gave financial assistance for some years to four hotels. One was in Bundoran, at the western extremity of the system, while the Beach Hotel at Warrenpoint and the Mourne and Woodside Hotels at Rostrevor were close to the picturesque Carlingford Lough on the eastern seaboard.

In 1899 the Great Northern bought these hotels outright, and in the next few years spent over £50,000 in modernising them. The Mourne Hotel at Rostrevor and the Warrenpoint and Bundoran Hotels were renamed 'Great Northern'. After a few years the Woodside was sold, and in 1922 disposal of the Warrenpoint Hotel brought in £11,332 to the company's capital assets. The Bundoran and Rostrevor hotels together continued to provide a high standard of accommodation.

The Bundoran Hotel was requisitioned by the military authorities from 3rd December, 1914 until 1st January, 1915. During this short occupation the building appears to have suffered something more than hob-nail marks on the polished floors, for the company received £277 compensation for billeting and £100 as compensation for damage. After the 1920 season, the hotel was closed

Mr Neill's long car for Kilkeel outside the Mourne Hotel, Rostrevor, 22nd July, 1897.

L.J. Watson

The Great Northern Hotel and golf links, Bundoran.   *Charles Friel Collection*

until Easter 1924 to allow it to be extensively rebuilt and improved. During this period the golf course was kept open as a tourist attraction.

The hotel venture promised well, and in 1902 the company's catering department became responsible for the station refreshment rooms and the dining cars, which until then had been leased. From 1912 until 1921 all the three activities were again leased, but the income which resulted was only around £1,000 per annum, a poor return for the capital investment which they represented. Working on its own account after 1921, the company was able to depend most years on an income of around £4,000 from this side of the business. The attraction of hotel meals during the rationing of World War II produced a spectacular rise in the profits, which totalled almost £29,000 in 1943.

The joint ownership with the Midland of the former Donegal Railway from 1906 has been mentioned. At the time of the vesting, there was under construction a branch to the old DR, destined to be the last passenger-carrying narrow gauge line to be built in Ireland. The owning company was an independent concern, named at first the Strabane, Raphoe & Convoy Railway Co., and later the Strabane & Letterkenny Railway Co., and it arranged for the line to be worked by the joint committee on a mileage basis. This arrangement continued until the end of 1959, when the line was closed along with the remainder of this narrow gauge system.

The healthy state of the traffic around the turn of the century is evidenced by the decision to double parts of the long single-track line between Portadown and Derry. The 10½ miles between Portadown Junction and Trew & Moy were doubled between 1899 and 1902, St Johnstown to Londonderry followed in 1902-7, and finally the shorter Dungannon-Donaghmore section was done in 1905-6. These works cost £38,000, £61,000 and £11,900 respectively.

Traffic working at the Belfast end was eased in 1907-8 by laying a 'third road' north of the down main as far out as Balmoral. Then close to Adelaide, 60 acres of marshy land forming part of the Bog Meadows were bought and after much filling used to accommodate a marshalling yard and a locomotive depot. The latter, with nine roads and able to hold 55 engines, cost £40,000 to construct and replaced the old Ulster shed close to the Belfast terminus. Withdrawal of engines from Belfast out to the new Adelaide depot took place in March 1911.

Evidence of the intention to extend the 'third road' out to Lisburn or beyond is shown by the three-arch masonry bridges built about this time, at Finaghy and on the site of the Lisburn-Ballinderry road level crossing. Due to war, and the changes which came after it, the scheme was not carried out. Other minor improvements may be briefly recalled: passing places made at Maguiresbridge (1904) and Dromore Road and Katesbridge (1905), halts for the railmotors at Derriaghy, Finaghy, and Hilden (1907), a fruit siding at Richhill (1911), wagon shops at Dundalk (1912), and a line from Barrack Street to the quays (1913). The Maysfields lairages on the Belfast Central line were laid out in 1913-4. A quarry was opened in grey granite on the hill scarp west of Goraghwood station in February 1911; its crushing plant put through around 50,000 cubic yards of stone for ballast each year, and the clean, sparkling product came to distinguish the Great Northern permanent way. To teem the ballast, Dundalk made new hopper wagons and plough vans.

In the spring of 1911 some interesting data on coal consumption was obtained when an interchange of engines took place with the Great Southern & Western Railway. The locomotives involved were GNR 'QL' class 4-4-0 No. 113 *Neptune* and GS&WR '321' class 4-4-0 No. 322. *Neptune* was shown to burn about 10 per cent less coal per mile than its rival.

Coal economy was soon to exercise the minds of the management in a less pleasing way; in 1912 a British miners' strike held up supplies and dislocated trade. By drawing on its own stocks, built up the previous winter, the Great Northern kept all important trains running. The ultimate result of the strike was, naturally, a sharp rise in coal costs, and in four years the locomotive fuel bill trebled.

Labour troubles within the company itself led to strikes in August, September and October 1911. Serious loss in traffic resulted, and the resulting expenses cost the company £8,800. In the following year, the rates of pay and conditions of service were considerably improved. In April of the same year, after about 50 years' service, Charles Clifford resigned his office as locomotive superintendent and was succeeded by George T. Glover who had been with the North Eastern Railway at Gateshead. Clifford died on 5th September, 1927.

The onset of war in 1914 saw the company at the height of its strength under the general managership of John Bagwell. Rolling stock, buildings, and permanent way were all in good condition, and the financial state of the company was sound. Four years of war affected the company as it did many others, and depletion of staffs, rising costs, and shortages of raw materials created their difficulties. For over two years the company worked as best it could under the prevailing conditions. Then on 22nd December, 1916, an Order in Council placed all the Irish railways under the control of the Government as from midnight on 31st December, 1916.

The main features of control were that the company received no direct payment for such Government services as naval and army transport, while the Government on the other hand guaranteed to the company the same net earnings as those of 1913. The control continued long into the ensuing peace, and the line was not handed back to the company until 17th August, 1921. Lengthy negotiations had taken place, as a result of which the Government paid a cash sum as compensation for arrears of maintenance. The Irish railways received a sum of £3 million, free of income tax, in full discharge of all claims which they might have made.

The Great Northern was faced with the urgent and complex task of overdue rehabilitation of rolling stock and permanent way. The task was difficult enough, but its accomplishment was complicated by the current Irish political troubles.

British rule in Ireland was grinding to a halt, and after years of strife, the country was declared in 1921 to be self-governing. Twenty-six counties formed the Irish Free State, with Dublin its capital; the remaining six counties grouped around Belfast constituted Northern Ireland. Internal tension and violence continued after the political division, and a state of civil war continued into 1923.

Arising out of 'the Troubles' the company suffered malicious damage and interference on numerous occasions. These took the form of derailments of trains, ambushes, raids on stations and trains, and seizures of mails. The detailed story of these attacks and the ways by which the company protected its property and passengers has yet to be told. Incidents small and large continued almost daily for nearly four years, yet throughout this time the company managed to give a remarkably good service under conditions of stress which no railway in Great Britain ever experienced. Even John Bagwell was kidnapped, though not because he was the General Manager, but on account of his position as a member of the Senate of the newly-constituted Government of the Free State. Some of the major incidents are listed in Appendix Three.

An explosion at Amiens Street on 28th April, 1923 seems to have signalled the end of sabotage, so far as it affected the Great Northern, and the company should have been able to start on a much-needed programme of rehabilitation. But the creation of an inter-state border the previous year had immediate repercussions on the operating conditions of the railways which happened to traverse the frontier. Apart from the Great Northern, the Sligo, Leitrim & Northern Counties (SLNC), the Dundalk, Newry & Greenore (DN&G), the Londonderry & Lough Swilly (L&LS), and the County Donegal Railways Joint Committee (CDRJC) lines attained the doubtful distinction of being international in their operation. The problems of these four minor lines were insignificant compared with the Great Northern's headache. Its ramifying lines entered all the six counties of Northern Ireland, and seven counties more in the Free State. The political frontier was crossed by the Great Northern track no less than 17 times, though six of that total were accounted for by the serpentine Monaghan-Fermanagh boundary between Clones and Cavan.

Customs examination of passengers' luggage and of goods became necessary as tariffs were introduced, and running times of trains had to be adjusted to suit this new requirement. Journey times were inevitably lengthened. Office accommodation was provided for preventive staff at 14 stations, seven on each side of the frontier. On the Dublin-Belfast main line, the customs stations were at Dundalk and Goraghwood; on the Clones-Portadown line, at Glaslough and Tynan; on the Dundalk-Enniskillen line, at Clones and Newtownbutler. (In each case, the Southern (Irish Free State, Eire, or Republic of Ireland) station is named first, the Northern station second.) On the Bundoran branch, Ballyshannon and Pettigo were the southern posts, Kesh and Belleek the northern. There were special arrangements for trains on the Londonderry line while trains stopping at the intermediate stations were examined at Strabane. Non-stop Dublin-Belfast trains, run after 1947, were examined at the terminals, and there were various special arrangements for particular traffics.

The pattern of business, such as attendance at cattle fairs, at towns near the border was radically altered, and as a result traffic on the comparatively new Castleblayney-Keady-Armagh section fell away. The Castleblayney to Keady portion was closed in April 1923 and the track was lifted shortly afterwards.

Because of its operation in two separate political areas, the Great Northern was excluded from the amalgamation of other railway companies that was effected in the Free State by the Railways Act of 1924. The SLNC, DNG, L&LS, and CDRJC were similarly unaffected. To the south of the Great Northern, the contiguous lines at Dublin, Navan, Belturbet, and Cavan became integrated into the Great Southern Railways.

No sooner had the company become accustomed to the novelty and irritation of working in two countries than even more serious problems loomed ahead in the form of road transport. This had been little more than a curiosity prior to 1914, but it had been forced in the hothouse of war. The motor industry, geared by the demands of war to a high rate of vehicle production, was able and willing to offer an interested public a new and attractive form of personal and freight transport. Motor omnibuses and cars began to flow from cross-channel factories on to the dusty Irish roads, a trickle that was soon to develop into a steady stream. Surplus army lorries and their new counterparts formed the complement to the passenger-carrying vehicles. Hire-purchase agreements enabled back-yard operators with little or no capital or experience to enter a new and apparently profitable field. A growing swarm of bus and lorry owners were free to put on the ratepayers' roads whatever sort of vehicles they thought the public might make use of. It was not long before cut-throat competition developed, first against that established and highly-regulated form of transport, the railway, and then among the individual road operators themselves. To survive in the resultant rat-race, standards of vehicle maintenance, safety, operators' wages, and working conditions were frequently sacrificed, but the public, aware only that a transport service had come to their own road-end, and one that was offering cheaper fares withal, accepted the new order of things. The buses and lorries had the merit of being more flexible in their working than the railways, and they were not slow to take full advantage of that. It was the exception to find the new road services complementing the railway, and rather than feed passengers into the railway stations at appropriate times, they indulged in unbridled competition on the basis of a fare war.

Linking the two largest Irish cities, and carrying into both of them a heavy suburban traffic, the Great Northern withstood the impact of the roads remarkably well. The company suffered on short country hauls, and the little market towns well inland from the busy coastal strip saw more and more of the country folk come in from the farms, first by bus and then by car. The two curves of gross receipts and expenditure, which had swept up through the war years to a peak in 1920, dropped steadily throughout the twenties and, more significant, showed a tendency to converge. Then in 1932, the net receipts tumbled to £29,000, and in 1933 a loss of £72,000 was incurred on the year's working. The tendency was reflected in the dividend on ordinary shares, which had been above 5 per cent since before 1900, for in 1925 a dividend of 3 per cent was declared. Four more years at 3 per cent followed, a feat maintained by scrupulous economies and careful housekeeping. The 1930s were ushered in by the declaration of a 1¼ per cent dividend, and then ½ per cent in 1931. Nine dark years followed during which no dividend was paid on ordinary shares. In 1932 no dividend was paid on preference stocks, and £54,000 had to be withdrawn from reserves to provide for the interest on the debenture and guaranteed stocks. The situation worsened until the outbreak of World War II, and in 1938-9 even debenture interest could not be met.

Against this gloomy financial background, which extended over the 15 years preceding the outbreak of war in 1939, the company continued to function in a way not only remarkably efficient but also outstandingly enterprising. The story of those years is, however, intimately linked with the growth of road transport.

During this time, the reconstruction of the great viaduct over the River Boyne at Drogheda was the outstanding civil engineering work. This wrought-iron three-span continuous-girder bridge carried two tracks of the main line and had been unrestricted as regards loading from 1855 until 1885. Around then, it was felt that corrosion of certain parts of the girder work made it advisable to allow only one train to be on the bridge at any one time, and signalling was introduced to enforce this rule. In spite of careful maintenance it became necessary to limit axle loads on the bridge, and this meant that heavy express engines, had they been in the company's stock, could not have crossed it. After 1920, the 'SG3' goods engines were thus affected.

By 1925, the restrictions imposed on traffic by the Boyne viaduct had become intolerable, and it was evident that wholesale renewal and strengthening was urgently required. A scheme was put forward which would have cost around £130,000, but action was deferred for some years. In 1929, George B. Howden of the North British and LNE railways came to Ireland as the Great Northern's Chief Engineer, and under his guidance a new plan was prepared. This was estimated to cost £30,000 and involved the building of a steel girder structure in three spans, resting on the original stone piers. This revised scheme was adopted and was done by contract. Construction took from 1930 until 1932, the old track was singled, and the new steel girders placed between the rails and the old bridge. Traffic meanwhile continued to use the bridge, and on completion of the new work, the old structure was removed piecemeal.

Inevitably, the new steel structure was rather narrower than its predecessor, and it was unable to accommodate orthodox double track. However, what was virtually single line working had been in force for many years, and the provision of gauntletted double track, thus avoiding points, was a welcome and satisfactory solution. Increased axle loads were permissible, and this was at once made use of by the 'SG3' engines and by G.T. Glover's new class 'V' compounds which played an outstanding part in accelerating main line trains in 1932.

By 1927 the Governments in North and South recognised that legislation to permit the railways to run their own ancillary road services was overdue. The Great Northern had meanwhile assessed the status of the road opposition, and once the Acts were passed it started upon the costly buying-out of its competitors and the planned establishment of integrated road services in their place. For some years the company was in the unenviable position of having to lay out capital on a new venture which would give only long-term benefits, and at the same time maintain and improve its railway services. To this systematic reorientation of its activities, the lengthy railway strike in 1933 delivered a cruel blow, and in that year both income and engine miles were cut back by about a third.

Initially, the road fleet was a miscellaneous collection of buses and lorries, culled from their previous owners. The vehicles were put into good order, and routes were settled which worked with and not against the railway services. By

GNR Leyland dropside lorry No. 120.   *Duffner*

GNR Dennis van No. 269.   *Duffner*

1929 the Great Northern possessed 60 buses, in 1930 91 buses and 33 lorries, and 124 and 49 in 1931. Buses rose to a maximum of 171 in 1934, lorries to their peak of 153 in 1935.

In the Free State up to 1932, any person could establish and run a road passenger service. The Road Transport Act of 1932 required a system of licensing; new entrants were limited, and better operating standards were enforced. The Act repealed the 1927 Act, but gave the railways in the South extra powers to acquire road undertakings. In the next year the Road Transport Act clamped down further on the private operators and largely succeeded in its object of reducing uneconomic competition and wasteful duplication. The Great Northern responded by acquiring road lorry undertakings and by further co-ordinating its road and rail services.

There was, be it noted, no parallel move in Northern Ireland, and there the situation continued to become more and more unrealistic as frantic competition was allowed to continue. By 1934 it was estimated that in Northern Ireland more goods were being carried on the roads than on the railways. Rail fares and charges were being brought down to compete, while wages and material costs were rising. It appeared that the survival of the railways in the north was at stake. The Northern Government at last took action and asked Sir Felix Pole to survey the position and report. His findings showed that the development in road services was not mirrored by losses in the railways' accounts; passenger journeys and freight carriage had not fallen greatly (though the rates had); and most of the road traffic was therefore of new origin. The railways' plight lay in their inability to attract new business. Pole recommended that road and rail services in the North be co-ordinated, and following his advice there was

A later GNR dropside lorry. *Duffner*

AEC single-deck bus No. 206 ZC1291 at Killybegs on 21st April, 1953.   *H.C. Casserley*

AEC Regent double-decker No. 65 ZC6981 at a customs point on the Northern Ireland/Irish Republic border.   *Duffner*

passed the Road & Rail Traffic Act (Northern Ireland), 1935. This Act established the Northern Ireland Road Transport Board (NIRTB) and charged it with the duty of taking over all road undertakings, co-ordinating road and rail, and pooling the joint receipts. As a result of the first of these requirements, a proportion of the Great Northern's vehicle fleet went to the NIRTB. The position therefore differed from that in the Free State, where the Great Northern was free to continue its road services. There, the total bus fleet began to grow again after the 1935 reduction, and the first of the double-deckers came in 1938.

In the North, the road freight fleet of the Great Northern was treated in the same fashion as the buses, and a proportion went to the NIRTB. The Great Northern's lorry fleet, having grown from a total of 33 vehicles to a maximum of 153 in 1935, was accordingly pruned by 27 vehicles in the 1936 return, the remainder working exclusively in the Free State or entering the northern province only in terminating runs started from south of the frontier.

The Great Northern, in common with the other railways in Northern Ireland, had been promised under the terms of the 1935 Act that, in return for the road vehicles it had surrendered, some form of sane collaboration between road and rail would be achieved. In practice, nothing of the sort took place; the pooling of receipts appeared to be unworkable, and the green road vehicles, uniform in livery and in purpose, worked in their wonted, but now more concerted, competition with the railways. This was the unhappy state of affairs at the outbreak of World War II in 1939.

After this brief review of the impact of road on rail, it is necessary to return to a consideration of less competitive matters. Since July 1880, the Great Northern had received an annual rent of £600 from the Dundalk, Newry & Greenore Railway for its use of the line and station at Newry (Edward Street). Apart from the use of a Great Northern express locomotive to work boat expresses from Greenore to Belfast, the two concerns worked independently, with the DN&G self-contained within its two end-on junctions against the GNR(I) at Newry and Dundalk. Since 1910 the DN&G had failed to earn anything for its owners (the LNWR and later the LMS), and although losses had been reduced by the ending in 1926 of the Greenore-Holyhead passenger steamer service, it was clear that the concern would never again earn a profit. The goods terminal services of the GNR(I) and the DN&G were amalgamated in November 1932, and from 1st July, 1933 the Great Northern took over the working and maintenance of the line. These arrangements resulted in a considerable reduction in the Greenore line's loss, but they did not submerge its individuality. Although the old custom of sending men specially from Wolverton to overhaul the carriages ceased and was replaced by the more logical use of the nearby Dundalk shops, the old LNWR livery of chocolate and off-white was perpetuated. Two railbuses, built at Dundalk, took over some of the passenger workings from 1935, but the old Crewe-built saddle tanks still ran, though assisted by Great Northern engines. Class 'JT' and class 'AL' were commonly used, and a maximum axle load of 13½ tons was imposed between Dundalk (Quay Street) and Greenore. The Greenore to Newry section was not similarly restricted, since the express boat trains to Belfast had used it many years earlier.

DN&G 0-6-0ST No. 2 *Greenore* has just arrived at Dundalk Quay Street with the 4.45 pm to Greenore on 23rd May, 1924.   *LCGB/Ken Nunn Collection*

DN&G 0-6-0ST No. 6 *Holyhead* at Dundalk Junction before departure for Greenore. Note the coaching stock carries London & North Western Railway livery.   *Real Photographs*

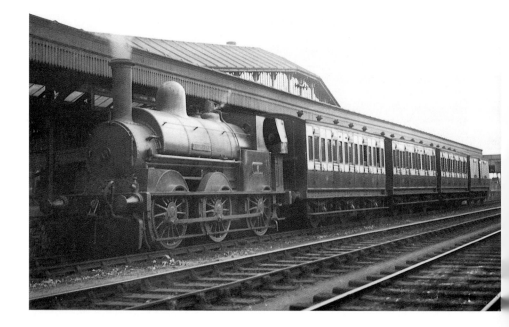

A general view of Greenore. The engine shed is on the right, and the steamer for Holyhead can be seen on the left. *G. Harrop*

In an effort to attract patrons from the scattered agricultural community on the flanks of the Carlingford mountains, four halts were opened in July 1935, at Crossalaney, Gyles Quay, Annaloughan, and Bellurgan Point, between Dundalk and Greenore. In addition, roadside stopping places at Dunstable's Crossing and White's Crossing were opened between Greenore and Newry.

World War II saw some revival of activity at Greenore, when from May 1941 until April 1943 two cargo sailings were run each week from Heysham. The Greenore railway hotel became a popular focal point for holidays and a convenient escape from the rigours of wartime food rationing a few miles distant. When the British Transport Commission assumed ownership of the DN&G in 1948, it was clear that closure of the line could not be long delayed. For four years the interesting position continued in which a British nationalised railway undertaking financed a losing portion of their system which was itself located in two other countries. All services ceased on 31st December, 1951, but the short spur from Windmill Road Junction to the Dundalk quays continued to be used by the Great Northern.

On the GNR (I) system itself, economy in maintenance resulted in the singling of certain sections of double track, rendered less essential as traffic declined. The 12¼ miles from Monaghan to Clones were so treated in 1932, St Johnstown-Londonderry in 1933, Armagh-Monaghan in 1934, and Dungannon-Donaghmore in 1936. After the line had passed out of Great Northern hands, the Portadown to Trew & Moy section was singled by the Ulster Transport Authority in 1959. This left the entire Portadown-Londonderry main line as single track.

World War II effected a dramatic change in the railway's fortunes. The conflict affected the company in a remarkable fashion, since to the south of the inter-state frontier one-third of the mileage lay in a neutral country (now the Republic of Ireland). Although the railways in Great Britain promptly came under Government control with the outbreak of war, no such steps were taken in Northern Ireland by the Government there, and in common with the other lines, the Great Northern found itself expected to contribute fully to the war effort but without the cross-channel guarantee of net revenue.

Wartime conditions produced some measure of traffic distortion on the system. In Northern Ireland military camps, aerodromes, and the dispersal of vital industries gave rise to much additional traffic in passengers and freight. Troop trains along the Antrim branch led to the LMS Northern Counties Committee (NCC) line and to the Larne cross-channel steamers, while off the same branch a 2¼ mile spur was made and opened in May 1942 to Gortnagallon, near the shore of of Lough Neagh, at the request of the Ministry of Aircraft Production. The depot at Gortnagallon consisted of an island platform for personnel and four lines of sidings. The contrast in activities between North and South was emphasised by the black-out conditions in Northern Ireland.

Inevitably much of the Great Northern's operating in the North was integrated with the LMS (NCC) and the Belfast & County Down concerns. For security reasons the three operating offices were in direct telephone communication with HQ Movement Control, so that secret conversations were kept clear of Post Office telephone exchanges.

An activity which particularly concerned the Great Northern was the use of Warrenpoint as one of the two ports for bringing in ammunition, and many thousands of tons were brought up the single NW&R line to Goraghwood for eventual dispatch to supply depots throughout the country. Scarva became one of the three petrol depots supplying WD and RAF requirements; much of the fuel was brought in tins into the port of Larne by coastal vessels and worked from there via Antrim and Knockmore.

Early in the war, a number of 25 ton wagons were taken over by the War Department and converted into steel-plate-sided mobile trolleys. Intended to patrol the lines in the event of invasion, they were powered by diesel engines and suitably camouflaged.

Some Great Northern bogie carriages were used along with ex-LMS and LMS (NCC) stock in the make-up of two ambulance trains. Both were stationed for a time at Whitehead, on the Belfast-Larne line of the NCC; one was later moved to Broomhedge where arrangements were made for water supplies and for charging the electric batteries.

Londonderry was one of the major naval bases, and through it were imported many of the WD stores. Although the principal berths were adjacent to the GNR(I) terminus, WD material in transit could not be sent on the line to Strabane since it would have passed through neutral Eire on the way. Wagons loaded on the quays had therefore to be capstan-hauled over the Craigavon bridge and on to the NCC's system at Waterside. Nissen hutting consigned from Londonderry to Omagh, 34 miles away, had to be worked via Coleraine

The GNR Ambulance train at Broomhedge on the down side. Note the temporary water
tank behind.   *Charles Friel Collection*

and the Derry Central line to Magherafelt, thence to Cookstown and on to
Omagh via Dungannon, a total distance of 121 miles.

The virtual cessation of private motoring rapidly changed the financial aspect
of the Great Northern's working. Both the 1938 and 1939 returns show very
similar passenger statistics, with just over 5 million passengers paying an average
fare of 1s. 7d. In 1944 almost 11 million passengers paid 2s. 4d. Season ticket
holders too rose from around 5,000 pre-war to a maximum of 12,292 in 1942.

The trend in goods traffic was similar, although the increase from the pre-war
3 million tons came more rapidly. In 1939 and 1940 the goods tonnage was
around the 1 million mark; thereafter it rose to a peak of 1¾ million tons in 1944,
falling slowly back to around 1¼ million tons in 1952.

Gross earnings rose from £1.3m in 1938 to £3.4m in 1944, and total net income
from £70,000 in 1938 to over 10 times that amount in 1942-3-4. It became
possible to pay modest dividends to ordinary stockholders for the seven years
1941-7. In 1946 a Government White Paper proposed a merger of the public
transport undertakings in Northern Ireland.

By 1947 the wartime boom was over, and although rising fares maintained
the gross receipts at around £3.5m, they were inexorably overtaken by
expenditure. This passed the £3m mark for the first time in 1946, and by 1949 it
was in excess of income by £118,000. The pre-war agonies of the company had
returned, and the position was a hopeless one. It was apparent that the days of
private ownership of the company were at an end.

By November 1950 the Directors announced that the company was at the end of its financial resources, and on 6th December, 1950 the shareholders authorised its Board to close the line as soon as possible. Forced with a situation that would have meant the speedy end of all rail transport in the Great Northern's area, the two governments entered into negotiations with the company.

Meanwhile, on 6th January, 1951 the company gave notice of its intention to discontinue all services in Northern Ireland about five weeks later. Two days later one week's notice was given to around 1,200 of the employees, to be withdrawn on the following day when it was announced that the governments were prepared to meet the deficits. An offer of £3.9m was received from the governments, and after protracted negotiations this was raised to £4.5m, divided equally between the two governments. On 1st October, 1951, pending formal acquisition, the two governments agreed to finance deficits incurred in current operations and the purchase of materials and equipment. The company had now ceased to be self-supporting, and the debit balance continued to grow until by the end of 1952 it had reached the appalling total of £1.9m.

Through two Acts, a statutory body termed the Great Northern Railway Board (GNRB) was constituted, one Act passed by the Oireachtas of the Republic of Ireland and the other by the Parliament of Northern Ireland. The Board consisted of 10 members, five appointed by the Republic's Minister for Industry and Commerce and five by the Northern Minister for Commerce, and it began operations on 1st September, 1953.

Before the story of the GNR(I) is left, it is necessary to notice how, in spite of dwindling resources, the company continued its progressive policy. The class 'V' compound locomotives were all fitted with Belpaire fireboxes between 1946 and 1950. Then on 11th August, 1947 the first regular non-stop run of over 100 miles in Ireland began with the 'Enterprise' express between Belfast and Dublin. During 1948, 15 new locomotives (classes 'U', 'UG' and 'VS') were added to stock and 20 AEC diesel railcars were ordered. Over five years ahead of their Western European counterparts, the company introduced 'two-class' travel on 1st January, 1951. Second class travel was abolished, and first class fares were reduced to slightly above the former second class rate.

Chapter Eleven

Gradients, Track and Signalling

Gradients

I. Main Line, Dublin to Belfast

Shortly after leaving Dublin, at 34 ft OD*, the line rises at 1 in 180/290 to near Raheny. It then falls past Howth Junction towards a level stretch near Portmarnock. Apart from minor humps at Malahide and Donabate the line is level out to the 13th mile post, when a 3½ mile climb at 1 in 163/173 to 131 ft follows. Thence a sharp fall at 1 in 150 takes one to Skerries. For the next 10 miles the line undulates, until at Laytown it again enters on a 3½ mile ascent, mostly at 1 in 300. Drogheda station lies ahead, at 106 ft, and the Boyne viaduct is crossed on a rise of 1 in 352.

From milepost 33, a 4½ mile climb, maximum 1 in 167, brings up Kellystown box at 227 ft. Afterwards there is a steady fall, mostly at 1 in 195, through Dunleer and nearly to milepost 46. Castlebellingham is sited on a 2 mile level stretch, after which the line falls again for a mile at 1 in 230. This 13 miles north of Kellystown summit was the scene of much of the fast pre-war running. From milepost 50 to milepost 52, the line rises at 1 in 180/167/206 and then falls 1 in 160 to Dundalk, 54½ miles out, and at 34 ft, identical with Dublin.

Once Dundalk is left, there comes 11 miles of stiff climbing, 3 miles at 1 in 100/91/100. The summit level at 422 ft lies near milepost 65½, with rough granite hills rising on each side. A long down grade follows at a limiting 1 in 100, over the Craigmore viaduct at Bessbrook and through Goraghwood Junction to milepost 74. Thereafter a mile rising at 1 in 216 brings in 14 miles of level running, broken by minor undulations, to Portadown. The disused Newry Canal lies alongside for much of the way.

At Portadown, 74 ft, the former Ulster Railway section is entered on a rise of 1 in 196. A dip of a mile near Boilie box intervenes before the climb takes the line to a summit at 193 ft, 96 miles from Dublin. Grades on the next 2½ miles down to Moira vary from 1 in 148 to 246. Easy running follows to Knockmore Junction, at 130 ft. From there, a gentle up grade into Lisburn is followed by mainly downhill sections into Belfast, where the terminus is at 20 ft OD.

II. Dundalk-Omagh

Leaving Barrack Street at 22 ft OD, a mile of level line prefaces a climb past the West Junction box. The line then steepens to 1 in 100 out to Kellybridge. After a brief fall, climbing continues past Inniskeen, at 173 ft, into Castleblayney. There is a small loss of altitude from there to Ballybay. From Shantonagh Junction a sharp ascent at 1 in 120/100 takes the line to the top of the section some 370 ft higher than Barrack Street and just past Monaghan Road. Minor undulations follow for 5½ miles; then from Newbliss to Clones come 4½

---

* Throughout this section, the heights are given above Ordnance Datum (OD), and for practical purposes may be regarded as the height above sea level. The present tense is used throughout to indicate the situation when the GN was working its full system.

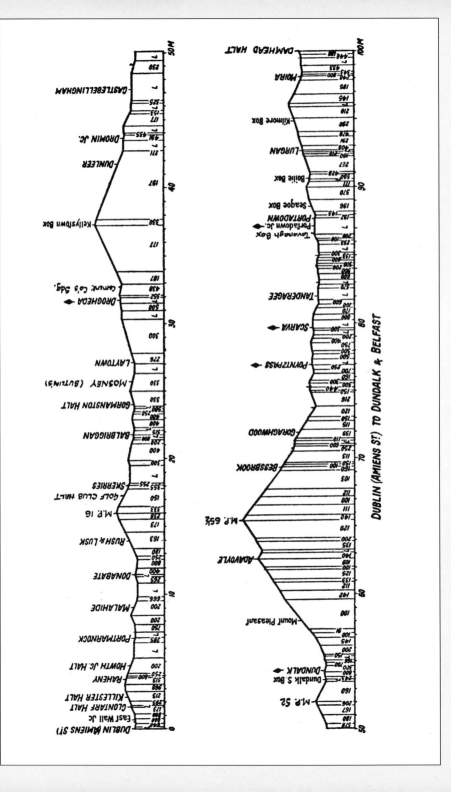

DUBLIN (AMIENS ST.) TO DUNDALK & BELFAST

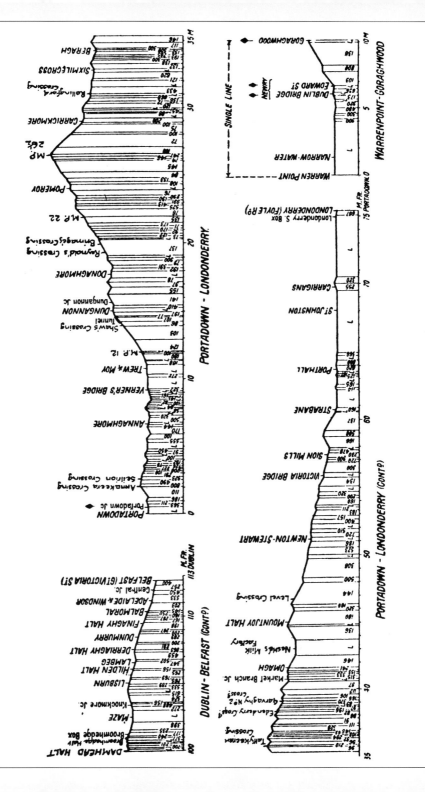

miles, mostly falling away at 1 in 90. Clones stands at 190 ft. Thereafter the only striking elevation is at Lisbellaw, flanked by short stretches of 1 in 100. Three miles of downgrades lead to Enniskillen, standing at 181 ft.

Shortly beyond Enniskillen a short rise at 1 in 76 offers variety in the next 7 miles. A vigorous ascent is started at 1 in 195 from milepost 67½ and continued past Bundoran Junction, 316 ft, to a summit at 335 ft at Trillick. Ten miles follow with little alteration in the general level, though with many stretches of 1 in 100. A second summit at 372 ft comes close to Fintona Junction, where the nearly level spur trails off to Fintona town, ¾ mile away. A 2 mile fall at 1 in 177 is followed by gentler gradients, though broken by a short 1 in 102 rise, down towards Omagh, which is at 257 ft.

III. Portadown-Londonderry

For 11 miles from Portadown the general height of the line varies but little, though there are many short fluctuations in grade. Noteworthy among these is a sharply graded summit 8 miles out, entered at 1 in 58 and quitted at 1 in 84. From Trew & Moy, the line rises at 1 in 168/180/124, with briefly 1 in 91/83/84, to a summit at 286 ft, 1½ miles beyond Dungannon. After a short descent, a climb at 1 in 155/97/78 takes the line to Donaghmore, where an 8 mile climb is commenced over the Sperrin Mountains watershed. The highest point is 561 ft, midway between Pomeroy and Carrickmore. Excepting the summit of the long abandoned CK&A line, this is the highest point on the system. Gradients between 1 in 70 and 80 occur on both sides of this summit. Minor uphill stretches interrupt a general downgrade into Omagh.

The line levels near the Milk Factory siding before rising for a mile at 1 in 136 into Mountjoy. Thereafter there is a steady loss of height down the valley into Strabane, which is at 23 ft. From there to Londonderry the track is laid close to the River Foyle, and apart from small humps near Porthall and Carrigans, it is virtually level, losing only 5 ft in height over the whole 15 miles.

IV. Portadown to Cavan

From the junction there is a steady climb out to Retreat Halt and the line gains 100 ft in altitude over 7½ miles. The gradients are generally between 1 in 150 and 200. From Retreat, half of a 2 mile descent is at 1 in 153. The line then crosses the valley of the Callan River, and at Armagh drops to 136 ft.

Rising gradients lie ahead towards Killylea, and a short section near milepost 12 is at 1 in 96. The climb is broken by a half mile down 1 in 163. A quarter-mile after Killylea station lies the summit of the section at 246 ft. Then, in a downhill run through Tynan, a mile is covered at 1 in 103/80/119. Towards the Eire border, wooded country by the River Blackwater and the disused Ulster Canal is threaded to Glasough, and the height drops to 137 ft. Thereafter there is a 6 mile climb with gradients varying from 1 in 1120 up to 1 in 100, until Monaghan is passed, 27¼ miles out.

The line from Monaghan to Smithborough and Clones lies around 200 ft; the country through which it passes is studded with small lakes and inter-drumlin marshland, and in consequence the gradient is forced to change frequently and is often as steep as 1 in 90/110.

Leaving Clones, the topography is similar to that seen in the previous 12 miles, though the proportion of bogland increases. The inter-state frontier here is very tortuous, and before Redhills is reached, the line actually crosses the border six times in 5 miles and is four times in County Monaghan and three times in County Fermanagh before entering County Cavan. Ballyhaise, where the Belturbet branch diverges, lies at the start of a sharp climb which includes a stretch at 1 in 74. Beyond it come marked undulations with short stretches around 1 in 100 for 4 miles. A final one mile ascent at 1 in 101 brings the line at 226 ft at its end-on junction with the former MGWR in Cavan station.

V. The Branches

(a) *Howth.* Leaving Howth Junction station at 54 ft, the line falls at 1 in 120/170 for a mile. Thereafter there are no noteworthy gradients to the terminus, which is at 25 ft.

(b) *Howth Tramway.* At Sutton, on the Howth branch, the tramway had one of its two termini. The line was very steeply graded and on each side of the summit of Howth Hill, 407 ft, there were long stretches of 1 in 20. The steepest bank was 1 in 16½, unbroken for almost half a mile on the initial ascent from Sutton.

(c) *Oldcastle.* This long branch leaves the main line at Drogheda at 106 ft and begins with 2 miles at 1 in 205/186. Duleek lies beyond this hill. A summit at 229 ft, before Beauparc, is flanked by 1 in 162 grades. Navan, in the valley of the River Boyne, is approached down a long bank at 1 in 154/375. The junctions with the former Meath line are passed on a 1 in 415 rise, which levels somewhat into Ballybeg. From there, the line enters on a long though unspectacular ascent, which ends at 383 ft after some 1 in 200 work. A fall of 23 ft over the last mile brings the track into Oldcastle.

(d) *Ardee.* This short branch shows only short stretches at 1 in 150, and much of it is less markedly graded.

(e) *Carrickmacross.* From 172 ft at Inniskeen the first mile rises at 1 in 129/240. Much of the branch is then on gentle down grades, with only the last mile rising 1 in 100/121/300. Carrickmacross is at 139 ft.

(f) *Cootehill.* Over its length this branch loses only 8 ft in height from 299 ft at Shantonagh Junction. There are however frequent changes in grade. The steepest rise is a short 1 in 75, 1¼ miles short of the terminus.

(g) *Belturbet.* Similar features to those described on the Clones to Cavan section are to be found on Ballyhaise to Belturbet line, and the limiting gradient is 1 in 100.

(h) *Bundoran.* This branch leaves the junction station at 316 ft and falls with fluctuating gradients for 12 miles. A stiff bank, 11 miles at 1 in 106, comes half way between Kesh and Pettigo. Two miles beyond Pettigo a 260 ft summit is approached at 1 in 113, after which there is a fall at 1 in 100 for 1½ miles. Ten miles of nearly level line follow, and a 3 mile drop down 1 in 106 takes the line into the Erne valley. Between Ballyshannon and Bundoran a 183 ft summit is flanked by 1 in 100 grades.

(i) *Warrenpoint to Armagh.* This section, scarcely a branch in the strict sense, is almost level into Newry, at around 22 ft OD. Thence a long climb, lasting for 6½ miles, is posted at 1 in 103/135/70 and levels only through Goraghwood. The Lissummon tunnel is driven on a rise of 1 in 75 and ends at the top of the climb. A rapid fall of 1 in 70/71 ensues, into Loughgilly. Soon afterwards, a mile up 1 in 80 brings the line to Markethill. There is a mile at 1 in 100 down to Hamiltonsbawn, after which a 1 in 80 portion is encountered in a climb to a summit. On the fall towards Armagh the site of the tragic 1889 accident is passed, on a 1 in 75 down grade, and the old Newry & Armagh section terminates at 136 ft.

(j) *Scarva*. Between here and Banbridge, an ascent towards Laurencetown is taken at 1 in 98/73/82 for a mile. Rising gradients, mostly about 1 in 300, though steeper sometimes, bring the line past Banbridge.

(k) *Newcastle*. The Knockmore to Banbridge part contains a 6 mile ascent to 410 ft, on which is the steepest gradient of the whole system (excepting the Hill of Howth Tramway), 1 in 57.4 at Hillsborough. This is followed by a general fall in height through Dromore, at 1 in 82/92. Some uphill work is met before Ashfield and also between Mullafernaghan and Banbridge. The latter place is approached down nearly 2 miles of 1 in 100. Knockmore stands at 130 ft, Banbridge 60 ft above this.

A long climb beyond Banbridge carries the line up to a 334 ft summit, 14 miles away. The following 8 miles into Newcastle, the latter half of it over Belfast & County Down line, fall away with many banks of 1 in 80/90/70.

(l) *Cookstown*. This branch starts on a rise at Dungannon Junction and climbs 60 ft over 1½ miles. Two miles downhill at 1 in 72/90 follow, and Coalisland is at 132 ft. The three miles into Stewartstown are on a rising gradient and the summit lies at 258 ft. Several downgrades at 1 in 75/80 follow, broken by a short rise. The Ballinderry River is crossed, and a climb out of the valley at 1 in 75/86 brings the line past the Killymoon estate and into the terminus.

(m) *Armagh-Castleblayney*. From 136 ft this section rises at 1 in 70 much of the road to Keady. The ascent continues for several miles across a range of hills to Carnagh, closely following the main road. This long bank brings the line to 613 ft, the maximum altitude attained on the GN system. Falling gradients supervene south to Castleblayney, where the track stands almost 250 ft higher than at Armagh.

(n) *Antrim*. The highest point is 3½ miles from Knockmore, by which time banks at 1 in 114/108/97 have brought the line to 265 ft. Over the next 9 miles the line undulates gently and from Aldergrove begins an unbroken drop towards Antrim. A short final rise at 1 in 106 brings in the junction with the old NCC main line.

(o) *Omagh Market and North Wall*. These two short branches are both built on falling gradients, being 1 in 71 and 1 in 100 respectively.

Track

The type and construction of the track* in pre-GNR (I) days showed distinct variations, due to the individual preferences of the various companies. Originally rails of the bridge, Barlow, and double-headed types were used, and changes were made as experience at home and elsewhere brought to light the defects of the early track.

There appear to have been several types of the bridge rails in use. The earliest were those laid by the Ulster company between Belfast and Lisburn, which weighed only 53 lb. per yard. Longitudinal sleepers supported them, and their life was short, for when this section was doubled on the regauging in 1846, they were replaced by 80 lb. rails of similar type. Rails of this weight were also laid between Lisburn and Portadown. Bridge rails were replaced between Belfast and Portadown by either double-headed or bullhead rail. The Ulster main line beyond Portadown used bridge rails to Monaghan, but the later extension to Clones came in time to be made with double-headed wrought-iron rails.

Between Portadown and Dungannon, bridge rails formed the original road when it was opened in 1858. Replacement was by double-headed iron or steel rails in 1875-85. By 1861, when the line was extended to Omagh, bridge rails were out of date and wrought-iron flange rails formed the original track.

Bridge rails were also standard on the Dublin & Drogheda's line. This company appears to have used at least three types, an early light section, and later 80 lb., 82 lb., and 82½ lb. weights. Bridge rails were also laid on the Drogheda-Navan line, where the original track was made up of 15 ft to 18 ft lengths, to be replaced in 1865-74 by Hardy's 82½ lb. bridge-section rails 21 ft, 24 ft and 27 ft in length. These were also laid up to Kells and were used there until around 1890, when steel flange rails were substituted. On the Howth branch, 12 ft bridge rails and later 24 ft bridge rails were used until about 1880.

The Dundalk & Enniskillen Railway adopted bridge rails from Barrack Street to Newbliss. From there to Clones both bridge and iron flange rails formed the original track. Around 1890 both types were lifted, and replaced by steel flange rails.

Part of the Dublin & Belfast Junction line was characterised by Barlow rails, but a good deal of it consisted of low bridge rails. The Barlow rail was bedded in ballast and weighed 90 lb. per yard. It appears to have been used exclusively between Castlebellingham and Mountpleasant. The Boyne viaduct was also laid with it, though 82 lb. high bridge rails formed the road from there to Dunleer and Castlebellingham.

Double-headed rails, intended to give long life with turning, did not give satisfactory service. Unlike their forerunners, they were seated in chairs, but these produced enough wear in the face of the rail to cause unevenness in the track once they were turned. Both iron and steel versions were in vogue for some years. Renewal of the Ulster's main line out to Portadown included both kinds.

---

* Much detailed information on the history of the track has been obtained from a manuscript diagram, formerly in the Civil Engineering section at Amiens Street and now in the possession of the UTA [*in 1962*]. This detailed diagram is drawn on a scale of 2 in. to 1 mile and gives complete information on the original track and on its successive renewals up to around 1910.

The Newry & Armagh Railway was laid in 14 ft 9½ in. double-headed rails between Newry and Goraghwood from 1854-74, though flange rails were used over the hill to Armagh.

Double-headed wrought-iron rails also formed the remarkable track of the Londonderry & Enniskillen Railway. The rails were carried on heavy iron supports, rather like massive chairs, and there were four of these along each 20 ft rail, with one below the rail joint. There were no sleepers, the chairs rested directly on the gravel ballast, and iron tie bars held the rails to gauge. This assemblage formed a hard, unyielding track, which punished the flimsy rolling stock. In frosty weather the great joint chairs, each weighing 2 cwt, were liable to crack as a result of shrinkage stresses. The permanent way of the L&E contributed in no small measure to the troubles that beset the line, which determined the decision to hand over operations to the INWR. Under the latter company, replacement by iron flange rails began in 1865-75, and these were followed by steel flange rails under the Great Northern, after 1880.

Iron flange rails, usually 75 lb. per yard, formed the original track of the Cootehill, Bundoran, and Antrim branches, and between Lisburn and Banbridge. By the time the Great Northern had engineered the Carrickmacross and Belturbet lines, a fall in steel prices had allowed the company to purchase 'at advantageous prices' a large stock of steel flange rails, and these formed the original track on these two small branch lines. Less fortunate was the Banbridge Extension line to Ballyroney, which had to do with second-hand iron flange rails, originating from the main line between Goraghwood and Portadown.

The 1876 amalgamation slowly produced uniformity over much of the system. On the main line 26 ft steel flange rails, weighing 79 lb. per yard, became standard, though on the conservative Ulster sections the earlier 75 lb. double-headed steel was slow to go. Flange rails gave way to 85 lb. bullhead rails on the main line: they were carried in cast-iron chairs with *inside* wooden keys, an unusual practice due to W.H. Mills, the Chief Engineer, who claimed that it assisted track inspection. Heavier section bullhead rail of British standard section, 90 lb. per yard and in 45 ft and later in 60 ft lengths, was adopted in stages for main line relaying.

The Howth tramway was laid latterly with chaired, inside-keyed, bullhead rail, 72 lb. per yard, with the exception of the half-mile from Sutton Cross to St Fintan's which was laid with standard grooved tramway track, sunk to road level.

On the secondary and branch lines, flange rails were brought up in stages to 85 lb. weight and 45 ft length. After 1933, 60 ft lengths were introduced.

Signalling

Before block working was brought in, train dispatching was done on a time-interval system whereby trains were permitted to follow one another at intervals which depended on the types of train involved and were from 5 to 20 minutes. This comparatively haphazard way of handling traffic led to the disastrous accident at Armagh in 1889.

Even before the time-interval system, an even less satisfactory method seems to have been in use; in May 1849 the Newry, Warrenpoint & Rostrevor Railway's *Regulations for Enginemen* state: 'All engines travelling on the same line shall keep 800 yards at least apart from each other'. Safety in these early days was largely in the hands of policemen, who operated along a 'beat' and had their own lineside 'sentry boxes' which are shown on the early Ordnance Survey maps. They were responsible for the safety and signalling of trains over their own beat, but they seem to have acted as permanent way inspectors as well. They were provided with a white flag and a lantern showing a white light, for use during the day and at night-time. Gatemen at level crossings were similarly equipped.

Broken rails seem to have been common in those early days, for to slow a train on the NW&R, the policeman was instructed to hold his flag down 'pointing to the defective spot', or at night to move his lantern in a 'horizontal direction over the defective spot'.

As well as the flag or lantern signals given by the pedestrian police or by the gatemen, there were what were called 'fixed signals' at the stations, fixed in the sense that they were fixed to a post. These were the early three-position semaphore type. They exhibited a red, green, or white light, for Danger, Caution, or All Right, corresponding to the signal arm being horizontal, at 45° to the horizontal, or vertical.

In its *Regulations for Enginemen* the NW&R also gave details of the procedure to be followed on entering the terminal stations and resulting no doubt from their forced economies which had left them without turntables:

> On approaching the terminal stations the engine must be disconnected from the train before coming to the switches, so as to enable it to go into the side line and allow the carriages to go on to the passenger platform. The enginemen must be careful to bring in the train at such a speed as to enable the outside guard to stop the carriages opposite the passenger platform and also to prevent the possibility of any injurious consequences arising even supposing the guard should be unable to manage the break [*sic*].

It is to the credit of the ever-watchful Board of Trade that, with widening experience, these dangerous if diverting practices were abandoned or made illegal.

On the double lines, modern signalling was* by means of the absolute block system, using Harper block instruments. Exceptions to this were however seen on the Third Line between the Belfast terminus and Balmoral, and on the Belfast Central section, in each of which permissive block working was in force. The up

---

* Although the past tense is used in this section, similar practices remain in use on those portions of line still operated by the UTA and CIE [*in 1962*].

and down lines from Central Junction to East Bridge were worked by permissive block instruments for goods alone, but for occasional special passenger workings to and from the Belfast & County Down line to Bangor absolute block working was brought into use. The Third Line was mainly used by locomotives between the sheds at Adelaide and the terminus, but to some extent also by goods trains in and out of the Grosvenor Road depot.

Single lines were controlled by electric train staff, and in its later years a single train staff was used between Goraghwood and Markethill. Mechanical staff exchange apparatus was in use at nine stations on the Portadown-Londonderry section.

When the Gortnagallon branch was in use between 1942 and 1945 an auxiliary staff instrument was sited at Siding Junction.

Long-section working was formerly applied between Dungannon Junction and Pomeroy (9 miles), between Armagh and Tynan (7 miles), and between Monaghan and Clones (12 miles). This allowed the boxes at Donaghmore, Killylea, and Smithborough to be closed.

Signals were of the lower quadrant type, with two-position semaphore arms 3 ft 6 in. in length and 10 in. in width. Distant signals were fish-tailed, and since 1945-6 were painted yellow and showed a yellow light; previously they showed red. Shunting signals were either of the dwarf or disc type.

The signal boxes had narrow-segment locking frames and operated the points by rodding and the signals by wires. There was no power operation of either points or signals, except on the north approach to the Boyne viaduct, where electric motors attached to the posts worked the signals.

Adherence to the strict speed limit on the Boyne viaduct by southbound trains coming off the Kellystown bank was ensured by the use of two warning hooters, which operated automatically as the trains entered the track circuits. The first of these hooters was one mile north of the up distant signal, the second on the distant signal post itself. Having passed both of these, the driver was further warned by an illuminated indicator showing the 25 mph limit in force from that point. These precautions were not necessary for northbound trains, as the approach to the viaduct was round the sharp curve of Drogheda station.

The Howth tramway was signalled by its own peculiar system. This consisted of bull's-eye electric lights, attached to the poles of the overhead wiring in the centre of each of the 11 passing loops. These lights were operated by the drivers, by means of a rotary two-way switch, which rendered it impracticable for two cars to approach on the same length of single line track. Several following cars were thus enabled to run through the sections in close succession, as demanded during spells of heavy traffic. In such circumstances, the leading car or cars carried prominent notices 'Car to Follow' in the driver's compartments, thus warning cars waiting to proceed in the opposite way not to leave the loop prematurely. The system worked admirably and was well suited to the comparatively slow speeds on the tramway.

Chapter Twelve

Locomotives

An extended description of the locomotives is beyond the scope of this volume. The constituent companies possessed about 190 engines, of which 128 were inherited by the GNR(I). Apart from these, the latter acquired 277 engines. This total, approaching 470, can be sub-divided into 121 distinct types or classes.

The lists of engines (*Tables One to Ten*) are arranged on the basis of the recognisable types, and the types are numbered chronologically using Roman numerals. This classification is chosen for convenience in reference and in the case of many of the Great Northern engines the numbered 'types' relate to the official classes. Thus type 'XVII' of these tables consists of the eight class 'QL' engines, and type 'XXXV' consists of the five class 'V' compounds.

Ulster Railway

This company possessed a total of 68 engines (*Table One*) and naming was general. Indeed the earliest engines, *Express* and *Fury* ('I') and *Spitfire* ('II') probably never carried their official numbers.

The bulk of the Ulster's passenger engines consisted for many years of 2-2-2 types, with either 6 ft or 5 ft 6 in. driving wheels. The company possessed well organised shops in Belfast, and in the 1860s rebuilt six of their Sharp standard singles ('V'). Two of these were *Pluto* and *Cerberus* ('Va'), but *Lucifer, Jupiter, Vulcan,* and *Spitfire* emerged as 2-4-0 engines ('Vb'). *Spitfire* had come from the Belfast & Ballymena Railway in 1847 and remained in use on the GNR(I) until 1890.

The first Beyer, Peacock products arrived in 1859 ('IX'); one of which, the 2-2-2 *Iveagh*, survived until 1905. Three 2-2-2 Fairbairn engines came in 1859-62 ('X'); all of them lasted into GN days, while one of them, *Blackwater*, went through an extensive rebuild in Belfast in 1881, to emerge as an 0-4-2 with 17 years' further life ('XIX'). The last 2-2-2 engines to be bought were *Ulidia* and *Dalriada*, coming from Sharp, Stewart in 1861 ('XI'); in 1877-9 Belfast converted them to 2-4-0s. *Dalriada* by 1914 was probably the last of the Ulster's double-frame engines, though *Leinster*, a Beyer 2-4-0 of 1863 ('XII'), lasted to the same year.

Goods trains were hauled by 0-4-2 locomotives until 1872. The first of these came from Sharp, Roberts in September 1842 and were named *Samson* and *Hercules* ('IV'). Sharp, Stewart built a second pair, *Callan* and *Neagh*, in 1852 ('VI'). These four engines had outside frames. The first inside-framed goods engines were a trio of Sharp, Stewarts ('VII'); after about 20 years' service two of them were rebuilt to 0-6-0 ('XVIII').

In 1872 the Belfast shops turned out the first 0-6-0 engines ('XVI'), after buying in the frames and boilers from outside makers.

Table I - Ulster Railway

Type	Wheel Arr.	No. in class	Builder	Built	Cylinders	Driving wheels	Total htg surface	Weight t. c.	Remarks
I	2-2-2	2	Sharp, Roberts	1839	13 in. x 18 in.	6 ft 0 in.	579 sq. ft	14 1	Rebuilt to 5 ft 3 in. gauge. Withdrawn 1859.
II	2-2-2	1	Sharp, Roberts	1839	14 in. x 18 in.	6 ft 0 in.	579 sq. ft	14 11	Rebuilt to 2-2-2WT in 1847, 5 ft 3 in. gauge 1848. Sold to B&BR in 1847.
III	2-2-2	4	Sharp, Roberts	1841	14 in. x 18 in.	5 ft 6 in.	600 sq. ft		Two sold 1849, two withdrawn 1854.
IV	0-4-2	2	Sharp, Roberts	1842	14 in. x 20 in.	5 ft 0 in.	480 sq. ft	14 15	Goods engines. Withdrawn 1872-73.
V	2-2-2	7	Sharp Bros	1846-47	15 in. x 20 in.	5 ft 6 in.	878 sq. ft	22 13	5 ft 3 in. gauge. Six rebuilt 1864-69.
Va	2-2-2	4	UR	1864	15 in. x 20 in.	5 ft 6 in.			Rebuilt from type 'V'. One rebuilt 16 in. x 24 in. in 1894.
Vb	2-4-0	4	UR	1867-69	15 in. x 20 in.	5 ft 6 in.		35 0*	Rebuilt from type 'V'. Withdrawn 1890-1906.
VI	0-4-2	2	Sharp, Stewart	1853	16 in. x 24 in.	4 ft 6 in.			Double frames, withdrawn 1875.
VII	0-4-2	3	Sharp, Stewart	1857-61	16 in. x 24 in.	4 ft 6 in.	1,076 sq. ft	27 0	Inside frames, withdrawn 1877-79.
VIII	2-2-2	3	Sharp, Stewart	1857-58	15 in. x 20 in.	5 ft 6 in.			Withdrawn 1886-877. Rebuilt as 2-4-0.
IX	2-2-2	3	Beyer, Peacock	1859-61	16 in. x 22 in.	5 ft 6 in.	960 sq. ft		Two to type 'XVII' in 1875. One withdrawn 1905.
X	2-2-2	3	Fairbairn	1859-62	15 in. x 20 in.	5 ft 6 in.	1,019 sq. ft	24 0	One to type 'XIX' in 1880.
XI	2-2-2	2	Sharp, Stewart	1861	15 in. x 20 in.	5 ft 6 in.			Rebuilt to 2-4-0 1877-79. Withdrawn 1906-14.
XII	2-4-0	4	Beyer, Peacock	1863	16 in. x 22 in.	6 ft 1 in.	979 sq. ft	31 12	Withdrawn 1909-14.
XIII	0-4-2	3	Sharp, Stewart	1866	16 in. x 22 in.	5 ft 0 in.	966 sq. ft	30 0*	Withdrawn 1906-09.
XIV	0-4-2	4	Beyer, Peacock	1866	17 in. x 24 in.	5 ft 0 in.	1,056 sq. ft	32 0	Withdrawn 1911-12.
XV	0-4-2	6	Sharp, Stewart (2) UR (4)	1871-76	16 in. x 22 in.	5 ft 0 in.	956 sq. ft	30 0	Withdrawn 1906-11.
XVI	0-6-0	2	UR	1872-73	?17 in. x 24 in.	5 ft 0 in.	1,045 sq. ft		Withdrawn 1939 and 1948.
XVII	2-4-0	2	UR	1874-76	16 in. x 22 in.	5 ft 6 in.		26 0	Withdrawn 1904 and 1913.
XVIII	0-6-0	6	Beyer, Peacock (2) UR (4)	1876-79	17 in. x 24 in.	4 ft 7 in.	983 sq. ft	32 0	Withdrawn 1924-25.
XIX	0-4-2	3	GNR (ND)	1880-82	16 in. x 22 in.	4 ft 6 in.			Withdrawn 1898-1907.

* As rebuilt later.

*Total number of engines: 68 (2-2-2, 27; 0-4-2, 23; 2-4-0, 10; 0-6-0, 8).
Engines transferred to GNR(I): 41.*

Dublin & Drogheda Railway

This company also purchased its early engines from Sharp who supplied 11 in 1843-4 (*Table Two*). At the opening date the company had one 0-4-2T ('I') and five singles ('II', 'III', 'IV'). The 0-4-2 tank engines ('I') were apparently used for both goods and passenger trains. One of the singles, *Faugh a Ballagh* ('III'), became a 2-2-2WT in 1846 and worked regularly out to Howth. *Alfred* ('III') was converted to a 2-4-0 engine in 1868 and renamed *Saturn* entered the GNR (I) stock.

Further 2-2-2 engines, to work the Drogheda passenger trains, came from the Drogheda works of Grendon in 1845-7 ('V'). This firm also made a 2-2-2T for the Howth branch, which was rebuilt as a 2-2-2 some time in the 1850s ('VI').

In its early days the Oldcastle line saw the two 2-2-2 Sharp, Stewarts ('VII'). They passed into the stock of the GNR (I) as Nos. 17 and 18 and were renamed *Apollo* and *Diana*.

Two 2-4-0 engines from Fairbairn (VIII) and Grendon (IX) came in 1855-6, and added to the variety of the stock. Four Beyer singles, taken into stock between 1859 and 1861, were the standard express engines up to the amalgamation. Goods haulage was reinforced by two batches of 0-4-2 engines from Beyer, Peacock (X, XIII). The first of these contained No. 20, which as No. 9 of the GNR (I) was the train engine involved in the Armagh collision of 1889.

Dublin & Belfast Junction Railway

This company followed the practice set by its neighbours by starting work with a bunch of Sharp singles ('I') (*Table Three*). Had the company's original order been fulfilled completely, they would have had no less than 16 of these, but the makers were asked to reduce the numbers originally contracted for.

From July 1849 until December 1852, the line was worked under contract by Dargan, apparently on the basis of Dargan supplying the motive power. He seems however to have been content to use the existing D&BJ engines, paying the company interest on their cost. Dargan probably used three Grendon engines in addition.

On their resumption of operations, the company ordered six 0-4-2 engines from Sharp, Stewart ('II', 'III'). These were for goods and passenger work and came at intervals between 1853 and 1857. The same firm supplied a brace of 2-2-2WT engines in October 1858 which were used on the Banbridge Junction Railway.

The second of the company's locomotive superintendents was named Harden, and when consideration was being given in 1865 to buying new passenger engines, he indicated a strong preference for Beyer, Peacock products. Three 2-4-0 tender engines were ordered from that firm, and all of them survived into GN days ('V'). One of this class was derailed with its train at Brackagh Moss, south of Portadown, in 1886, killing six passengers.

It was not the practice of the D&BJ to name its engines. Its workshops, which were situated at Dundalk, close to the Square Crossing, were small; although they were capable of effecting major repairs, no building was attempted.

Table II - Dublin & Drogheda Railway

Type	Wheel Arr.	No. in class	Builder	Built	Cylinders	Driving wheels	Total htg surface	Weight t. c.	Remarks
I	0-4-2	4	Sharp Bros	1843-44	15 in. x 20 in.	5 ft 0 in.		23 0	Two to GNR(I) (Nos. 1 and 6)
II	2-2-2	1	Sharp Bros	1843	15 in. x 18 in.	5 ft 0 in.		16 0	Withdrawn 1885.
III	2-2-2	6	Sharp Bros	1844	14 in. x 18 in.	5 ft 6 in.			One to GNR(I) (No. 0), withdrawn 1885.
IV	2-2-2?	1	Butterley	1844	?	?			Withdrawn 1853, bought second-hand.
V	2-2-2	4	Grendon	1845-47	14 in x 18 in.	5 ft 6 in.	797 sq. ft		One to GNR(I) (No. 7), withdrawn 1891.
VI	2-2-2T	1	Grendon	1847	14 in. x 18 in.	5 ft 6 in.			Withdrawn 1861.
VII	2-2-2	2	Sharp, Stewart	1854	15 in. x 20 in.	5 ft 0 in.			Both to GNR(I) (Nos. 17 and 18). Sold 1886.
VIII	2-4-0	1	Fairbairn	1855	?	5 ft 0 in.	1,005 sq. ft	26 10	Withdrawn 1887.
IX	2-4-0	1	Grendon	1856	15 in. x 20 in.	5 ft 6 in.	998 sq. ft	28 2	GNR(I) No. 4/22. Withdrawn 1888.
X	0-4-2	3	Beyer, Peacock	1858-62	16 in. x 22 in.	5 ft 6 in.	964 sq. ft	28 0	All to GNR(I), withdrawn 1903-15.
XI	2-2-2	4	Beyer, Peacock	1859-61	15 in.x 20 in.	6 ft 0 in.	964 sq. ft	23 16	To GNR(I), No. 13-16, withdrawn 1896-1901.
XII	2-2-2T	1	Neilson	1862	12 in. x 18 in.	5 ft 0 in.	730 sq. ft	21 16	GNR(I) No. 8, withdrawn 1891.
XIII	0-4-2	1	Beyer, Peacock	1863	16 in. x 22 in.	5 ft 0 in.	964 sq. ft	25 16	GNR(I) No. 21 rebuilt 0-6-0, withdrawn 1906.
XIV	2-2-2	2	Sharp, Stewart	1863-64	15 in. x 20 in.	5 ft 6 in.	879 sq. ft	24 6	Withdrawn 1885-92.
XV	2-4-0	1	Beyer, Peacock	1871	16 in. x 22 in.	6 ft 0 in.	950 sq. ft	28 13	GNR(I) No. 12, withdrawn 1911.
XVI	0-6-0	1	Beyer, Peacock	1872	17 in. x 24 in.	5 ft 0 in.	999 sq. ft	31 0	GNR(I) No. 5/29, withdrawn 1911.

Total number of engines: 34 (2-2-2, 20; 2-2-2T, 2; 0-4-2, 8; 2-4-0, 3; 0-6-0, 1).
Engines transferred to GNR: 21.

Table III - Dublin & Belfast Junction Railway

Type	Wheel Arr.	No. in class	Builder	Built	Cylinders	Driving wheels	Total htg surface	Weight t. c.	Remarks
I	2-2-2	9	Sharp Bros and Sharp, Stewart	1848-54	15 in. x 20 in.	5 ft 6 in.	879 sq. ft	22 13	Six to GNR(I), withdrawn 1873-85.
II	0-4-2	2	Sharp, Stewart	1853-57	16 in. x 24 in.	4 ft 6 in.	1,204 sq. ft	26 7	To GNR(I), Nos. 35 and 36.
III	0-4-2	4	Sharp, Stewart	1854-57	16 in. x 22 in.	5 ft 0 in.	988 sq. ft	24 0	To GNR(I), Nos. 31-34.
IV	2-2-2WT	2	Sharp, Stewart	1858	12 in. x 18 in.	5 ft 0 in.	656 sq. ft	23 7	To GNR(I), Nos. 28-29.
V	2-4-0	3	Beyer, Peacock	1866-68	16 in. x 22 in.	6 ft 0 in.	1,077 sq. ft		To GNR(I).
VI	0-6-0	2	Beyer, Peacock	1872	17 in. x 24 in.	5 ft 1½ in.	1,030 sq. ft	33 10	Withdrawn 1934 and 1937.

Total number of engines: 22 (2-2-2, 9; 2-2-2WT, 2; 0-4-2, 6; 2-4-0, 3; 0-6-0, 2).
Engines transferred to GNR(I): 19.

Dundalk & Enniskillen Railway

From its opening until the end of 1850 the company arranged with Dargan to operate its line under contract. After this Grendon's of Drogheda worked the line for a short time (*Table Four*). The earliest engines, 2-2-2 for passenger and 0-4-2 for goods work, came from this firm ('I', 'II'). Three Sharp singles came to assist passenger workings in 1852-4 ('III'). Shortly afterwards Grendon's supplied two powerful, long-boiler 0-6-0 goods engines, one of which lasted with the GNR (I) until 1902 ('IV').

Sharp, Stewart supplied two 0-4-2 engines in 1858 for goods trains ('V'). These were identical with Type 'III' of the D&BJR. It was one of these which, leading a double-headed train 3¼ miles north of Mountjoy on 16th November, 1871, was derailed because of excessive speed, killing the driver.

With the line opened to Enniskillen in 1859, a Beyer, Peacock 2-2-2 engine came and was followed two years later by two more ('VI'). They lasted until 1907-4. Two, as GNR (I) Nos. 13 and 14, finished their days in Dublin and were held for running the Mail Specials on days when the Kingstown boat was late. They sometimes ran the 22½ miles from Drogheda to Dundalk in 22 minutes. They were the last single engines on the GNR(I) and the last single tender engines in Ireland.

Londonderry & Enniskillen Railway

The rapid changes in the staff of this line were reflected in its engines, which were a varied and unsatisfactory collection (*Table Five*). The Longridge 2-4-0 and 2-2-2 long-boiler engines were reasonably useful ('I', 'II', 'III'), but the later Adams patent well-tank engines were notoriously under-powered, and were compared by Ahrons to 'steam perambulators'. An unhappy acquisition was a pair of second-hand 2-2-2 engines ('VI') which had started in 1841 as Sharp, Roberts 6 ft 2 in. gauge jobs on the Ulster's line. That company sold them at the regauging, and got £1,150 for the pair from the Belfast firm of Coates & Young, who promptly converted them to run on the 5 ft 3 in. The L&E took delivery of them in November 1852, but Robert Dods, the locomotive engineer, complained of their imperfect condition. The bill, for £1,741 each, was not settled until June 1853. After only four years' work, the L&E was glad to be rid of them as scrap metal and took £150 for the pair.

A pair of 2-2-0WT engines was supplied by Robert Stephenson in 1852 ('VII'). Both were involved in the Trillick derailment in 1854, but in spite of that they had a life of 27 years.

Two engines, known as 'The Long Backs', were bought from John Jones of Liverpool in 1855 ('VIII') and were probably the only Irish engines to come from that firm. Ordered in February 1855, three months later it was found that they would be too long for the 15 ft turntables. By then it was too late to make alterations. Once taken into stock, complaints were made to the builders that they were using excessive quantities of coke, and after nearly a year of negotiation, the makers offered to knock £100 off the agreed price. They lasted for about 18 years under the GN, one finally working the Cootehill line while the other finished its days on the construction of the new Dundalk station.

Table IV - Dundalk & Enniskillen Railway

Type	Wheel Arr.	No. in class	Builder	Built	Cylinders	Driving wheels	Total htg surface	Weight t. c.	Remarks
I	2-2-2	2	Grendon	6/1848	14 in. x 18 in.	5 ft 6 in.	687 sq. ft	15 0	One to GNR(I), withdrawn 1874 and 1887.
II	0-4-2	2	Grendon	1849	14 in. x 18 in.	4 ft 4 in.	687 sq. ft	17 0	One to GNR(I) (No. 45), withdrawn 1850 and 1885.
III	2-2-2	3	Sharp, Stewart	1852-54	15 in. x 20 in.	5 ft 7 in.	878 sq. ft		GNR(I) Nos. 46-48, withdrawn 1880-85.
IV	0-6-0	2	Grendon	1855-56	16 in. x 24 in.	5 ft 0 in.	1,090 sq. ft	26 0	GNR(I) Nos. 49-50, withdrawn 1886 and 1902.
V	0-4-2	2	Sharp, Stewart	4/1858	16 in. x 22 in.	5 ft 0 in.	943 sq. ft	22 15	GNR(I) Nos. 51-52, withdrawn 1883-85.
VI	2-2-2	3	Beyer, Peacock	1859-61	15 in. x 20 in.	5 ft 6 in.	955 sq. ft	24 0	GNR(I) Nos. 53, 55, 56, withdrawn 1907-14.
VII	2-4-0	1	Longridge	1846-7	15 in. x 24 in.	4 ft 9 in.			GNR(I) No. 54, bought 1860, scrapped 1890.
VIII	0-4-2	4	Neilson	1861-63	16 in. x 24 in.	5 ft 3 in.	979 sq. ft	26 0	GNR(I) Nos. 57-58, 70-71, scrapped 1901-1907.

Total number of engines: 19.   Engines transferred to INWR: 17.

Table V - Londonderry & Enniskillen Railway

Type	Wheel Arr.	No. in class	Builder	Built	Cylinders	Driving wheels	Total htg surface	Weight t. c.	Remarks
I	2-4-0	2	Longridge	1846	15 in. x 24 in.	4 ft 11 in.			Long boiler. GNR(I) Nos. 59-60, withdrawn 1879, 1892.
II	2-2-2	1	Longridge	1846	15 in. x 24 in.	6 ft 1 in.			Rebuilt to 2-4-0 in 1854. Sold in 1860 to D&ER.
III	2-4-0	1	Longridge	1847	15 in. x 24 in.	5 ft 6 in.			Transferred to L&CR in 1851, withdrawn 1875.
IV	2-2-0WT	1	Adams	1850	9 in. x 15 in.	5 ft 0 in.	417 sq. ft	23 12	No. 4: INWR No. 19, withdrawn 1873.
V	2-2-0WT	4	Kitson, Thompson & Hewitson	1852	10 in. x 16 in.	5 ft 2 in.	481 sq. ft	?10 0	Adams patent 'Steam perambulators'. Two to GNR(I), withdrawn 1871-1877.
VI	2-2-2	2	Sharp, Roberts / Coates & Young	1841	14 in. x 18 in.	5 ft 6 in.	600 sq. ft	11 0	Bought second-hand in 1852. Ex-6 ft 2 in gauge on UR, withdrawn 1857.
VII	2-2-0WT	2	Stephenson	1852	11 in. x 18 in.	5 ft 2 in.	544 sq. ft	14 0	GNR(I) Nos. 66-67, withdrawn 1879.
VIII	2-4-0	2	John Jones	1855	15 in. x 20 in.	4 ft 7 in.	830 sq. ft	25 0	The 'Long Backs', withdrawn c.1894.

Total number of engines: 15.   Total engines to GNR: 8.

Table VI - Irish North Western Railway

Type	Wheel Arr.	No. in class	Builder	Built	Cylinders	Driving wheels	Total htg surface	Weight t. c.	Remarks
XVII	0-6-0ST	2	Manning, Wardle	1859	11 in. x 17 in.	3 ft 3 in.	392 sq. ft	16 10	Bought 1866 second-hand, withdrawn 1892.
XVIII	2-4-0	2	Dübs	1866	15 in. x 21 in.	6 ft 0 in.	994 sq. ft	27 17	Withdrawn 1904-06.
XIX	0-4-2	1	Dübs	1867	16 in. x 24 in.	5 ft 3 in.	1,016 sq. ft	28 0	Withdrawn 1909.
XX	0-6-0	3	Dübs/INWR	1871-76	17 in. x 24 in.	5 ft 0 in.	1,109 sq. ft	35 11	Withdrawn 1948 (class 'E', GNR(I)).
XXI	2-4-0	1	INWR	1873	15 in. x 21 in.	5 ft 6 in.	987 sq. ft	29 0	Withdrawn 1891 or 1895.
XXII	2-4-0	1	INWR	1874	16 in. x 21 in.	6 ft 0 in.	1,024 sq. ft	31 0	Withdrawn 1921.

Total number of engines: 17 ex-D&ER → 17 to GNR(I)
11 ex-L&ER → 8 to GNR(I)
10 of new stock → 10 to GNR(I)
17 + 8 + 10 = 35

Engines to GNR(I):

Irish North Western Railway

At its formation, this company found itself managing 16 different types of engine. Pemberton, the locomotive engineer, proceeded to make confusion more confused (*Table Six*) by picking up a pair of second-hand 0-6-0 saddle tanks of Manning, Wardle origin, from Brassey, who was building the Enniskillen, Bundoran & Sligo Railway ('XVII'). He had originally got them while he was making the Worcester & Malvern Railway in 1859-60: *Rutland* fell into Lough Erne when being shipped by the contractors; it was salvaged and with its sister *Malvern* it finished its days shunting in the Barrack Street yard.

The Glasgow firm of Dübs sent over two passenger engines in 1866 ('XVIII') and a goods engine the next year ('XIX'). These three were all initially paid for by Brassey and did not actually enter the Irish North stock for some years.

Under Charles Clifford's superintendence, some degree of rationalisation at last came to Barrack Street. Reliable and powerful 0-6-0 goods engines were needed, and two were bought from Dübs in 1871-2 ('XX'). Boilers and wheels were purchased to build a third at the INWR works under Clifford's supervision. These three engines survived until mid-1948. Two were loaned to the MGWR during the 1931 strike, and one, as GNR (I) No. 193, went to the SLNC in 1947.

Barrack Street turned out two further engines, both 0-4-2, in 1873-4 ('XXI'-'XXII').

Newry & Armagh Railway

There are serious gaps in the history of this line, since many of the company's minute books are missing. Moreover, from February 1870 until August 1872, there are no reports, and since during much of this time the line was in the hands of creditors, it seems likely that no reports were issued or meetings held (*Table Seven*).

The first of the N&A's engines was a 2-2-0WT which was bought second-hand from the Londonderry & Coleraine Railway (L&CR) in 1853. It was rebuilt to 2-2-2WT in 1866 and sold for £450 in 1874 ('I').

Little is known of the next two engines ('II', 'III'). The first was by Hawthorn's of Leith, and it appears to have been altered from 0-4-0T to 0-4-2T. The second engine was a Fairbairn; it was sold to John Watson in 1864. In its place came a pair of 0-6-0 Stephenson engines, already five or six years old ('IV'). A solitary 2-4-0T ('V'), which was a shunter at Dublin in its later years, is thought to have been built by Sharp, Stewart and to have been originally built for an Indian line.

The final additions to this unsatisfactory stock were two new engines ('VI', 'VII'). The Sharp, Stewart 0-4-2 arrived at a time when the unfortunate company could not pay for it; it eventually was bought by J.B. Cooper of the Belfast Central, from whom it went to the Belfast & Northern Counties Railway.

Table VII - Newry & Armagh Railway

Type	Wheel Arr.	No. in class	Builder	Built	Cylinders	Driving wheels	Total htg surface	Weight t. c.	Remarks
I	2-2-0WT	1	Sharp, Stewart		11 in x 18 in.	5 ft 3 in.			Bought ex-L&CR 1853. Rebuilt to 2-2-2WT 1866. Withdrawn 1874.
II	0-4-0T?	1	Hawthorn		13 in. x 18 in.	4 ft 6 in.	478 sq. ft		Bought ? second-hand 1854. Rebuilt to 0-4-2T. Withdrawn 1884.
III	?	1	Fairbairn	1858-59	16 in. x 24 in.	4 ft 7½ in.	874 sq. ft	25 10	Taken over by Watson in 1864 and withdrawn.
IV	0-6-0	2	Stephenson	1864	15 in. x 22 in.	5 ft 0 in.	952 sq. ft	32 1	Bought 1864. Withdrawn 1881 and 1886.
V	2-4-0T	2	?Sharp, Stewart	1864	16 in. x 22 in.	5 ft 0½ in.	1,138 sq. ft	31 0	*The Buck*. Withdrawn 1895.
VI	0-4-2ST	2	Vulcan	1864	16 in. x 22 in.				Rebuilt 0-4-2. Withdrawn 1887 and 1893-95.
VII	0-4-2	1	Sharp, Stewart	1878	16 in. x 22 in.	5 ft 0 in.	955 sq. ft	27 2	Sold to BCR 1880, thence BNCR.

Total number of engines: 9.   Engines transferred to GNR(I): 6.

Table VIII - Newry, Warrenpoint & Rostrevor Railway

Type	Wheel Arr.	No. in class	Builder	Built	Cylinders	Driving wheels	Total htg surface	Weight t. c.	Remarks
I	?2-2-2	3	BC&K	1848-49 ?	15 in. x 20 in.	25 ft 8 in.			Sold in 1850 to Dargan.
II	2-2-2T	2	Forrester	1834-36	11 in. x 18 in.	5 ft 0 in.			Ex-D&KR. Probably used from 1850 by Dargan.
III	2-2-2T	1	Grendon	1850	10 in. x 15 in.	4 ft 0 in.	351 sq. ft		No. 3 *Victoria*. Withdrawn 1885. Scrapped 1886 or 1887.
IV	2-2-2T	1	Fairbairn	1850-51		5 ft 0 in.	450 sq. ft	13 0	Used by Dargan.
V	2-2-2T	2	Grendon	1858-59	11 in. x 16 in.	5 ft 0 in.			Scrapped 1886, and 1892 by GNR(I).
VI	?2-2-2T	1	Grendon	1866	9 in. x 13 in.				Withdrawn ?1882.
VII	2-4-0T	1	Beyer, Peacock	1882		?4 ft 0 in.	600 sq. ft	28 10	Withdrawn 1898.

Total number of engines: 11.   Engines transferred to GNR(I): 2.

Table IX - Belfast Central Railway

Type	Wheel Arr.	No. in class	Builder	Built	Cylinders	Driving wheels	Total htg surface	Weight t. c.	Remarks
I	0-6-0ST	2	Black, Hawthorn	1868, 1874	14 in. x 20 in.	3 ft 6 in.			Both withdrawn 1894-95 by GNR(I).
II	0-6-0T	1	Fossick & Hackworth	1862	13 in. x 24 in.	4 ft 0 in.		24 0	Ex-L&LS 1885. Owned by Kelly.
III	2-4-0T	1	Beyer, Peacock	1878	14 in. x 20 in.	5 ft 0 in.		20 9	Similar to NW&R type 'VII'. Withdrawn 1898.
IV	4-4-0T	1	Beyer, Peacock	1880	15 in. x 20 in.	5 ft 0 in.		42 6	Dundalk Pilot, 1904. Withdrawn 1950.
V	0-4-2	1	Sharp, Stewart	1878	16 in. x 22 in.	5 ft 0 in.	955 sq. ft	28 0	Ex N&A in 1880. To BNCR in 8/1886.

Total number of engines: 6.   Engines transferred to GNR(I): 4.

Newry, Warrenpoint & Rostrevor Railway

This company began operations with three Bury, Curtis & Kennedy engines, probably of the 2-2-2 type (*Table Eight*). Shortly afterwards they were bought by Dargan under the terms of his contract, and as owner he probably transferred them to the Waterford & Limerick Railway. They never returned to the NW&R. There is only slender evidence to connect a pair of 2-2-0T engines ('II') with the line. These were Forrester-built in 1834-6 for the Dublin & Kingstown, and were named *Kingstown* and *Victoria*. They were sold to the contractor McCormick in 1846, who resold them to Dargan. Around 1846 they were regauged from 4 ft 8½ in. to 5 ft 3 in. and in this form they may have run between Newry and Warrenpoint. Dargan also used a ('III') and a Fairbairn 2-2-2T ('IV') on the line.

A pair of Grendon 2-2-2T engines ('V') named *Rostrevor* and *Mourne* may have dated from 1858-9; they appear to have worked up to the time of amalgamation. A further Grendon engine, named *Drogheda*, is of uncertain type ('VI'). Finally a 2-4-0T came from Beyer, Peacock in 1882 ('VI'), becoming No. 90 in GN stock. It had a short life of 16 years, due to the standardisation policy.

Belfast Central Railway

Until 1874 this company contracted for engine supplies with the firm of Kelly & McFarlane. The locomotive stock position of the company is obscure until 1879. The Board of Trade returns list no engines in 1874, but one in the following year (*Table Nine*). This was probably the first of the Black, Hawthorn pair ('I'). A hired engine, which was probably a Fossick & Hackworth, came from the 5 ft 3 in. gauge L&LS to Kelly & McFarlane from 1868 to 1874 ('II').

Beyer, Peacock supplied a 2-4-0T in 1878 ('III'), similar to the NW&R type 'VII'. A second Beyer ('IV') was the Dundalk pilot from 1904 until its withdrawal in 1950. The Sharp, Stewart 0-4-2 from the N&A ('V') has already been noted.

Great Northern Railway (Ireland)

At the amalgamation, the GNR(I) inherited 118 engines, 41 from the Ulster, 35 from the Irish North, 21 from the D&D, 19 from the D&BJ, while another couple had been built during the short life of the Northern Railway. This total was serviced by five workshops, which were under four locomotive superintendents. The best-equipped of the shops were those of the UR, situated at Belfast and run by John Eaton. Next to them came the Barrack Street (Dundalk) shops of the Irish North; this company also had the old Londonderry shops of the L&E, and both were managed by Charles Clifford. The old D&D shops were down at Dublin, under William Curry. Finally, Thomas Armitage was in charge of the small Dundalk workshops of the D&BJ, which were sited somewhere about the position of the later Great Northern works.

Table X - Great Northern Railway (Ireland)

Type	Wheel Arr.	No. in class	Builder	Built	Cylinders	Driving wheels	Total htg surface	Weight t. c.	Remarks
I	2-4-0	8	Beyer, Peacock	1875-83	16 in. x 22 in.	5 ft 7 in.	950 sq. ft	27 18	Class 'G' (Passenger).
II	0-6-0	4	Sharp, Stewart	1877	16 in. x 24 in.	4 ft 7 in.			Class 'B' (Goods).
III	0-6-0	5	Sharp, Stewart	1879-80	17 in. x 24 in.	4 ft 7 in.	1,005 sq. ft	31 12	Class 'B'.
IV	2-4-0	4	Beyer, Peacock	1880-81	16 in. x 22 in.	6 ft 1½ in.	1,063 sq. ft	32 10	Class 'H'.
V	0-6-0	15	Beyer, Peacock (13) / GNR(I) (2)	1882-91	17 in. x 24 in.	4 ft 7¾ in.	989 sq. ft	32 0*	Class 'A'. * The two GNR(I) built engines had a weight of 31 t. 10 cwt. *Victoria* No. 88, *Albert* No. 99.
VI	4-2-2	2	Beyer, Peacock	1885	16 in. x 22 in.	6 ft 7 in.	970 sq. ft	34 0	Class 'J'. Withdrawn 1921-24.
VII	4-4-0	12	Beyer, Peacock	1885-89	16 in. x 22 in.	6 ft 7 in.	943 sq. ft	34 12	
VIII	4-4-0T	13	Beyer, Peacock (3) / GNR(I) (10)	1885-93	14 in. x 18 in. or 15 in. x 18 in.	4 ft 7 in.	595 sq. ft	31 0	Class 'BT'. One rebuilt to 0-6-0T (No. 100/1/119 in 1920).
IX	4-4-0	4	Beyer, Peacock (4)	1892-95	17 in. x 24 in.	6 ft 7 in.	1,110 sq. ft	39 6	Class 'P'. 6 ft 6 in.
X	4-4-0	8	Beyer, Peacock (4) / GNR (I) (4)	1892-1906	17 in. x 24 in.	5 ft 7 in.	1,110 sq. ft	39 0	Class 'P'. 5 ft 6 in. GNR(I) built engines weighed 41 t. 9 cwt. with a heating surface of 1,256 sq. ft.
XI	0-6-0	11	Beyer, Peacock (7) / GNR(I) (4)	1893-96	17 in. x 24 in.	4 ft 7 in.	1,130 sq. ft	34 10	Class 'AL'.
XII	2-4-2T	6	GNR(I)	1895-1902	16-17 in. x 22 in.	5 ft 7 in.	961/1,069 sq. ft	44 18#	Class JT. # Some members of the class were 45 t. 13 cwt.
XIII	4-4-0	17	Beyer, Peacock (15) / GNR(I) (2)	1896-1911	18 or 18½ in. x 24 in.	6 ft 7 in.	1,128 sq. ft (1896)	42 0	Class 'PP'. Mostly superheated when rebuilt, two superheated originally (1911).
XIV	4-4-0	13	Beyer, Peacock (2) / North British (2) / Neilson (9)	1899-1904	18½ in. x 26 in.	6 ft 7 in.	1,357 sq. ft	45 15	Class 'Q'.
XV	0-6-0	7	Neilson (3) / GNR(I) (4)	1899-1904	18½ in. x 24 in.	4 ft 7 in.	1,262 sq. ft	39 10	Class 'PG'. All superheated in 1921-29.
XVI	0-6-0	4	North British	1903-04	18 in. x 26 in.	4 ft 7 in.	1,357 sq. ft	41 10	Class 'QG'. Superheated in 1926-28.
XVII	4-4-0	8	North British (7) / Beyer, Peacock (1)	1904-10	18½ in. x 26 in.	4 ft 7½ in.	1,531 sq. ft	49 10	Class 'QL'. Superheated in 1919-28. The Beyer, Peacock locomotive had 18 in. x 26 in. cylinders.
XVIII	0-6-2T	2	Stephenson	1905	18½ in. x 26 in.	4 ft 7 in.	1,266 sq. ft	55 6	Class 'QGT'. Superheated in 1932-35.

Class	No.	Builder	Year	Cylinders	Driving wheels	Heating surface			Remarks
XIX	3	North British	1905	12 in. x 16 in.	3 ft 7½ in.	623 sq. ft			Lisburn Railmotors. Withdrawn 1913.
XX	4	Manning, Wardle	1906	12 in. x 16 in.	3 ft 9 in.	653 sq. ft			Howth Railmotors. Withdrawn 1913.
XXI	11	North British (9) GNR(I) (2)	1906-08	18½ in. x 26 in.	4 ft 7½ in.	1,520 sq. ft	45	3	Class 'LQG'. Superheated in 1921-30 to class 'LQGs'.
XXII	4	Beyer, Peacock	1908-11	17 in x 24 in.	4 ft 3 in.	1,087 sq. ft	56	8	Class 'RT'. Unsuperheated.
XXIII	5	N. Wilson	1911	18 in. x 26 in.	4 ft 7 in.	1,332 sq. ft	45	16§	Class 'NQG'. Superheated in 1930-31. § Some engines were 47 t. 9 cwt.
XXIV	1	N. Wilson	1911	18½ in. x 26 in.	4 ft 7 in.	1,430 sq. ft	46	0	Class 'NLQG, later 'LQGs'.
XXV	2	Stephenson	1911	18½ in. x 26 in.	4 ft 7 in.	1,257 sq. ft	60	0	Class 'QGT2'.
XXVI	8	Beyer, Peacock	1913-15	19 in. x 26 in.	6 ft 7 in.	1,209/1,240 sq. ft	52	2	Class 'S' and 'S2'. Rebuilt to type 'XXXVII'.
XXVII	15	Beyer, Peacock (10) N. Wilson (5)	1913-24	19 in. x 26 in.	5 ft 1 in.	1,284 sq. ft	48	19	Class 'SG' and 'SG2'.
XXVIII	1	Hunslet	(1913)	10 in. x 15 in.	2 ft 8½ in.	? 275 sq. ft	16	0	Built 1904, sold 1930.
XXIX	1	Hunslet	(1913)	15 in. x 20 in.	3 ft 4 in.		28	10	Ex-CK&AR contract, withdrawn 1930.
XXX	5	Beyer, Peacock	1913	18 in. x 24 in.	5 ft 9 in.	1,092 sq. ft	65	2	Class 'T'. Superheated 1923-26.
XXXI	5	Beyer, Peacock	1915	18 in. x 24 in.	5 ft 9 in.	1,056 sq. ft	44	6	Class 'U'.
XXXII	15	Beyer, Peacock	1920-21	19½ in. x 26 in.	5 ft 1 in.	1,600 sq. ft	52	10	Class 'SG3'.
XXXIII	20	Beyer, Peacock (10) N. Wilson (10)	1921-29	18 in. x 24 in.	5 ft 9 in.	1,056 sq. ft	65	15	Class 'T2'.
XXXIV	1	H. Leslie	1927	14 in. x 20 in.	3 ft 4 in.	637 sq. ft	45	0	Crane locomotive.
XXXV	5	Beyer, Peacock	1932	(1) 17¼ x 26 in. (2) 19 in. x 26 in.	6 ft 7 in.	1,528 sq. ft	65	1	Class 'V'. Compound express passenger.
XXXVI	10	GNR(I) (5) Beyer, Peacock (5)	1937-48	18 in. x 24 in.	5 ft 1 in.	1,022 sq. ft¶	45	12	Class 'UG'. ¶ Beyer, Peacock engines had a heating surface of 1,031 sq. ft.
XXXVII	8	GNR(I)	1938-39	19 in. x 26 in.	6 ft 7 in.	1,240 sq. ft	53	6	Class 'S' and 'S2'.
XXXVIII	5	Beyer, Peacock	1948	18 in. x 24 in.	5 ft 9 in.	1,032 sq. ft	44	6	Class U (modified).
XXXIX	5	Beyer, Peacock	1948	15¾ in. x 26 in.	6 ft 7 in.	1,531 sq. ft	66	6	Class 'VS' (3 cyl).

Classes 'P', 'PP', 'Q', 'PG', 'QQ', 'QL', 'LQG', 'QGT', 'LQG', 'NQG' had a small 's' added to title when superheated.

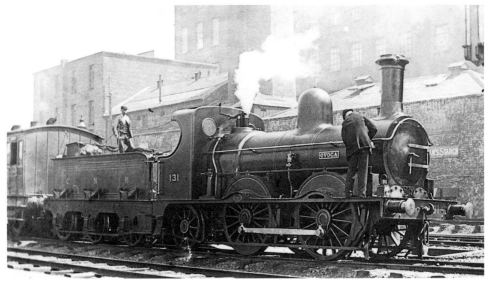

0-4-2 No. 131 *Ovoca* at Belfast. This locomotive was built for the Ulster Railway by Sharp, Stewart in 1866. This view shows the engine after being rebuilt by the GNR in 1882.

0-4-2 No. 134 *Liffey* was also built for the Ulster Railway. It was supplied by Beyer, Peacock and was delivered in 1866. It is seen here after rebuilding in 1890 and remained in service until 1911.

John Alsop Collection

Simplification was clearly needed, but it was slow to come. The first stage was Armitage's departure to the Waterford & Limerick line in 1875, which left Curry to manage the engine stock of the original Northern Railway. When the INWR joined in, Clifford remained at Barrack Street, but was subordinate to Curry, who was in charge of the Southern Division of the company. At Belfast the reluctance of the Ulster to submerge its individuality extended to Eaton's domain; the engine renumbering was deferred for some years, and the striking brick-red Ulster livery stayed for nine years. It was not indeed until Eaton's retirement in 1885 that the Northern Division of the GNR(I) came under Dundalk's control.

It was soon decided to centralise heavy locomotive work at Dundalk, in new buildings. James C. Park came from the Great Northern of England to take command. Curry was transferred from Dublin to be Park's assistant, and Clifford went to Dublin as district locomotive superintendent. As we have seen, Eaton remained aloof in the north.

The earliest additions to the locomotive stock (*Table Ten*) perpetuated existing practice as 2-4-0 passenger engines ('I') and 0-6-0 goods engines ('II', 'III'). About this time, the old D&D works built, as their swan-song, its only engine; a complete renewal of old No. 15 (D&D type 'XI') for use on the Limited Mails. Four 6 ft passenger 2-4-0 engines of 1880-1 were a follow-on of old D&BJ practice, and one of them was the primary cause of the Armagh disaster, when it failed on the Markethill bank.

Park's training and influence were soon evident when the first class 'A' goods engines arrived in 1882 ('V'). Their livery, chimney, and cab followed upon Pat Stirling's Doncaster practice, and there began the well-known external resemblance between the engines of the two Great Northerns that was to continue for over half a century.

The traditional use of single-driver engines on the Limited Mails was maintained when Beyer, Peacock sent over, in 1885, the only 4-2-2 engines to run in Ireland ('VI'). With inside cylinders, and named *Victoria* and *Albert*, their main line work was only to last 12 years after which they were demoted to work locals out of Dublin.

The first of the long line of 4-4-0 engines, a type that was to personify GNR (I) passenger train haulage, came as class 'J' in 1885. With others delivered up to 1889 ('VII'), their 5 ft 7in. driving wheels reflected the earlier 2-4-0 engines.

After the Armagh disaster, fitment of the automatic vacuum brake in place of the earlier simple vacuum brake began. The increased steam usage called for the provision of larger boilers, and in consequence enlarged versions were designed of both the passenger and the goods engines. The class 'P' 6 ft 6 in. ('IX') and the 'P' 5 ft 6 in. ('X') passenger 4-4-0s were the first to come; they were followed by the class 'AL' goods ('XI'). The construction of these was shared between Beyer, Peacock and the new Dundalk works.

By the mid-1880s, passenger tank engines were arriving from Beyer, Peacock, in the shape of three 4-4-0T types, to replace some of the small engines acquired from the constituent companies. Named *Lisburn*, *Balmoral*, and *Dunmurry*, these precursors of the large class 'BT' worked the Belfast suburban traffic. There followed 10 more, all built at Dundalk between 1887 and 1893. The class was withdrawn for the most part in 1920-1, but one engine, the first to be built at Dundalk, became an 0-6-0T in 1920 and in this form lasted a further 15 years as the Derry shunter.

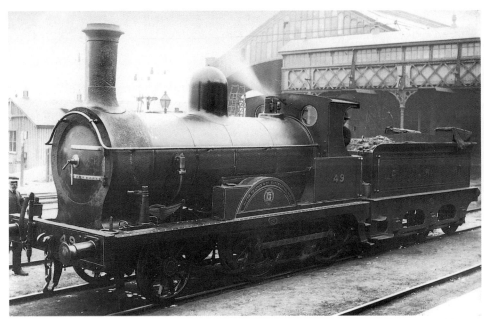

'G' class 2-4-0 No. 49 was built by Beyer, Peacock and delivered in 1877. It is seen at Dublin Amiens Street after its rebuild of 1899. It was to be rebuilt again in 1915 and continued in service until 1921.   *John Alsop Collection*

'JS' class 4-2-2 No. 89 *Albert* was one of a pair (the other being No. 88 *Victoria*) delivered in 1885. These engines had been withdrawn by the end of 1904.

0-6-0 No. 21 was built by Beyer, Peacock and originally delivered to to the Dublin & Drogheda Railway in 1863. This view shows the engine after its rebuild of 1887. Withdrawal came in 1908.
John Alsop Collection

0-6-0 No. 103 at Londonderry on 12th July, 1931. This locomotive was originally built by Neilson, Reid and was delivered in 1901 when it was classified as 'PG' class and carried the name *Dunleer*. No. 103 was the last of the class to receive a superheater (in April 1929) when it was reclassified 'PGs' class. *L&GRP*

The machine shop in Dundalk works.   *Duffner*

The erecting shop, Dundalk works *c.* 1910. Beyond 'AL' class No. 35's cab is 'QG' class 0-6-0 No. 154, another locomotive end and a 'JT' class 2-4-2T. This view is looking towards the main line, note the narrow gauge track on the right.   *Duffner*

LOCOMOTIVES 141

The next tanks to be designed were the more powerful class 'JT', with much increased steaming capacity compared to the little 'BT' class boilers. Park's death took place on 27th May, 1895, before the first of these engines was completed, and his place at Dundalk was taken by Charles Clifford. *Sutton*, *Howth*, *Aster* and *Crow* came in turn and were assigned to the local Dublin-Howth and Dublin-Malahide trains. *Viola* and *Tulip* in 1902 were the final additions to the class ('XII').

Clifford's first design was for main line passenger express working, and there arrived from Beyer's in 1896 the first of the 17 class 'PP' engines ('XIII'), all of which were named. These new engines had 18 in. by 24 in. cylinders, 6 ft 7 in. coupled wheels, and boilers 4 ft 2 in. by 10 ft 2 in. Later engines had 4 ft 3 in. boilers, and many were eventually given 4 ft 6 in. boilers with superheaters. The maximum axle loading of this class rose, with rebuilding, to 15¼ tons.

There followed within the next few years larger named 4-4-0 engines of similar appearance, classes 'Q' and 'QL' ('XIV' and 'XVII'). The delivery of the latter class, which had boilers 4 ft 9 in. in diameter, was spread over 1904-10, and during this period the smaller 'PP' engines continued to be built for branch line working.

Although Clifford was nominally responsible for locomotive design, there is no doubt that a large measure of credit in Clifford's later years must be given to L.J. Watson, who became chief draughtsman at Dundalk.

In December 1910, the Great Northern suggested to the Great Southern & Western that an experimental interchange of engine power might yield useful results. The GS&W agreed, and GNR (I) No. 136 *Minerva*, of class 'Q,' manned by driver Robert Bruce and fireman William Wallace, ran during the spring of 1911 on the GS&W, while their No. 322 came over to the Great Northern. *Minerva* proved to be the more economical engine of the two, burning 34.2 lb. of coal per mile compared to the GS&W's 38.9 lb.

Clifford's final passenger design was the highly successful class 'S' engine ('XXVI'), of which five came from Beyer, Peacock in February 1913. Schmidt superheaters and 8 in. piston valves with rocker arms were an innovation on the GNR (I). Before they arrived from the makers, Clifford had retired. He was succeeded by G.T. Glover, from the North Eastern Railway of England. Soon after coming, Glover made detail changes in the 'S' class, extending the cab roofs backwards and replacing the green livery with black. The nameplates were removed about 1920.

A further batch of three large passenger engines, class 'S2', came in February-March 1915 ('XXVI'). Much like the 'S' engines but never green, they had direct motion driving inclined piston valves, and Robinson superheaters.

From 1911, Clifford had experimented on some of the 'PP' engines with the Phoenix superheaters. They were unsuccessful and were removed within a few years. Under the Glover regime, superheating began in earnest at the end of the first war, and the smaller 4-4-0 engines were so modified, a gradual process that was not completed until 1932.

The 4-4-0 passenger engine stock built up by Clifford and Glover included five of class 'U' with 5 ft 9 in. driving wheels ('XXXI'), and they served the company well into the 1930s.

Beyer, Peacock-built 'PP' class 4-4-0 No. 71 *Bundoran* of 1896 at platform 4, Great Victoria Street station, Belfast in original condition. The carriage in the background provided conveyance to the Imperial Hotel in Donegall Place.   *John Alsop Collection*

Neilson, Reid-built 'Q' class 4-4-0 No. 133 *Apollo* of 1899 at Amiens Street Shed, Dublin also in original condition.   *John Alsop Collection*

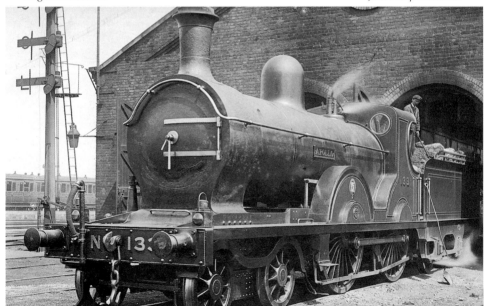

The rebuilding of the Boyne viaduct, completed in 1932 by G.B. Howden, allowed axle loads to be raised from 17 to 21 tons across the river, and new and heavier engines were introduced to handle accelerated train services. These were the three-cylinder compounds of class 'V' ('XXXV'). They were akin in some ways to the famous Midland compounds of England, but they were larger, and with their 250 lb. boiler pressure both their high and low pressure cylinders were 2 in. smaller than those of the LMS engines. Another difference was the fitment of balanced slide valves to the lp cylinders, though these were removed in 1933. The axle was the maximum allowable, 21 tons. Numbered 83-87, they were named *Eagle, Falcon, Merlin, Peregrine* and *Kestrel* respectively.

The compounds coped easily with the new schedules, and it is noteworthy that in 1932 the average overall time of the main line trains, five each way, including all stops and the customs, was 2 hr 28 min. The mean running time, inclusive of restarting and stopping an average of five times per train, was 129¾, min., which is just under the present non-stop diesel allowance of the 'Enterprise' express. Timings were eased in 1934, and the boiler pressure was reduced to 200 lb., though this was later raised to 215 lb. Belpaire boilers were fitted in 1946-7, working at 220 lb.

The next innovation came in 1938-9, when after 25 years of service it was decided to renew the class 'S' engines. The light frames had kept the engine within the 17 ton limit; new and heavier frames brought this up to 18 tons. Other changes were increase of the valve travel from 3. in. to 5 in. and the provision of exhaust injectors. The 'S2' engines were similarly renewed and were named for the first time (*Appendix Five*). The resulting engines retained the old class 'S' and 'S2' titles, but they were virtually new construction ('XXXVII').

The last additions to the passenger stock came in 1948, when five more of the 'U' class engines, *Meath, Louth, Armagh, Antrim* and *Down* (Nos. 201-205), came from Beyer, Peacock in January ('XXXVIII'). Compared to their 1915 precursors, their cylinders were 21 in. closer, their boilers pitched 21 in. higher, while their cabs had side windows.

Towards the end of 1948, the five 'VS' class engines completed the Great Northern's steam stock; they were the last main line 4-4-0 engines to be built, a feature probably forced on the designers by the limited space in the Dundalk erecting shops. Its design was based on the well-tried 'V' class compounds, but it had three-cylinder simple propulsion with Walschaerts valve gear. The Belpaire boilers were identical with those used on the compounds, and certain other parts were interchangeable. Shortly after arrival, smoke deflector plates were fitted. With greatly eased schedules compared to the pre-war days, they had little chance to prove themselves in any spectacular fashion in the dozen years that passed before the diesels took over the running ('XXXIX'). Numbered 206-210, they were named *Liffey, Boyne, Lagan, Foyle* and *Erne* after Irish rivers.

In tracing the evolution of the passenger engines, we have neglected the goods and tank engines. Clifford began the practice of building goods engines with the same boiler and firebox as the current passenger engines. Thus the 'PG' goods class ('XV') paralleled the 'PP' passenger locomotives, though they had a larger boiler. Class 'QG' ('XVI') corresponded to the 'Q' and the 'LQG' ('XXI') to the 'QL' classes. All of them carried names.

'V' class 4-4-0 3-cylinder compound No. 87 *Kestrel* as delivered by Beyer, Peacock in 1932. The tender was built at Dundalk works.   *Duffner*

'VS' class 4-4-0 3-cylinder simple No. 206 *Liffey* was the first of the class to be delivered by Beyer, Peacock in 1948 and is seen here before smoke deflectors were fitted. It was withdrawn in 1960.
Duffner

The backplate and footplate of a 'V' class 3-cylinder compound.   *Duffner*

'QGT2' class 0-6-2T No. 169 was built by Robert Stephenson & Co. and was delivered in 1911, it was last used in 1953, seen here at Strabane on 30th June, 1937.   *L&GRP*

A 1933 view of 'T2' class 4-4-2T No. 21. It was built by Nasmyth, Wilson in 1924 and was withdrawn in 1959.   *L&GRP*

Until 1908, tender engines had performed nearly all the shunting work. Clifford then produced the first tank engines to be built specifically for yard work: two 0-6-2T engines of class 'QGT' ('XVIII') in which were combined the 'QG' cylinders and firebox with the 'PG' boiler. Two class 'QGT2' engines with larger fireboxes came in 1911 ('XXV'). Four 0-6-4T class 'RT' engines came from Beyer, Peacock in 1908-1911 ('XXII'); their apparent powerfulness was deceptive, for they were small engines with 'AL' class cylinders and boilers.

The 0-6-0 'NQG' and 'NLQG' goods engines ('XXIII', 'XXIV') were Nasmyth, Wilson modifications of the earlier 'QG' and 'LQG' types. Tentative experiments with Phoenix superheaters were unsatisfactory.

The five 'SG' engines that came from Beyer's in 1913 departed from previous goods practice in having 5 ft 1 in. wheels rather than 4 ft 7 in. ('XXVII'). Later members of this class, 'SG2', had as their source both Beyer, Peacock and Nasmyth, Wilson, and in place of rocking arms had inclined valves and direct motion. Schmidt superheaters replaced the earlier Robinson type of the 'SG' engines. The 'SG3' engines ('XXXII') had boilers increased in diameter by 5 in. up to 5 ft, and cylinder diameters up from 19 in. to 19½ in. Heavy engines resulted, and because of their axle loading they were prohibited from crossing the Drogheda viaduct until after 1932.

The first five 'UG' class engines ('XXXVII') came at a time when H.R. McIntosh was effectively in charge of the mechanical engineer's department; they were Dundalk built. Wheels were 5 ft 1 in. but their light axle loading allowed them to go almost anywhere on the system. Five more were added to the class in 1948, being Beyer built, and differing from their precursors in having a sliding side window to the cab.

The most numerous class of engines to be seen on the GNR(I) were the 4-4-2 tanks. Strictly speaking, their total of 25 is subdivided into the 'T' (later 'T1') and 'T2' types ('XXX', 'XXXIII'). The 'T1' engines were the first design to come from G.T. Glover and had 'PP' saturated boilers. Their driving wheel diameter of 5 ft 9 in. was new to the line. At first, they were not much used on suburban work, the original allocation being two engines at Clones and one each at Derry, Dundalk, and Belfast. Their successors, the 'T2' engines, came from Beyer's or Nasmyth, Wilson between 1921 and 1930. All were built with superheaters. The 'T1' engines were superheated and converted to piston from slide valves between 1923 and 1927.

The seven small railmotor engines were all of the 0-4-0T type with attached carriage, and worked the Lisburn ('XIX') and Howth ('XX') suburban traffic between 1905-6 and 1913. Like their contemporaries on other lines, they were not popular, but they may be regarded as the precursors of the light diesel railcars.

Two odd engines came via the CK&A Railway, which was absorbed by the Great Northern in 1911. These had been the property of the contractor Robert Worthington, who had made an unsuccessful start on the line and from whom the work was taken over in May 1908. The smallest driving wheels on the GNR (I) were possessed by the 0-4-0ST *Kells* ('XXVIII'), Hunslet-built in 1904; it was transferred to departmental use in 1921 and sold in 1930. The 0-6-0T engine ('XXIX') *Mullingar* had been bought new by Worthington in 1889 and saw service on the Kanturk to Newmarket and on the Mallaranny to Achill contracts. After lying for some years at Newport, it arrived on the CK&A contract in 1903. These two engines were not recorded as bought by the GNR(I) until 1913.

The final class to be noticed consists of the Dundalk works crane engine ('XXXV'), a standard 0-6-0T from Hawthorn, Leslie in 1927.

Locomotive sheds were located at Belfast, Portadown, Dundalk, Drogheda, Dublin, Newry, Oldcastle, Clones, Cavan, Enniskillen, Bundoran, Omagh, Londonderry, Antrim, Belturbet, Cookstown, Carrickmacross, Cootehill, and Armagh. At Newcastle, the Belfast & County Down shed was shared.

The extant details of pre-Great Northern engine liveries is very scanty. It is known that the D&D, D&BJR, and INWR engines were green, but nothing appears to be known of the lining. Ulster engines were brick-red, with black lining and brass nameplates which were smaller than those used later on the Great Northern. Ulster engines were always officially referred to by names rather than by numbers, and the plates were situated on the front ring of the boiler.

As might be expected, the dominant green was continued after amalgamation by both Park and Clifford. On his appointment in 1912, Glover ordered that goods engines were to be black, and from July 1914 this also affected the passenger engines. Nameplates were removed, though the 'QL' class kept them for a time.

The first change from Glover's black livery came in 1935, when G.B. Howden introduced a splendid sky-blue scheme, lined out with black and white, for the class 'V' compounds. This striking livery was later given to the 'S', 'S2', 'U' and 'VS' classes as well.

Fuller details of the three Great Northern liveries are contained in Appendix Four.

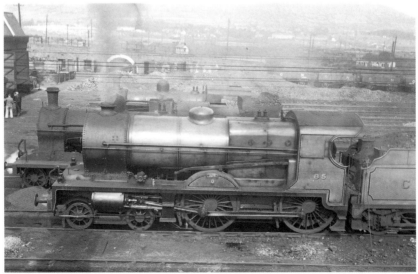

'V' class 4-4-0 3-cylinder compound No. 85 *Merlin* at Belfast's Adelaide Shed on 6th August, 1950. This locomotive had recently been rebuilt with a Belpaire firebox.

H.B. Priestley

Chapter Thirteen

Railcars and Railbuses

As an antidote to rising road competition in the 1920s the County Donegal Railways Joint Committee decided to introduce light railbuses similar to those in use on the roads. Since the Donegal narrow gauge line was jointly owned by the LMS (NCC) and the GNR(I) it was logical that railbus design and construction should be done at Dundalk works. With the experience thus gained, the next step was to build similar vehicles to run on the Great Northern's gauge. This was done successfully, and the Great Northern (Ireland), more than any other railway in the British Isles, pioneered and organised a diesel-propelled service on those minor lines whose light traffic merited them. This development was twofold and comprised both railcars and railbuses. It naturally graduated into the adoption in 1950 of multi-unit diesel trains for main line working.

The railbuses were conversions from existing road vehicles. In contrast, the railcars were of new construction. Although the first railcar was running two years ahead of the first railbus, the development of the former followed a more gradual course.

The traffic department initially laid down certain requirements in railcar design: a speed of up to 50 mph, seats for 32 persons, and the ability to drive them from either end and thus avoid the use of a turntable. The first pair of railcars, titled 'A' and 'B', emerged from Dundalk works in 1932. Careful stress assessment had enabled the frame and body weights to be kept well below those of orthodox steam coaching stock, and fuel consumption was only 8 to 10 mpg. Operating costs were a little less than 4*d*. per mile.

Railcar 'A' was a diesel-mechanical unit with a 130 hp AEC engine, later replaced by a 100 hp Gardner. Railcar 'B' had a 120 hp Gleniffer engine, later a '6L3' Gardner, and drove electrically via a Tilling-Stevens generator. Both cars worked mainly in the Portadown area. In October 1946 'B' was converted to a passenger trailer numbered 500 and was hauled by a steam locomotive on the Irish North section. This procedure was not economic, and the vehicle was scrapped in 1949.

In 1934, two years after 'A' and 'B' came railcar 'C'. Its engine and driving compartment were separate from the main body but were articulated to it through a bellows connection and door. A 96 hp Gardner diesel engine provided the power, driving through a four-speed gear-box to four wheels which were linked by side-rods. Unlike 'A' and 'B' it could be driven from one end only, and small turntables were provided where necessary. One class of seating was provided for 50 passengers. It went into service on Enniskillen-Bundoran work and covered almost 1,000 miles a week, at 12 mpg of fuel.

The need to turn railcar 'C' after each journey had obvious disadvantages on shorter runs, and in the next pair of vehicles this was avoided by running them in tandem with the driving cabs at the ends. Thus railcars Nos. C.2 and C.3 came out in 1935 as a combined unit, capable of separation if necessary. At the same time 'C' was renumbered C.1. Cars C.2/C.3 ran as a two-coach train but used only one of the power bogies at a time. The unit worked principally from Amiens Street to Howth and to Balbriggan. The two units ran separately from August 1937.

Railcar 'A' on the 6.08 pm local to Omagh train at Strabane in 5th August, 1958. A 'PP'-hauled Londonderry-Strabane local train stands behind.   *Author*

A portrait of railcar 'C' at Dundalk works.

In 1936 a more advanced design was evident in railcars 'D' and 'E'. These consisted of two light-weight coach bodies, articulated to a central power bogie. Seating initially was for 8 first, 50 second, and 101 third class passengers; later second and third class were merged. A 153 hp Gardner engine propelled the car, and its exhaust gases provided heating. The power bogie had three axles, driven through an electro-pneumatically controlled four-speed gearbox. The driving wheels were coupled, and the two driving cabs were sited terminally.

The triple-unit formation of 'D' and 'E' gave excellent service and was further developed in railcars 'F' and 'G', which were placed in service in early 1938. Their central power bogies ran on two axles. The driving wheels were not coupled, but a 102 hp Gardner engine drove each axle through a hydraulic coupling and five-speed gearbox.

By the mid-1930s it was apparent on certain sections of the line that something smaller than the railcars would be needed if services were to be maintained economically. The answer was provided by the conversion of a road bus in 1934, the resulting vehicle being noteworthy in having pneumatic tyres successfully applied to rail running, as the patented Howden-Meredith wheel.

The Howden-Meredith wheel was the result of collaboration between these two Dundalk engineers and the Dunlop Rubber Co., and it had some similarity to an Austro-Daimler design used on Austrian railcars. The Irish version had a steel rim or tyre between the pneumatic tyre and the rail surface. The outer part of the steel tyre was profiled in accordance with orthodox railway practice, but its inner surface was machined to correspond with the tread of the pneumatic tyre. By making the inside diameter of the steel tyre slightly less than the outside diameter of the inflated rubber tyre, the two were held firmly together. Puncturing was practically obviated, and the rubber tyre suffered no tread wear. Since the steel tyre distributed the load over the pneumatic inner, the safe axle load could be considerably more than in the case of a similar road vehicle. A final gain was the maintenance of the low rolling friction characteristic of steel wheels on steel rails. To safeguard against the risk of accidental deflation of the pneumatic tyre, a safety brake block was sited above the wheel. It not only applied braking power but also held the wheel rim vertical and switched off the engine ignition in emergency.

The pneumatic tyre scheme was first tested in 1933-4 on two permanent way vehicles, converted from Leyland lorries. One of these operated between Omagh and Londonderry and covered 4,200 miles in its first year. As a result of these tests it was found desirable to have a squatter shape of tyre on passenger-carrying vehicles. A special offset steel inner wheel was made by Dunlop to take the pneumatic tyre, which was of a size suitable to use with scrap steel tyres from locomotive bogies.

Altogether six railbuses were made for Great Northern working. The Dundalk works also built some for use on the Sligo, Leitrim & Northern Counties Railway and the Dundalk, Newry & Greenore Railway.

The first railbus was lettered 'D' and came into use in September 1934. It was renumbered D.1 when railcar 'D' appeared, and was sold to the SLNC in mid-1939. While on Great Northern work it operated between Dundalk and Clones.

Railbus 'E', later E.2, followed in October 1934 and enabled the Scarva branch to be reopened to passengers. It was again renumbered 1 in 1947, and later

Railcars Nos. C2 and C3 alongside Dublin Shed in 1936. Note the radiator shield.   *L&GRP*

Railcar No. C3 with trailer at Portadown platform 3. One of the AEC multiple units, No. 612, can be seen in the background, 3rd July, 1957.   *Kelland Collection*

converted to a civil engineer's vehicle and renumbered 8178. This vehicle was fitted with a reverse gearbox so that it could run equally well in either direction. No. 1 passed to the Ulster Transport Authority in 1958.

In January 1935, railbus 'F' appeared, becoming 'F.3' in 1938. It was damaged beyond repair in an accident at the Square Crossing, Dundalk, on 26th April, 1944. A replacement, also numbered F.3, went into service later in the same year. Renumbered 2 in 1947, it went into CIE stock in 1958.

Two railbuses, numbered 1 and 2, were made for the DN&G in 1935. They were taken into GN stock in 1947 and renumbered 3 and 4. No. 3 was scrapped in 1955, No. 4 was transferred to the permanent way department and numbered 8177 in 1956. It went to the CIE in 1958.

The usual power unit in these railbuses was the Gardner '4LW' diesel, of 60 hp, although in most of them petrol engines were installed when built. They all originally had Howden-Meredith wheels front and back. Complaints arose that the vehicles were not operating the track circuits, and this was traced to the grease in the wheel bearings, which prevented proper current transfer from rail to rail. It was felt that this could be overcome by fitting solid wheels with a solid connecting axle in front, although at some cost in riding comfort. However further experience showed that whilst there was an improvement, a railbus could not be considered as completely reliable in track-circuit operation. Signalmen were therefore ordered to treat railbuses as not operating track circuits and to handle their passage accordingly.

Certain of the railbuses originally had a full front cab, but to simplify engine access they were later made with half-cabs. Some of the bodies had the original front entrance doors, but later it was found that the most suitable place for a door was at the trailing end, with a side step just below platform height and steps up from the back to facilitate entrance at the various conditional level crossing stops.

Mileage records of the railbuses were not separately kept between 1934 and April 1936, but in that early period D.1, E.2, and F.3 aggregated a total of 132,800 miles. Between April 1934 and its transfer to the SLNC, D.1 covered 94,500 miles, while its 1937 total of 41,700 miles was the greatest ever to be run by a Great Northern railbus in a single year.

The total of 374,000 miles of railbus E/E.2/1 between 1934 and 1958 was the highest recorded in the series, and was equal to an annual average of 17,000 miles. The second F.3/2 railbus clocked 317,900 miles between 1944 and 1958, an annual average of 23,000 miles.

The yearly totals recorded for the two DN&G vehicles were more variable. In the later 1930s they usually covered between 15,000 and 20,000 miles per year, but in 1945 and 1946 DN&G No. 1 is credited with only 421 and zero miles respectively, while No. 2 had corresponding figures of 4,200 and 15 miles. The grand totals for these two buses between 1935 and 1955 were 266,800 miles and 285,500 miles.

Railcars and railbuses were painted in the same fashion as the road buses: dark blue lower and cream upper panels.

The railbuses and railcars played an important part in retaining branch line services and traffic in the face of increasing road competition, and they effectively paved the way for the introduction of the post-war multi-unit diesel trains.

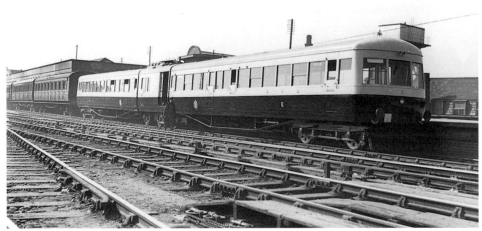

Railcar 'E' at Dublin on a Howth working   *Kelland Collection*

Railbus No. 2 at Clones on 7th June, 1957.

Chapter Fourteen

Multiple Unit Railcars and the MAK Diesel Locomotive

There is no doubt that, but for the war, the development of diesel railcars that had taken place between 1932 and 1939 would have proceeded earlier beyond the stage of the triple-unit cars. As it was, there was ample time for consideration of the next stage. In England AEC Ltd and the Great Western Railway had together produced successful designs of multiple-unit railcars, and these provided the Great Northern with a basis for their post-war plans. By the late 1940s it was clear that the sooner diesel traction took the place of steam the better, if the system was to survive. This, however, begs the question why the GNR took delivery of a further 15 steam locomotives (five 'UG' class 0-6-0s, five 'U' class 4-4-0s and five 'VS' class 4-4-0s) in 1948!

Early the same year it was decided to purchase 20 diesel railcars and to substitute them for steam-hauled trains both on main and on certain branch lines. About six months later an order for them was placed with AEC Ltd of Southall.

Unlike the triple-unit vehicles, these new railcars were individually powered, and although they could run singly, the intention was to marshal them in three-coach formations, two power cars on each side of a standard coach.

Each railcar was of the double-bogie type with two independent AEC 9.6 litre, 6 cylinder, direct injection compression ignition engines. These were symmetrically placed on each side of the frame, and each had a power output of 125 bhp. Transmission was by a fluid flywheel and five-speed, preselector, epicyclic gearbox. Engines, transmission, and a pair of 50 gallon fuel tanks were situated below the floor.

The railcar bodies were made by Park Royal and were divided into four compartments, containing driver, 12 first class seats, 32 third class seats, and guard and luggage. There were two vestibules, one with a toilet. The length over headstocks was 62 ft 6 in. and over buffers 66 ft 6 in., while the overall width was 9 ft 6 in.

The AEC railcar stock was numbered from 600 to 619 inclusive. A Vapor-Clarkson oil-fired heating boiler was installed in each of the even-numbered cars, its steam output being enough to heat a three-coach train. The livery was royal blue, with cream upper panels and grey roof.

The intermediate coaches, which were intended to run between even and odd-numbered railcars, were built at Dundalk. Their bodies were 58 ft long and 9 ft 6 in. wide. Four entrances opened directly into the car, which was open, with 54 third class seats. The centre of the vehicle was occupied by a bar. The coaches were linked by orthodox gangway connections, and the overall length of the three-coach train was 195 ft.

Provision was also made for these railcars to run with a non-powered coach in a two-car set, and for this purpose modifications were made to some standard third class coaches at Dundalk, a driving compartment being placed at one end. This type of train was well suited for small branch line working and had 12 first class and 104 third class seats.

AEC railcar No. 601 inside Dundalk works in May 1950.   *Kelland Collection*

AEC railcar No. 612 is signalled away to Belfast at Portadown platform 3 on 3rd July, 1957.

Kelland Collection

Two interior views of the AEC railcars. *Above:* view from first class towards the driver and cab. *Below:* view through one of the intermediate carriages, second class open with bar.

(Both) Duffner

As a result of an engine seizure at Drogheda on 11th September, 1952, railcar 614 was destroyed by fire. It was replaced by a new car, similarly numbered, in the autumn of 1953.

Almost seven years passed before the successful operation of the AEC railcars was to be extended. The Great Northern Railway Board decided in March 1954 to purchase 24 more railcars. Government sanction was necessary for the expenditure; it was not forthcoming until the following December. The design of these railcars differed considerably in detail from the earlier series. The chassis and the unassembled structural sections of the bodies were to be supplied by BUT Ltd and construction done at Dundalk. Owing to the shortage of steel, delivery did not start until September 1956, and the first three cars were not ready for service until June 1957. By September 1957 eight of the railcars were in service. It was not until October 1958, four and a half years after the decision to purchase, that the programme of delivery and construction was completed. Since control of the once-great Dundalk works had passed from the GNRB in January 1958, the final stages of the work were done by the Dundalk Engineering Co.

The BUT railcars were of two distinct types, and the differences between them permitted unusually flexible working. Sixteen, numbered 701 to 716, were full second class with 56 seats and driving compartments and corridor connections at each end. The remaining eight, 901 to 909, were first and second composites, seating 12 and 40 respectively and with a driving compartment at one end only and a corridor connection at the other end.

In both types of BUT car, larger AEC diesel engines were used than in the earlier railcars; they were of 11.3 litres capacity and developed 150 bhp at 1,800 rpm. The gearbox was four-speed and was not pre-selective. The nominal top speed was 85 mph. While both could run independently, the extra power and the versatile double-ended '701' cars enabled intermediate non-powered coaches to be marshalled in the train sets. These non-powered cars were built at Dundalk from existing coaching stock. The first train to run consisted of three powered and three intermediate cars and formed the Belfast-Dublin 'Enterprise' express.

Heating of the BUT cars was by means of the engine cooling water, necessarily supplemented by steam from a 500 lb. per hr boiler located in an intermediate car.

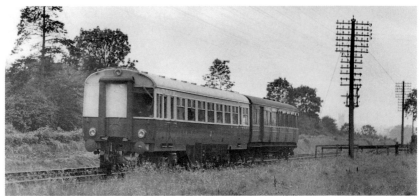

BUT car No. 705, with 'D3' class trailer, brake third No. 396, on the 8.50 am Enniskillen to Belfast working near Portadown on 18th September, 1957.   *C. Hogg*

Diesel-hydraulic No. 800 built by Maschinenbau A-G, and seen at the locomotive weighbridge shed, Dundalk works.

The GNR Board's modernisation scheme included not only multiple-unit railcars but also diesel-engined locomotives. Several types of these were considered, and in April 1954 the Board invited tenders for three types of diesel locomotives, 350 to 400 hp, 800 hp, and 1,000 hp. The German firm of Maschinenbau A-G, Kiel, offered to construct and ship at their own expense an 800 hp diesel-hydraulic locomotive. The offer was accepted, and the MAK locomotive arrived at North Wall on 14th December, 1954. It ran on four axles and had a wheel arrangement of O-D-O. Voith hydraulic transmission was fitted, and the total weight was 57½ tons. The maximum speed was 53 mph.

Five days before its arrival, the Tolka viaduct had been washed away by floods, and the MAK engine had to run to Dundalk by way of Clonsilla Junction, Navan Junction, and Drogheda. Satisfactory trial runs were made with heavy goods trains on the Dublin-Belfast and the Belfast-Londonderry lines and with local passenger trains from Dublin. Some experience was also gained on the UTA's system before the Board decided to purchase it for £29,500. It became No. 800 in the Board's books, the number not only indicating the engine power but also ranking it among the collection of railcars.

If the Board's recommendations had been followed by the two governments, there is no doubt that further diesel locomotives would have been ordered. Despite continued pressure by the Board for a decision on their proposals, the governments would not sanction the necessary expenditure, and as a result the MAK engine remained as a solitary example of its type of motive power on the GNR.

The colour scheme for the multiple unit railcars followed upon the established practice for railbuses and single unit railcars, namely, dark blue lower and cream upper portion, and black roof. The MAK locomotive was finished in essentially the same livery as the blue steam locomotives.

'Y3' 4-wheel parcels van No. 283.   *L.J. Watson*

'Q2' 6-wheel lavatory second No. 131 of 1898, photographed in 1948.

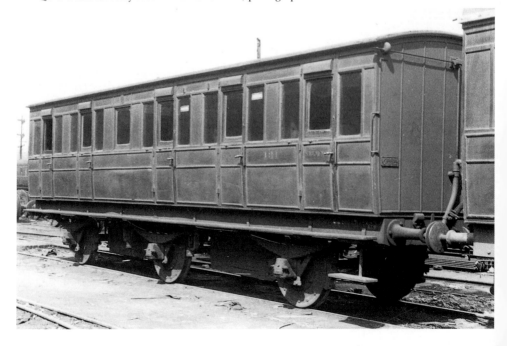

Chapter Fifteen

Coaching Stock

At the time of amalgamation in 1876, the total coaching stock of the constituent companies was made up as follows:

Great Northern Coaching Stock, 1876

	UR	D&DR	D&BJR	INWR
First	15	10	6	-
Second	10	9	6	-
Third	40	27	11	23
First/Second compos.	16	21	11	25
Luggage, brake, and mail vans	24	15	7	22
Horse boxes	10	12	10	8
Carriage trucks	5	12	10	10
Post Office sorting vans	3	1	-	-

This miscellaneous collection of coaching stock appears to have been regarded, even in 1876, as antiquated, with four-wheelers in the majority. Under the Great Northern, systematic scrapping of the four-wheelers was started, and six-wheelers were built to take their place. The first bogie carriage was built in 1889 and the last six-wheeler in 1896.

Great Northern coaching stock was classified by index letters, and the 28 classes thus denoted were each subdivided by numbered suffixes. All the vehicles in each sub-class were more or less identical. Each vehicle carried its class letter and number on a small cast metal plate at each end. Bogie vehicle classes ran from A to P, six-wheelers from O to Z, while Y was reserved for certain four-wheeled vans. The Fintona horse tram was in a class by itself, in more senses than one.

Great Northern Coaching Stock, 1944

Bogie vehicles
A	Saloons	3
B	Dining and kitchen cars	9
C	First class	1
D	First and brake *or* first, second and brake *or* second and brake	10
E	Second class	3
F	First and second composites	42
G	First, second and brake	11
H	Second and third composites	7
I	Tri-composites	15
J	Tri-composites and brake	27
K	Third class	134
L	Third and brake	41
M	Guards' Brake Van	10
N	Post Office sorting van	2
O	First, third and brake	2
P	20 ton parcel van	13

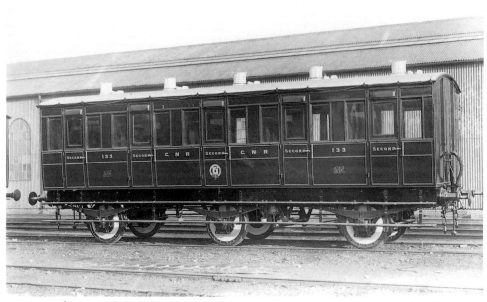

'Q3' 6-wheel second No. 133.   *L.J. Watson*

'V3' 6-wheel brake third No. 364.   *Duffner*

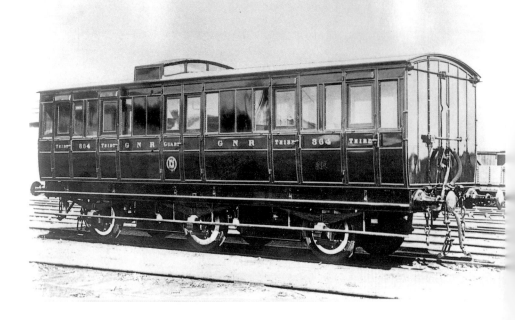

'W2' 6-wheel guard's brake van No. 301. *Duffner*

The interior of the carriage shop at Dundalk works. *Charles Friel Collection*

Great Northern Coaching Stock, 1944 (continued)

6-wheel vehicles

O	First class saloon	0	U	Third class	30
P	First class	0	V	Third and brake	6
Q	Second class	3	W	Brake van	18
R	First and second composites	12	X	Mail and parcel van	11
S	Second and third composites	0	Z	Refreshment van	3
T	Tri-composites and brake	2			

4-wheel vehicles

Y	Parcel, etc., Van	26

In addition to this letter/number classification, each vehicle carried its own serial number, at waist level on the side of the body.

Four roof shapes were officially recognised. The 'flat roof' was in fact curved, but differed from the others in overhanging the sides. Elliptical roofs were of both 'low' and 'high' types, and merged smoothly into the vehicles' sides. Clerestory roofs formed the fourth shape. Building of the stock was practically all done at the Dundalk shops, once centralisation had been decided upon.

The earliest six-wheeler classification included 'O^1' to 'O^6' and 'P^1' to 'P^2'. The 'O' saloons became extinct around 1922, some being converted into brake vans. There were 13 class 'P' coaches in all, seating 30 or 32 and varying in length between 25 ft and 33 ft 6 in. By 1928 only four were left, but in that year Nos. 3, 22, and 30 were scrapped and No. 358 converted to a third class.

The class 'Q' seconds seated 38 to 52. No. 339 was the sole member of class 'Q^1', 33 ft 6 in. long and weighing 14½ tons. It had a small brake compartment. It ended its days as a brake third and was one of the last six-wheelers to be broken up.

Originally the 'R' coaches were first and second composites, but later they were made tri-composites. Most of them had 16 first and 20 second seats, and there were nine sub-classes. No. 4 of 'R^3' was unusual; it had a large brake compartment and only half the usual quota of passenger seats.

Largest of the six-wheeler classes was naturally the thirds, which were sub-classed from 'U^1' to 'U^9'. Length varied from 27 ft to 31 ft, and seating from 40 to 60. There were altogether 126 of them. Thirty survived World War II, and the last regular six-wheeled workings were on the Gortnagallon branch.

Class 'X' contained 5 general purpose vans, 3 stores vehicles, 2 vacuum cleaning vans, and a speed test van. Most of them were taken into the stock of the engineering department, in which they were renumbered in the 8000 series.

Class 'Y' were the four-wheeled versions of class 'X'. Among them were 2 mortuary vans and 3 refrigerated vans. The majority were luggage and parcel vans with louvred sides.

The first bogie coach emerged from the shops as No. 382 in 1889. In the next year No. 383 followed it. Both were first and second composites, 38 ft 6 in. long in the body, and with 8 first and 34 second class seats. The transition away from six-wheeler building was gradual; thus in 1891 9 six-wheelers and no bogies were built, and in 1892 two bogies. The latter were numbered 397 ('F^{10}') and 398 ('F^{11}') ; these together with the 1889-90 bogies were the only ones to have flat roofs.

The first catering vehicles, Nos. 338, 401, and 402, were put into service in 1895. In 1896, four bogie vehicles were built, No. 409 (restaurant car), two 'I⁶' tri-composites, and the first of the 'K¹' thirds. These forerunners of the large class of bogie thirds had 10 compartments, each seating 10, and were non-corridor; altogether 19 'K¹' coaches were built, the bulk in 1899-1900. They packed their cargo into a body 51 ft 3 in. by 8 ft 9 in., and with their production third class bogie travel began, albeit in cramped conditions.

Three years after the last 100-seater 'K¹' came the solitary 'K²', a 90-seater of similar dimensions, numbered 160, and with a clerestory roof. Classes 'K³' and 'K⁴', more generously dimensioned than their forerunners, followed in 1904-10; they totalled 19 and one respectively and held 82 passengers in a 48 ft by 9 ft body.

The first vestibuled third ('K⁵') came in 1911 and was followed by three 'K⁶' coaches in 1913. The 'K⁶' vehicles were 56 ft long, and held 90. A fourth 'K⁶', No. 261, came in 1915 and was for a time a 12-wheeler. Three of them were altered to class 'L¹¹' and worked with three 'G⁶' coaches on push-and-pull trains. Later still they were used as brake vans on the Bundoran expresses.

Various sub-classes augmented the total of bogie thirds up to 1932. A noteworthy departure from tradition was the introduction in 1935 of the open-centre 'K¹⁵' class, some of which had steel panels. Tubular frame seats held 70, in a body 58 ft by 9 ft 6 in. The total weight was 31 tons. Some later additions to the class came by the conversion of wartime 'K²³' workmen's coaches. The sole 'K¹⁹', No. 3, was built in 1936 for the Banbridge branch. It held 60 passengers within a 43 ft 6 in. body, which also had a small luggage and brake compartment.

Wartime acquisitions were the 15 members of classes 'K²⁵' to 'K³⁰', originally built by the LNWR and bought from the LMS. Three 'G⁷' coaches had similar histories.

The last coaches to be built by the Great Northern were Nos. 8 and 9 of class 'K³¹'. They came from Dundalk in 1954 and were built specifically as trailers, with driving controls, to run with the AEC railcars.

The first steel-panelled coaches were made in 1935; of these the four 'K¹⁵' have been mentioned, and in addition in the same year five 'F¹⁶' vehicles were produced.

Catering services were introduced in 1895 on the main line only. Their extension to other routes came slowly. Greenore boat trains had a restaurant car from 1906 until 1912. A Sunday restaurant car service on the main line was begun in 1913; the Derry road got catering in 1920, the Irish North in 1927, and the Belfast to Cavan trains in 1930. Tea-cars were introduced in 1914, based on 'K⁷' thirds which had corridors; they had small cramped kitchens in which tea was brewed over a paraffin stove. Although primitive, and a tray on the knee had to deputise for a table, they gave meal facilities to the thirds for the first time.

In 1916, despite war restrictions, restaurant cars 401 and 402 of class 'B¹' were produced. They were much in advance of anything the Great Northern had operated previously, with high elliptical roofs, end kitchens, and chair seats in a 58 ft by 9 ft 6 in. body. Seats for 15 firsts were sited centrally, and the 19 seconds were placed at the end away from the kitchen.

Certainly the most primitive of the catering vehicles were the three 'Z¹' six-wheeled refreshment vans, which were produced in 1939-40 from older vans. They were nothing more than travelling bars for occasional use on excursion trains. Two station seats, back-to-back in the middle of the floor, provided the

Interior of a first class dining car.

Charles Friel Collection

Interior of 'B1' class first/second dining car No. 401 of 1916. Note the distinctive oval windows.

Duffner

'P2' parcels van No. 777. *Duffner*

'I10' class tri-composite (16+20+40) No. 404 at Clones on 7th June, 1957. On the left is clerestory-roofed 'I8' tri-composite (13+25+30)

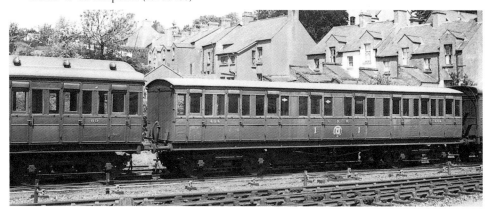

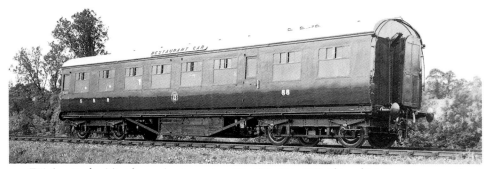

'B6' class 8-wheel first/second restaurant car No. 88 built in 1938. This vehicle is now preserved and running on Railway Preservation Society of Ireland (RPSI) trains. *Duffner*

'K9' third, a former railmotor, No. 214 on 25th June, 1952 at Great Victoria Street, Belfast.

R.H. Fullagar

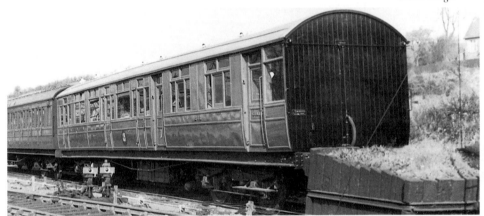

'J3' tri-composite and brake (17+18+42) another former railmotor No. 202. Seen at Clones on 18th April, 1955.

H.C. Casserley

This converted railmotor coach, No. 8485, is seen in the service of the Locomotive Department in Dundalk in February 1955.

Charles Friel Collection

only 'comfort', and drinks were dispensed from a bar counter placed along one side of the coach.

Heat for cooking *en route* was provided at first by coal-fired ranges, or by oil stove. Gas, adopted in the 1930s, was carried as highly compressed town's gas in small cylinders which were filled by a special plant at the Belfast Corporation's works. An explosion caused its abandonment, and reversion to coal, but as low-pressure gas fuel came on the market it was adopted, initially as Calor gas and later as Kosangas.

Counting the tea-cars, the Great Northern put into service altogether 31 catering vehicles. Tray service at passengers' seats was introduced in connection with the BUT railcar sets in 1957.

Slip-coach working was in use at Drogheda, Goraghwood, and Lisburn at various times. The first coaches to be fitted for slip working were Nos. 15 and 38 of class 'G¹' in 1910, followed by No. 2 of 'G²' in 1911. Fifteen coaches in all were available for this use.

Sleeping coaches were not listed as such in the official stock returns, but about 1908 the contemporary public timetables stated:

> The public are respectfully informed that sleeping accommodation is now provided for First Class Passengers on the night mail trains, leaving Dublin for Londonderry and Belfast at 8.20 pm, and Londonderry and Belfast for Dublin at 9.30 and 10.0 pm respectively. The charge for this convenience is 5s. per passenger, irrespective of distance in addition to the ordinary First Class fare. The carriage will be placed in a convenient place after arrival at the destination so that passengers can leave it at any time up to 8.0 am.

The sleeping-car service ran to the end of World War I. The three coaches involved were Nos. 444 and 445 ('I²') and 446 ('F13').*

The Manning, Wardle steam railmotors which came into use at Howth in 1906 had coach portions by Brush. After withdrawal in 1913 the coaches were converted to No. 207 ('J¹') and Nos. 204-6 ('J²'). These were the longest coaches in service, 61 ft and 61 ft 2 in. over body. Similar conversions were made to the North British/Pickering railmotors which ran between Belfast and Lisburn between 1905 and 1913, and Nos. 201-3 of class 'J³' resulted. Associated with them were the 'Lisburn bogies', whose numbers ran from 208 to 216. These were made up of two sets of four (two 'K⁹' plus two 'F¹²'), while a single 'L⁷' (No. 210) was a spare vehicle.

The Great Northern's coaching stock, considered altogether, consisted of 294 six-wheelers of 55 types, 30 four-wheelers, and 345 bogies of 120 types. All were GNR(I)-built with the exception of 34 bogie vehicles. Building at Dundalk was continuous from 1888, with breaks in 1933-4 and 1950-4. The last coaches were built in 1954.

In September 1958, at the end of the GNRB era, out of a total stock of 297 bogies only about 200 were in good order; 62 were awaiting scrapping, and about 35 were fit only for slow workings.

No complete description appears to exist of the pre-amalgamation carriage liveries. Carriages of the D&D were of dark varnished wood; those of the other

* The details of this announcement were a slight overstatement: to provide the services mentioned, four coaches would have been required but in fact only three were ever used. What happened was: two coaches were on the 8.20 ex-Dublin, one for Derry and one for Belfast; the other was on the 9.30 ex-Derry, and passengers from Belfast desiring to sleep joined this coach at Portadown. The coach which went to Belfast on the 8.20 from Dublin returned the following morning as an ordinary coach. *R. McAdams, JIRRS*

'J6' tri-composite brake (12+12+38) No. 463. At one time this vehicle was fitted for slip working.
Ellis

'L2' Brake third No. 418 photographed in June 1952 at Great Victoria Street, Belfast. This vehicle had a huge van section (30 ft 4 in.). There was still room for some 40 seats in an overall length of 55 ft 3 in!   *R.H. Fullagar*

lines were either varnished or dark red. It seems that the Ulster Railway carriages had white upper panels.

In early Great Northern days dark red may have been the standard, but by the end of the century all new carriages were being turned out in varnished mahogany. The colour has often been referred to as teak. Lining was in gold and blue, and numbering and lettering were in gold figures, blocked blue. All the carriages bore the company's coat of arms. Class designation was by word, on each door.

Mahogany-coloured paint, with a grained finish, appears to have replaced varnish some time around 1910. During World War I new coaches were panelled in oak, and probably at this time the blue lining was first omitted and the gold replaced by a straw colour. In a 1923 carriage specification only stain and varnish are called for; no paint is mentioned, and each carriage was to bear two GNR monograms and two coats of arms. Carriage roofs were white.

Steel-panelled stock, introduced in the mid-1930s, was at first painted a grained oak colour, in imitation of varnished wood. The colour was later altered to ungrained, orange-brown mahogany colour. About 1950 the class wording was replaced by large figures, in yellow colour.

With the introduction of blue and cream AEC railcars in 1950, about 16 carriages were fitted to work with them and were similarly painted. Seven years later, 23 more were similarly treated to work with the BUT railcars. A similar livery was chosen for the Royal Train of July 1953, of which six carriages were Great Northern and four UTA. Most of the royal train GNR (I) vehicles were later equipped for working with railcars, but a few remained to work on steam-hauled trains and were marshalled along with mahogany carriages.

In the earliest days the carriages were not provided with lighting, and passengers, who after all had known nothing better, were content to sit in the dark. Paraffin oil lamps, usually suspended from the roofs, provided the first form of illumination and lasted on many of the branch line six-wheelers until well into the 20th century. The Great Northern did not adopt acetylene or oil-gas lighting but graduated instead directly to electric lighting. This was first introduced on main line stock in 1896, and its use extended until all the coaching stock, including the vans, was electrically lighted.

Although the Howth tramway was on the 5 ft 3 in. gauge, its vehicles were confined to their own 5½ miles of line, and other railway vehicles were excluded from it. Rolling stock consisted of 10 double-deck passenger cars (Nos. 1-10) and a single-deck works car (No. 11), used for repair work. The passenger cars cost about £750 each. Nos. 1 to 8 dated from the 1901 opening; they had bodies 31 ft by 7 ft 6 in. by the Brush Engineering Co., on Brill maximum traction bogies. Each car seated 30 in the lower saloon and 37 on the upper deck. Cars 9 and 10 were two years younger, and slightly larger; they were bodied by Milnes, 33 ft by 7 ft 6 in., and had seats for 33 below and 40 above. They ran on Peckham maximum traction bogies. No additional vehicles were introduced during the life of the line, but towards the end cars 5 and 8 were withdrawn, and Nos. 9 and 10 were placed in reserve. Both classes had an open top deck, surrounded by railings and a wire-mesh screen.

Current for the Howth tramcars was taken from overhead wire at 550 volts dc. Until the 1930s the company had its own generating station at Sutton; thereafter power was bought in at 10,000 volts ac from the Electricity Supply

These two views of the interior of 'A4' class Director's saloon No. 50 were taken near Dundalk South cabin. This vehicle is now preserved by the RPSI.   *(Both) Duffner*

Board and rectified. The cars were powered by 35 hp motors. Braking equipment on the Howth trams consisted of regenerative, air, and hand brakes. Shedding and maintenance were done at Sutton.

The tramcar livery was originally lake, lined in blue and gold. Deck screens were white, lined brown. The teak finish of the carriages came later and was on Nos. 9 and 10 to the end. The other cars finished their careers in blue and cream colours.

It is uncertain what the original Fintona tramcar, in use for 29 years, was like, since neither drawings or photographs of it are known to exist. There is, however, a possibility that the double-deck carriage, mentioned in connection with the Londonderry & Enniskillen Railway's stock, did in fact run on the branch. In 1877, Mr Callaghan, the GNR (I) carriage superintendent, reported that a new carriage was required for the Fintona branch, and in due course a tender of the Metropolitan Co. was accepted at £205. There seems to have been a delay in the delivery, for the car did not arrive until 1883. It ran on four wheels and had a 10 ft wheelbase. Structurally, it was double-decked, the lower deck being divided by a partition into two compartments for the first and second class. The seats ran longitudinally, and the access was gained through sliding doors from the end platforms. These platforms gave the car a symmetrical appearance, which was heightened by the narrow spiral stairways that communicated with the upper deck. This deck was unroofed and was for the third class. It had a distinctly convex floor and two longitudinal slatted seats, placed back-to-back on top of the clerestory. The car was numbered 74 at first, but at some date, now unknown, the number was altered to 381. For most of its career it was finished in the standard varnished mahogany colour, but when the blue and cream livery was adopted for the railcars this was used for the tramcar. The motive power, one horse, was uncoupled at the end of each journey and shedded in a wooden hut from the elements, and at the junction from the noise of passing steam trains, until required for the return trip.

On 17th January, 1953 the Fintona tramcar was damaged against a wagon when the horse shied at a piece of paper and bolted. It remained in service for some weeks and was then hauled by a steam engine to Dundalk for repairs. Until it was returned to service on the branch, passengers' luggage and light goods were taken along the branch in a covered wagon, hauled by the horse. Officially, the passenger-carrying service was suspended during this period, but a seat was thoughtfully provided in the van for those unable to manage the walk along the side of the track.

A second car for the Fintona branch was constructed at Dundalk, and it was to have been numbered 416. Whether it was intended to replace the older car or to act as a standby is uncertain, but it never reached Fintona. Just before it was completed it was burned in the fire which destroyed the carriage shops in 1913. The second Fintona tram (No. 381) thus saw service behind a succession of horses from 1883 until 1957, when the branch was closed.

Immediately after the end of services at the end of September 1957 the tramcar was brought to Belfast, where it is preserved in the Transport Museum. Its last run was made from Fintona at 10.15 am on 1st October. Hauled by an engine that had come up light from Enniskillen, it went at a scheduled 19-20 mph, and with stops at Omagh, Pomeroy, and Dungannon it reached Belfast at 3.35 pm. Subsequently it was taken over the Belfast Central line to the museum near Queen's Quay station, the first time it had been off GNR (I) metals.

10 ton open wagon No. 4913 at Foyle Road, Londonderry on 12th July, 1931.   *L&GRP*

8 ton van No. 1799 at Foyle Road, Londonderry on 12th July, 1931.   *L&GRP*

Chapter Sixteen

Goods and Service Vehicles

The contributions of the companies which amalgamated in 1876, and those which joined the Great Northern later, to the railway's wagon stock are conveniently summarised in tabular form. The stock was largely made up of the usual open wagons, some of which dated from the earliest days and had a capacity of around four tons, with some covered wagons and cattle trucks. The remarkably high proportion of open wagons in the stocks of the N&A, NW&R, and Belfast Central companies is of interest:

Great Northern Constituent Companies' Wagon Stock

	D&DR 1875	D&BJR 1875	INWR 1875	UR 1876	N&AR 1879	NW&RR 1884	BCR 1885
Open wagons	28	106	190	339	71	63	183
Covered wagons	183	125	371	411	69	12	25
Cattle wagons	54	20	10	60	12	3	-
Timber trucks	14	6	16	31	12	-	17
Ballast wagons	27	16	-	20	-	-	-
Ballast brake vans	1	-	-	11	-	-	-
Boiler trucks	-	-	-	2	-	-	-
Lime wagons	-	8	-	-	-	-	-

The growth of the Great Northern's stock as given in successive half-yearly reports can be similarly tabulated. The steady growth in livestock traffic was noteworthy, as shown by the increase in the number of cattle wagons. These rose in number until around the end of World War I. A rapid fall occurred under the GNR Board, the 1954 total of 535 being cut to 406 in 1958. This trend coincided with a serious decline in the livestock traffic from July 1954 when the marketing of fat stock in Northern Ireland was freed from government control. Previously all fat stock marketed in Northern Ireland in the Board's area was carried by rail, under arrangements with the Ministry of Agriculture.

GNR(I) - Progress of Wagon Stock (I)

	1876	1880	1885	1890	1895	1900	1905	1910
Open wagons	706	915	995	1,387	1,608	1,808	2,027	2,169
Covered wagons	1,101	1,477	1,513	1,560	1,592	1,742	1,910	1,985
Cattle wagons	144	266	306	333	333	500	540	560
Goods brake vans	-	29	37	50	60	71	81	87
Ballast wagons	63	63	63	88	70	70	70	85
Rail wagons	-	25	25					
Ballast brake vans	12	6	6	6	6	9	9	9
Boiler trucks	2	-	-	2	2	2	2	2
Timber trucks	67	81	81	98	98	98	98	98

175

Vacuum-fitted cattle wagon No. 2242.   *L&GRP*

9 ton van No. 4646, 12th July, 1931.   *L&GRP*

8 ton butter van No. 847 in 1931 at Foyle Road, Londonderry. *L&GRP*

25 ton 6-wheel drovers' brake van No. 95 at Antrim in April 1957.

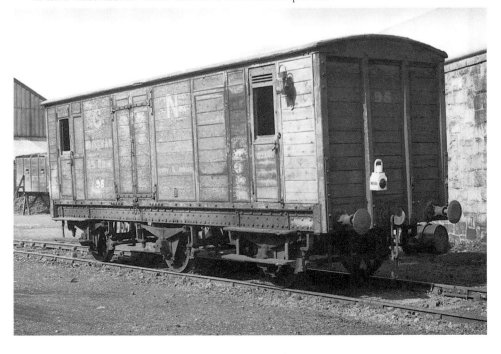

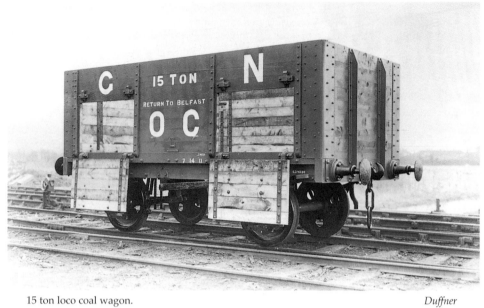

15 ton loco coal wagon.   *Duffner*

The weedkiller train and crew at Banbridge.   *Paddy Mallon*

As on other railways, the half-yearly reports were replaced in 1913 by the larger annual reports, and the more detailed statistics in the latter illustrate how the small wagons, both open and covered, were rapidly replaced by vehicles of greater capacity. Nevertheless the majority were in the 8 to 12 ton range, since the Great Northern had practically no need for wagons of larger capacity.

GNR(I) - Progress of Wagon Stock (II)

Merchandise and Mineral	1910	1930	1940	1950	1958
Open wagons, less than 8 tons	174	11	9	-	-
Open wagons, 8-12 tons	1,899	2,054	1,916	2,030	1,857
Open wagons, 12-20 tons	1	-	-	-	-
Covered wagons, less than 8 tons	134	32	25	10	9
Covered wagons, 12-20 tons	25	12	12	12	162
Cattle wagons	626	624	560	535	406
Rail and timber trucks	119	50	50	50	50
Brake vans	106	105	85	98	89
Miscellaneous	12	12	12	136	26
Hopper wagons	-	-	-	-	6
Boiler trucks	-	-	-	-	2
Glass wagons	-	-	-	-	2
Container trucks	-	-	-	-	191
Railway Service					
Locomotive coal wagons	234	251	242	205	192
Mess and tool vans	2	6	10	17	22
Breakdown cranes	2	2	2	2	2
Travelling cranes	13	13	13	15	13
Miscellaneous	32	56	75	80	93

The total of 93 miscellaneous service vehicles in use at September 1958 was made up of 27 different classes:

Breakdown vans	20	Omnibus trucks	2
Ash wagons	27	Creosote tank car	1
Diesel fuel tank wagons	6	Matisa tamper	1
Match wagons for cranes	5	Auto shunter	1
Refuse wagons	3	Inspection car	1
Weed sprayer	1	Speed test van	1
Weed sprayer tank cars	2	Drivers' instruction van	1
Road roller trucks	2	Crane fitters' van	1
Vacuum cleaning vans	2	Air compressor wagon	1
General stores vans	2	Clothes drying van	1
Electrical stores vans	2	Locomotive stores van	1
Welding vans	1	Weighbridge vans	2
Diesel rail buses	2	Guard trucks for breakdown cranes	3
Petrol railcar	1		
		Total	93

By 1958 a total of 447 vehicles were fitted with the vacuum brake, representing 81 per cent of the total freight stock. The figures were: covered wagons 120, cattle wagons 256, ordinary container trucks 25, bread container

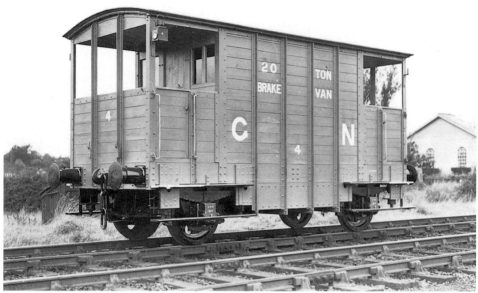

20 ton brake van No. 4.   *Duffner*

25 ton 6-wheel brake van No. 50 at Omagh in 1933.

Gypsum hopper wagons in the paint shop at Dundalk works in July 1944. *Duffner*

Gypsum hopper wagon No. 6016, July 1944. *Duffner*

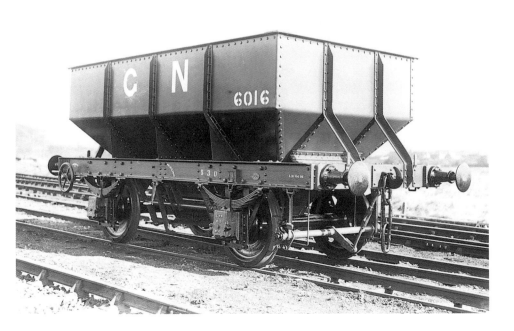

A general view of Drogheda cement factory with the River Boyne beyond. The Boyne viaduct is just visible in the distance.

Duffner

trucks (four-wheel) 43, bread container trucks (bogie) three. The largest proportion of vacuum-fitted vehicles were in the cattle wagon and container truck classes. None of the open wagons had vacuum brakes.

The establishment of a large cement works near Drogheda in 1938 resulted in the development of a large specialised traffic in this commodity. In 1954-5 the railway designed and built 150 wagons of 16 tons capacity exclusively for cement haulage. Twelve of these were of the hopper type for bulk traffic, and the remainder were modern covered wagons for bag traffic. The hopper wagons were loaded at the works through roof openings and discharged from bottom chutes by gravity, assisted by aeration, the cement being led by a large diameter hose to the consignee's storage silo. The original experiments in gravity/aeration discharge were made on cement containers on the Great Northern's road vehicles.

Container traffic developed mainly after World War II, and the total of 191 container trucks, given in the table above at September 1958, was a constant figure during the years of the GNRB. The total of containers in use reached 299 in 1957-8. In 1958, 225 of these were exclusively for bread. They carried the name of the originating bakery, and each had a capacity of two tons. The bread traffic from Belfast to the provincial towns ran largely on vacuum-braked, four-wheeled trucks each taking two containers. In addition there were three bogie trucks each carrying six containers; these were actually the underframes and bogies of scrapped dining cars which were suitably trussed and re-sprung for the extra loading. Apart from the bread containers, the remaining 74 were for general goods, bicycles, and bricks. In recent years there has been an increasing amount of traffic in Guinness stout in bulk, conveyed from Dublin in the firm's own container drums.

The Great Northern was never very well equipped for heavy vehicles. There were only 12 bogie trucks, 46 ft long, of 30 tons capacity, and one bogie well wagon of the same length and 40 tons capacity. The 30 ton trucks were strengthened by trussing to take 40 tons during World War II and were used for the conveyance of British army tanks.

Vehicles belonging to private owners were tank cars of the various oil companies, and coal wagons confined to use on dock sidings at owners' premises. The traffic in petrol and oil was never of great magnitude and tended in recent years to give way to road deliveries.

Goods wagons were originally painted dull red, and this colour was retained for vacuum-fitted vehicles. For non-fitted wagons, grey became the standard colour. Lettering was in white.

Breakdown crane No. 2 at Belfast.

16 ton covered wagon for cement traffic No. 286 (built in November 1954) for transporting bagged cement.   *Charles Friel*

16 ton hopper bulk cement wagon No. 2107 built in 1955.   *Duffner*

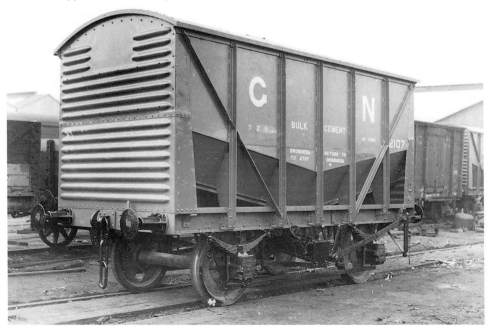

Chapter Seventeen

Train Services

Until the gaps between the extending lines of the three systems that originally joined Dublin and Belfast were eliminated, passengers made their way with the help of road coaches. Through running between the two cities was not possible until the Boyne viaduct was completed in 1855; before that the journey was made piecemeal. Thus, in 1849, it was made in six stages over the lines of four different railways:

		1st Class		2nd Class		3rd Class	
		s.	*d.*	*s.*	*d.*	*s.*	*d.*
UR	Belfast-Armagh	4	0	3	0	2	0
Omnibus	Armagh-Castleblayney	3	4	3	4	3	4
D&ER	Castleblayney-Dundalk	3	4	2	6	1	8
D&BJR	Dundalk-Drogheda	4	0	3	0	1	11
Road through Drogheda							
D&DR	Drogheda-Dublin	5	0	4	0	2	0

Once the Boyne was spanned, through running became possible, but engines were changed at Drogheda and Portadown.

On the main line, passenger services fall into two contrasted groups: inter-city traffic and local services in the city hinterlands.

In 1844, when the Ulster's broad gauge line had reached Portadown, the company ran six trains each way on weekdays and three on Sundays. Two of the weekday trains were mixed, the 2 pm ex-Belfast and its up counterpart. These two trains crossed at Moira and made very leisurely trips, no doubt because of the time spent handling 'goods and merchandize'; their times were 120 and 110 minutes for the 25 miles. Other trains took 75 minutes.

Unlike the Dublin & Drogheda, the Ulster did not run a frequent local service at first. Belfast was still comparatively small, and urban development towards Lisburn had scarcely begun. Dublin, on the other hand, was larger, and suburbs to the north justified the D&D's construction of the Howth branch to draw in commuter traffic.

By the late 1850s, the D&D was running seven trains to Drogheda on weekdays, and three on Sundays. The fastest of the former left Amiens Street at 5 pm, called only at Malahide, and was in Drogheda at 6.05 pm. The 7.15 pm down mail took 70 minutes, with stops at Malahide and Balbriggan. By contrast, the 10 am Parliamentary, with nine intermediate stops, needed 120 minutes to reach Drogheda. In the up direction, the first class Mail left Drogheda at 4.35 am and was into Dublin at 5.25 am.

Before the complication of the border customs stops, Dublin-Belfast express trains generally called at Drogheda, Dundalk, and Portadown. Apart from the Limited Mails, which had connections (and later through carriages) to and from Kingstown Pier, the timings were not particularly rapid. There were usually five through trains on weekdays in each direction and two on Sundays.

'QL' class 4-4-0 No. 114 *Theseus* with a Dublin-Belfast mail train *c.* 1905.

A posed photograph of 'S' class 4-4-0 No. 172 *Slieve Donard* with a Dublin-Belfast mail train *c.* 1917.

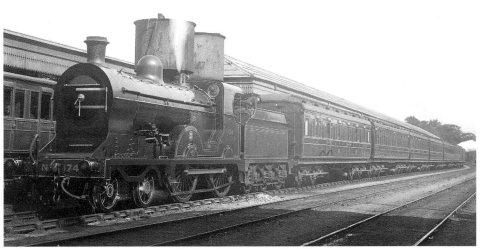

'S' class 4-4-0 No. 174 *Carrantuohill* at Dundalk on a Dublin-Belfast express.

'Q' class 4-4-0 No. 125 *Daphne* works a rake of 6-wheel coaches empty stock to Belfast at Knockmore Junction in 1912.
Sir Cecil Smith

In 1874, shortly before amalgamation, the Limited Mails, with first class accommodation only, had the following timings:

		Down	Up	
Dublin		8.10 *am*	6.15 *pm*	D&DR
Drogheda	*dep.*	9.07	5.20	
Dundalk	*dep.*	9.46	4.41	D&BJR
Portadown	*dep.*	10.47	3.40	
Belfast		11.30	2.55	UR

This end-to-end timing of 200 minutes was improved upon after amalgamation, and at the same time second class passengers were admitted. By the 1880s the journey time was 180 minutes, and increased engine power brought it down to 150 minutes.

The political division of Ireland in 1921 was followed by the introduction of compulsory stops at Dundalk and Goraghwood for customs examinations. Depending upon the amount of work to be done, these stops might take anything from five minutes to fifty, and they effectively brought the smart work of the Limited Mails to an end. Before that took place two noteworthy performances were recorded by special trains. In March 1914, No. 173, of class 'S', took a dining car and seven bogies 110¼ miles non-stop from Amiens Street to Balmoral in 121 minutes, an average speed of 54.6 mph, a fine effort with a 2,500 gallon tender and 165 lb. boiler pressure. Then, on 22nd July, 1924, driver Bruce with No. 190 of class 'S.2' took a single tri-composite brake carriage ('J⁴'), weighing 33 tons, from Belfast to Dublin in 97 minutes. This run was timed to the nearest quarter-minute, and it included a half-minute stand at the Lisburn home signal. The 105 miles from there to Dublin were run in 89 minutes, at an average speed of 70.8 mph.[*] The full details of this remarkable run have been published elsewhere, but merit repetition in a condensed form:

	Miles	Minutes
Belfast	0	0
Portadown	25	24
Goraghwood	40 ¾	38 ¼
Bessbrook	43 ¼	40 ½
Dundalk	58 ¼	52 ½
Kellystown Box	75 ¼	66 ½
Drogheda	80 ¾	71
Howth Junction	107 ¾	92 ½
Dublin	112 ½	97

On the ascent and descent of the Wellington bank, a minimum of 60 mph and a maximum of 89 mph were recorded.

Before the renewal of the Boyne viaduct, the up Mail's running time from Belfast to Dublin was 133 minutes, with three stops. Glover's new compound engines produced striking accelerations in the summer of 1932, and the 3.15 pm down express introduced the first booked run at over 60 mph in Ireland; 54 minutes for the 54.3 miles between Dublin and Dundalk. This timing included the Drogheda service slack, where a coach was slipped, and on occasions it was

---

[*] The recorded stop-to-stop time of 7½ min. from Belfast to Lisburn has been criticised by R.N. Clements, and it is certain that this is an underestimate, perhaps by 1½ min. (*Journ. IRRS*, 5, 152).

cut appreciably. Times as low as 52 min. 34 sec. between Dublin and Dundalk were recorded during that memorable summer. Running times between Dublin and Belfast in the same summer were scheduled at 125 minutes, two minutes less southbound. In the winter, Drogheda was added as a stop.

These fast timings represented the heyday of express operation on the Great Northern, but they probably brought the running to the limit of safety, and they could only be kept at the expense of a high coal consumption. The long 1933 strike forced the company to economise, the boiler pressures of the compounds were brought down from 250 lb. to 200 lb., and the fast 1932 schedules were eased. Notwithstanding, smart running continued between the two cities right up to the outbreak of World War II. During, the war, customs stops, especially at Goraghwood, were lengthened, and the inter-city journey times were stretched out to 190-200 minutes.

After nearly a quarter of a century of customs stops at Goraghwood and Dundalk, it was at last found practicable in 1947 to eliminate them on non-stop trains. The innovation was well received by the public, coinciding with a heavy southbound traffic of ration-weary folk. At 10.30 am on 11th August, 1947, the first 'Enterprise' express, hauled by No. 83 of class 'V', started from Belfast on its inaugural run, non-stop to Dublin. The down working left Dublin at 5.30 pm.

On the 'Enterprise' trains, customs examination of passengers' luggage was made on suitably guarded platforms in the terminal stations. For a short time, heavy luggage in the van was examined, northbound, during the journey, passengers being brought along to the van in batches of five or six. This procedure speeded dispersal at Belfast and involved a brief halt at Dundalk to pick up northern customs men.

'V' class 4-4-0 No. 83 *Eagle* prepares to leave Belfast with the first 'Enterprise' on 11th August, 1947 viewed from the Boyne bridge. *Cecil Sleator*

'S2' class 4-4-0 No. 192 *Slievenamon* leaves Dublin with a down 'Enterprise' in May 1950.
Kelland Collection

The 'Enterprise' had only first and third-class seating, and this was limited with seats bookable in advance. The timing was 135 minutes, a comparatively easy schedule when compared to the 1932 bookings, which were equivalent to non-stop runs of 115 minutes.

On 31st May, 1948, a second 'Enterprise' service was begun and has continued, winter and summer, the two trains generally passing each other between Drogheda and Dundalk.

From 1950 until 1953 the 'Enterprise' train was run through to Cork. This service began on 2nd October, 1950. The complete set of carriages of the 10.30 am from Belfast, due into Amiens Street at 12.45 pm, left there at 1.30 pm hauled by a CIE engine of the '800' or '400' class. Cork was reached at 5.15 pm with a seven-minute call at Limerick Junction *en route*. In the northbound direction the train left Cork at 1.15 pm, called at Limerick Junction from 2.26 to 2.33 pm, and arrived at Amiens Street at 4.45 pm, leaving there at 5.30 pm for Belfast. The working of the complete train to Cork ended on 27th June, 1953, though from 29th June until 19th September of that year a through coach from the 'Enterprise' set was handed over to CIE to be attached to a Dublin-Cork train.

The development of Belfast's suburban traffic began around the 1850s. Ten trains were run each weekday to Lisburn, stopping at Balmoral and Dunmurry, and five of these continued to Portadown. Slow trains took 25 minutes to Lisburn. By the end of the 1880s, Lisburn had 16 trains from Belfast on weekdays and six on Sundays, and of these nine and three went to Portadown.

The fasts took 14 minutes to Lisburn, slows 30 minutes with stops at Balmoral, Dunmurry, and Lambeg.

The turn of the century witnessed a great extension of this short-haul traffic up and down the Lagan Valley. Railmotors were brought in to handle it, but these were soon replaced with orthodox push-and-pull trains. In 1915, Lisburn was served by around 40 weekday trains in each direction. The total had grown to around 50 by the mid-1920s and to almost 60 by the outbreak of World War II. A peak of nearly 70 trains per day was reached late in the war. This exceptionally frequent service naturally included Dublin and Londonderry trains, and also trains making for the Warrenpoint, Newcastle, Antrim, and Clones lines.

After 1945 the frequency declined, being affected to some extent by branch and secondary line closures. By the summer of 1958, at the end of the GNRB administration, 50 weekday trains ran from Lisburn to Belfast. Counting all the trains listed in the last GNRB public timetable and including those running Saturdays only and Saturdays excepted, the city-to-Lisburn connections show the following distribution of stops:

13 trains were non-stop Lisburn to Belfast
6 trains stopped at one intermediate station
1 train stopped at three intermediate stations
4 trains stopped at four intermediate stations
8 trains stopped at five intermediate stations
5 trains stopped at six intermediate stations
21 trains stopped at seven (all) intermediate stations

Of the intermediate stations, Dunmurry received the most frequent service and Balmoral the least.

The Dublin suburban traffic divided at Howth Junction and extended along the main line to Malahide and Donabate. The service had been excellent since the earliest days. The 1859 timetable shows seven trains to Howth on weekdays, and nine on Sundays. The last train left Amiens Street at 9.30 pm, arrived at Howth at 10 pm, and returned to Amiens Street at 10.05 pm. The timetable contains the encouraging note that 'Special Trains from Howth or Malahide at a later hour may be secured, without extra charge, by application to the Dublin and Howth Agents.' It might be thought that the young company could do little more than that to attract traffic, but as further inducements it was stated that '1st and 2nd class Return Tickets to Howth, entitle the Holders to the privilege of a Cold Bath in the Company's Bathing Boxes at Howth during the Bathing Season', and 'The New Path Way round the Eastern Cliffs of the Hill of Howth is now open to the Public, free of charge . . . '

By the 7.30 am train from Amiens Street, due in Howth at 8 am in the year 1859, morning return tickets at single fares were advertised 'returnable by any Train during the day'. The eager city bather could ask for nothing more than a second-class eightpenceworth as an aperitif to his breakfast.

Housing developments throughout the years produced urban conditions most of the way to Howth, and the branch line flourished accordingly. Being off the main line, Howth never received the intensive train service that Lisburn did, but 20-23 trains on weekdays and 12-14 on Sundays were typical for many years. All the trains had connections with the Great Northern electric trams both at Howth and at Sutton.

Steam railmotor No. 3 at Dundalk works.   *L.J. Watson*

Steam railmotor No. 5 with trailer No. 13.   *R. Welch*

'JT' class 2-4-2T No. 94 on a local train, possibly near Baldoyle on the Howth branch, made up of six-wheel stock. *John Alsop Collection*

'BT' class 4-4-0T No. 7 waiting to depart Belfast Great Victoria Street platform 1 with a motor train comprised of ex-steam railcars. *John Alsop Collection*

'Q' class 4-4-0 No. 131 *Uranus* on an up passenger train near Balmoral. This locomotive was withdrawn in 1963 and is now preserved.

'V' class 4-4-0 No. 85 *Merlin*, now preserved, waits to leave Dublin Amiens Street with a passenger train for Belfast. It is in post-1936 blue livery, but still with round top firebox.

Real Photographs

'VS' class 4-4-0 No. 209 *Foyle* is seen leaving Dublin Amiens Street. Note the 'P' van immediately behind the locomotive.

Real Photographs

Malahide, lying nine miles out of Dublin, was more like Lisburn in its situation; while expresses passed it by, it was served by both purely local and Dublin-Drogheda slow trains. The total of trains was of the same order as at Howth, but Sunday services were considerably less frequent.

Stations between Howth Junction and Amiens Street were purely suburban in nature, and Killester in particular enjoyed an excellent service almost comparable to that of Dunmurry. Clontarf's traffic was taken away by road services, and it was closed in 1956. Population movement, based on new post-war housing, resulted in the opening of Harmonstown in 1957.

For seven months, from 27th October, 1941 until 1st June, 1942, a number of joint suburban workings across the city of Dublin were worked by the Great Northern and Great Southern companies. The bulk of the workings were done with Great Northern engines and carriages. The arrangement ended because of fuel shortage. The timings and terminal stations were:

Southbound		*Northbound*	
7.40 am	Drogheda-Westland Row	4.15 pm	Greystones-Donabate
8.05 am	Drogheda-Westland Row	5.32 pm	Westland Row-Howth
8.25 am	Howth-Dalkey	5.35 pm	Dalkey-Drogheda
8.30 am	Malahide-Westland Row	6.20 pm	Westland Row-Howth*
9.02 am	Howth-Dalkey		
4.25 pm	Donabate-Dalkey		
7.10 pm	Howth-Greystones*		

* Worked by GSR engine and train.

Apart from the main line, long distance through working was mainly on the Belfast-Londonderry and Belfast-Clones routes, 100¼ and 64¼ miles in length respectively. The first of these began as a combination of the Ulster and the Londonderry & Enniskillen trains, with a change at Omagh, but through running began in Great Northern days. On neither of these routes was there justification for true express workings, though the pre-war Derry Mail could be classed as such.

In pre-amalgamation days on the Belfast-Londonderry road, the Ulster ran five trains on weekdays, and one on Sundays to Omagh. The Great Northern maintained this service. Apart from the through trains, of which the best took 187-190 minutes from city to city, there were also a few 'all stations' trains from Belfast to Dungannon, Dungannon to Omagh, Omagh to Londonderry, and Strabane to Londonderry, these locals acting as feeders to the 'expresses'. Since Strabane and Londonderry were largely self-sufficient, no commuter traffic developed between the two; indeed for many years the earliest arrival at Londonderry was the Omagh local, at times which varied from 9.15 to 9.55 am throughout the years. It was followed by the Belfast, about two hours later.

The Ulster Railway reached Monaghan in 1859. Initially three trains ran there from Belfast both on weekdays and on Sundays, taking 142-47 minutes for the 52 miles. Ten years later, five trains connected Belfast with Armagh, and four ran from Portadown through Armagh to Clones. Armagh continued to offer more traffic than the stations beyond it, and as the years went on most of the trains terminated there, a state of affairs doubtless fostered by the secondary line to Newry.

Seven miles beyond Armagh, Tynan achieved the distinction of being a junction station from May 1887 until December 1941, as the eastern end of the 3 ft gauge Clogher Valley Railway (CVR) ran alongside the Great Northern. The western extremity of the CVR was at Maguiresbridge. At both Tynan and Maguiresbridge, the CV trains made connections with the Great Northern services.

In the latter decades of the 19th century, Armagh had seven arrivals from Belfast, but only four of these went on to Clones. Thereafter services to Armagh improved, reaching 15 trains on weekdays and five on Sundays in 1948, although Clones continued to have only four and one arrivals respectively. The last summer's working to Armagh, before the 1957 closures, consisted of 11 trains per day, plus two railbus services from Portadown.

Between Dublin and Londonderry two routes were available: 162¾ miles via Portadown and Omagh and 175¾ miles via Dundalk, Clones, Enniskillen, and Omagh. Except for a day through coach connection both ways, until 1939, travel between the two places involved changes either at Portadown or at Dundalk. The longer route, taking in the length of the old Irish North Western Railway, was considerably slower, and the inevitable 'all stations' train took between six and seven hours. Around two hours could be saved by going through Portadown.

Part of the longer Dublin-Londonderry route was used by the 'Bundoran Express', a summer train really run for Lough Derg pilgrimage traffic but giving reasonably good connection between Dublin and the fashionable little west coast resort, where the Great Northern had one of its hotels. This named train was started during World War II and ran both on weekdays and Sundays. It called at Drogheda and Dundalk, where it reversed on to the Irish North line. A single intermediate stop, the location depending on the particular day of the week, was made before Clones. It ran on to the Bundoran branch without stopping at either Enniskillen or Bundoran Junction. The down train crossed with the up at Pettigo which was the station for Lough Derg, and was just across the border in Co. Donegal. The total distance covered by the 'Bundoran Express' was 159¾ miles. Departure times from Dublin were 8.45 am and 10 am on Sunday. The speed of the train rather belied its name. In both directions, a 20 to 30 minute stop was made at Clones, where for a time the Dublin buffet car was exchanged between the down and up trains. The non-stop run from there to Pettigo avoided the nuisance of customs stops, since the train passed uninterruptedly through Northern Ireland *en route* to the Republic. The journey time was from 315 to 330 minutes on weekdays, and 295 minutes on Sundays. Belfast passengers were able to connect with the express at Clones.

The trains which ran between Dundalk and Enniskillen in 1859, under the D&E, were remarkably similar, in frequency at least, to those offered at the closure. Originally there were four through trains each day: two of these took first, second and third class passengers only and needed 165 minutes to cover the 63 miles. The 5 am from Enniskillen and the 7.35 pm from Dundalk carried goods as well and were another 55-65 minutes on the road. Slowest were the 5 am from Dundalk and the 12.15 pm from Enniskillen, which included Parliamentary passengers in their mixed load and took 310 and 295 minutes on the down and up trips.

Through carriages between Dublin and Londonderry were advertised in the 1859 timetable, showing that reciprocal arrangements had been entered into with the neighbouring companies.

In addition to the trains mentioned, the Mails in 1859 were conveyed on a first and second class train between Dundalk and Castleblayney, with rail connections to Dublin and road coach connections at Castleblayney, where the trains terminated. In the down direction the Mail left Dublin at 7.15 pm, and Dundalk at 9.35 pm. With one call at Inniskeen, the train was into Castleblayney at 10.25 pm. A coach connection arrived at Enniskillen at 6 am the next morning, and Londonderry was reached at the same time by coach to Omagh and the L&E train forward from there. The up service, with similar connections, left Castleblayney at 2.10 am, and was into Dublin at 5.15 am.

Ten years later, with the Irish North Western company in charge, four trains per day were still the rule, but the Sunday service had gone. The fastest run from Dundalk to Enniskillen took 130 minutes, the slowest 240 minutes. The Mail train in the dark, and the nocturnal bustle at Castleblayney, had gone for ever.

Under the Great Northern, the four trains per day were maintained, and running times altered but little. The falling-off in passenger traffic made itself felt in the 1920s and 1930s, and the line provided a testing ground for railcars and railbuses. These economical vehicles were enabled to beat the buses to some extent by picking up and setting down at the numerous level crossings. These stops, not listed individually in the public timetable, were made on request. The working book shows that a maximum of 14 such stops existed between Dundalk and Clones, 12 between there and Enniskillen, and 11 more between Enniskillen and Omagh.

During part of World War II, a railcar ran at 1.15 pm from Dundalk to Omagh, and was scheduled to make the request stops at crossings. Clones and Enniskillen were reached at 2.36 pm and 3.53 pm respectively and the car was due in Omagh at 5 pm. Passengers making for Belfast could connect with the Londonderry-Belfast express, due out at 5.04 pm; they must have often been perturbed when the crossing stops caused the railcar to run late.

Those proceeding to Londonderry had little to fear, as their connection left at 6.43 pm.

As demand fell away, so did the services on the Irish North road. During 1948, the first train out of Dundalk was the 8.50 am railbus. This stopped at eight stations before Clones, which was reached at 10.25 am. Enniskillen passengers disembarked and went on by a railcar, which left at 10.40 am and took 53 minutes to complete the run.

After World War II, the earliest service on the Irish North section was the 7.30 am up steam train from Ballybay. This purely local working survived until the closure of passenger services, but towards the end a railcar replaced steam. The railcar left Dundalk at 6.25 am and worked back from Ballybay after a 20 minute stop. During that last year, only two trains ran through from Dundalk to Enniskillen, though a third service was available by making a change at Clones.

The Omagh-Enniskillen section, originally the southern part of the L&E's line and later worked as part of the INWR, became in Great Northern days merely a secondary line, albeit with through trains using it, but with a marked lack of a good local service. The usual four daily trains in each direction called at all the five intermediate stations, and there was no Sunday service. The impact of World War II brought about a considerable increase in traffic, six daily trains in 1944, seven in 1945, and eight in 1946, with two on Sundays. The improvement was well maintained up to the date of closure.

At a distance of 6¾ miles from Omagh was Fintona Junction, where the small branch diverged for ¾ mile to Fintona. Trains in both directions were met at the junction by the horse tram. Its official time for the branch in recent years was 10 minutes to Fintona, and 15 minutes to the junction, the difference probably being accounted for by the slight uphill gradient. In 1921, the timetables show 10 minutes each way. The steam-hauled goods was timed to take five minutes.

Clones and Cavan, respectively railway crossroads and county town, were linked by a service of four to six local trains on weekdays only. The convolutions of the inter-state border were such that, although both the towns were in the Republic, the line entered Northern Ireland twice *en route*. Customs examinations at each border crossing would have made train operation over the 15¼ miles of line a farce, but since all the stations were in the Republic and much of the intervening district was marshy and thinly populated, the line was treated for practical purposes as being entirely in the south. Traffic density was light, except on market days, and railbuses and railcars made their contribution towards maintaining services.

Midway along this stretch of line was Ballyhaise, formerly Belturbet Junction, an impressive three-platform station complete with overbridge. Trains on the 4½ mile branch to Belturbet generally ran as a shuttle service, connecting with Clones-Cavan trains, and the Great Northern maintained a small engine shed at Belturbet. In its heyday the Belturbet branch carried up to seven weekday trains each way, with a journey time that started at 15 minutes and was cut to eight at the best. No trains worked into Belturbet on Sundays. After World War II, two trains a day sufficed, and GN road buses from Cavan supplemented the waning rail service.

At Cavan, Belturbet, and Enniskillen the Great Northern made contact with other companies' lines. At the first two, CIE latterly owned lines that had been previously Great Southern and before that Midland Great Western and Cavan & Leitrim property. Cavan station was a typical MGWR building, of grey limestone and deep eaves, into which the GNR (I) had running powers. Belturbet was a Great Northern station, with the narrow gauge Cavan & Leitrim line running into a bay on the north side of the single platform. At Enniskillen, the standard gauge Sligo, Leitrim & Northern Counties line came in from Sligo.

While passenger services lasted over CIE's long branch up from Inny to Cavan, one or two daily connections were usually provided with northbound Great Northern trains. Mullingar to Belfast could be done in 5¼ to 6¼ hours in the 1920s, with a 50-55 minute wait at Clones on the way. Galway-Belfast via Cavan figured in the timetables of that era, 10½ hours northbound and 9 southbound, a tiresome voyage during which travellers must have wished they had gone round by Dublin, if only to see the lights.

At Enniskillen, connections to Belfast via Omagh or Dundalk or to Derry via Omagh were reasonably good off the SLNC line, but there normally was no need for passengers from Sligo to Dublin to consider this routeing since they were well served by the direct line. However, in 1944-7 it came into its own, when trains ran only twice weekly on the Midland route, and for a time there were no passenger trains that way.

Services on the other secondary and branch lines naturally depended on their location. The quiet country branches usually offered four trains per day, an early morning, mid-morning, early afternoon, and evening train with perhaps a late one in on a Saturday night, and none on Sunday.

The Cootehill and Carrickmacross branches, diverging from the Irish North line and served from Inniskeen and Ballybay respectively, had the usual four trains per day during most of their existence. Generally trains on these lines were mixed. Inniskeen had a three-platform layout rather like Ballyhaise, and at Carrickmacross there was shed accommodation for the engine which worked the branch. Apart from the workings to and from Carrickmacross, one mixed train worked through from Dundalk in the morning.

The Cootehill branch diverged from the Irish North line 1½ miles west of Ballybay. Before the line was finally closed, deferred maintenance had caused the speed to be restricted to 20 mph, later reduced to 10 mph. The last passenger workings were scheduled to take 32 minutes for the nine miles, including a ticket stop at Rockcorry.

Oldcastle's long branch had generally three trains to and from the terminus. The timing for the 39½ miles from Drogheda was originally 90-95 minutes, including seven intermediate stops. During World War II, when railbus working enabled level crossing stops to be made, request halts were made at Factory Crossing (16¼ m.), Newgate Crossing (18¾ m.), Ardbraccan (20 m.), Castlemartin (21½ m.), and Phoenixtown (22¼ m.), the last four of these between Navan Junction and Ballybeg. In spite of these, the time along the branch was kept at around 80 minutes. Steam-hauled trains were sometimes mixed. Apart from trains running to the terminus, where the single-road shed could hold two engines, the comparative importance of Navan and Kells, respectively 17 miles and 26¾ miles from Drogheda, justified running some railcars only as far as these towns.

The Bundoran branch, in length much like that to Oldcastle, differed in being remote from the main line. Although ending 22 road miles from Sligo, it carried no traffic to that county town, which had two railways of its own. The Bundoran branch had no Sunday trains apart from excursions until the advent of the 'Bundoran Express', but once the fashion was established after World War II, Sunday trains became quite a feature in summer, generally one from Omagh which ran 20 minutes behind the 'Bundoran Express' and like it omitted the junction and Irvinestown, and another from Enniskillen which stopped at all stations. The three returned from Bundoran at hourly intervals in the evening. Apart from Sundays, three trains formed the usual weekday service to Bundoran for many years, until the arrival of the railcars enabled an extra service to be provided.

The co-existence for some years during the 1940s of double summer times in Northern Ireland with ordinary summer time in the Republic affected all the cross-border trains, but nowhere so markedly as on the Bundoran branch. There apparently the down trains took nearly four times as long as the up trains, as the following extract from the summer 1944 working timetable illustrates:

m.					
0	Bundoran	*dep.*	3.50 *pm*	*arr.*	8.45 *pm*
4	Ballyshannon	*arr.*	3.58	*dep.*	8.35
		dep.	4.11	*arr.*	8.23
8	Belleek	*arr.*	5.19	*dep.*	9.15
		dep.	5.27	*arr.*	9.05
12 ¾	Castlecaldwell	*arr.*	5.36	*dep.*	8.56
		dep.	5.37	*arr.*	8.55
20 ½	Pettigo	*arr.*	4.50	*dep.*	7.43
		dep.	4.53	*arr.*	7.41
25 ¾	Kesh	*arr.*	6.03	*dep.*	8.31
		dep.	6.10	*arr.*	8.21
32	Irvinestown	*arr.*	6.23	*dep.*	8.09
		dep.	6.27	*arr.*	8.07
35 ½	Bundoran Junction	*arr.*	6.35	*dep.*	8.00

Newcastle was reached in 1906 via Banbridge and Ballyroney; the last four miles were over the Belfast & County Down line. Nineteenth century timetables show that while Ballyroney was the terminus it was reached by four or five trains on weekdays, and none on Sundays. Once the breakthrough to Newcastle was complete, three trains were found to suffice, but the service improved during World War II to five weekday workings, with one on Sunday.

Lying halfway between Belfast and Newcastle, Banbridge had something in common with Armagh's situation on the Clones line. Like the latter it was a busy market town, and similarly it enjoyed a considerably better service of trains to and from Belfast than the stations beyond. Soon after the opening of the BL&BR, the Ulster Railway, working the line for its owners, ran four trains up to Banbridge on weekdays, stopping at Hillsborough, Dromore, and Mullafernaghan. For a time there were three trains on Sundays. Then, as we have seen, Ballyroney became the terminal station, and the Sunday trains vanished.

World War II caused and witnessed a dramatic increase in the traffic to Newcastle and beyond. Following the 1941 air raids on the city, many families were evacuated to towns and villages along the branch, resulting in an unprecedented number of journeys. By 1940, wartime demands for labour brought up the traffic to nine weekday and five Sunday trains, some of which ran on to Ballyroney. By the next year, the situation demanded a still heavier service, and 14 weekday trains were needed to cope with the requirements, with nine on Sunday. Only by 1954 had the weekday service fallen back to the 12 daily trains, though Sunday needs had diminished so that three trains were enough, and only one of them continued to Newcastle.

The 6¾ mile link between Banbridge and Scarva, a product of the D&BJR, had a virtually separate existence from the Belfast-Newcastle section, though it joined it at Banbridge station. The Scarva branch trains either worked a shuttle service or came up from Warrenpoint or Newry to Banbridge and terminated there. In spite of these traffic arrangements, the line was mileposted from Scarva to Castlewellan and not, as one might have expected, from Knockmore.

On the Scarva line in the early days, Laurencetown was the sole stop, and five trains ran on weekdays with one on Sundays. Lenaderg came later (1904), and apart from stops there, a few Saturday workings were added between Banbridge and Laurencetown. Motive power was centred on Banbridge, where there was a two-road shed. Falling traffic, aided by the 1933 strike, closed the branch, but it was reprieved and reopened on 15th October, 1934 using a railbus. This was soon found to be insufficient for the traffic, and Railcar 'A' was substituted, remaining a feature there until closure in 1955. With railcar workings, it became possible to introduce five additional level crossing halts (Millmount, Hazelbank, Chapel Row, Uprichard's, and Drumhork). In 1940, the railcar ran five trips each weekday, plus four on Saturdays only and two out to Laurencetown only. Later in the war, the intensity increased to 10-11 runs, with two steam train workings on Sunday. The Uprichard's crossing stop was dropped in 1946. For four summers after the war, Sunday trains were continued; there were four railcar and two steam workings in 1949, but they stopped during the winter. During the last year when the branch was open, the former good service was maintained, using both a railcar and a railbus, with five summer runs on Sundays worked entirely by the railcar.

The link opened in 1910 between Armagh and Castleblayney was ill-considered and short-lived. The service was understandably thin, and local demand was slight, so a morning and an evening train, timed through in 56 minutes, were provided. Closure south of Keady was the natural outcome of the political division, and Carnagh and Creaghanroe stations had a life of little more than 10 years. Keady had the distinction of being a passenger terminus for a similar period, and received three to four weekday trains from Armagh, with another on Wednesdays and Saturdays. No Sunday service was provided.

Running east from Armagh, the old N&A railway led up the ill-fated bank to the cluster of houses at Hamiltonsbawn and the village of Markethill. After plunging through the two long tunnels at Lissummon, it ran across and alongside the main line at Goraghwood and continued down to the water at Newry. Early workings would have started from what was later Newry Edward Street station, but the Great Northern recognised the unity of the Newry lines and worked through from Armagh to Warrenpoint, where the horse tram connected to Rostrevor. The section from Armagh to Goraghwood followed the Scarva branch into limbo after the 1933 strike, surviving merely as a goods line. While the Armagh-Newry section continued as an entity, the service was limited to four trains on weekdays.

The Warrenpoint train service originally consisted of eight trains each way on weekdays and on Sundays. After a month, the number rose to 11. Once connection was established between Newry Edward Street and Newry Dublin Bridge stations, some traffic emanated from Armagh, but a local service came in from Portadown, Goraghwood, and the two Newry stations. With the disappearance of traffic from Armagh, Belfast-Warrenpoint workings became established. Nine trains on weekdays and three on Sundays were characteristic up to World War II. Thereafter, the service improved to 14 on weekdays. The Sunday trains were markedly seasonal in frequency. In post-war summers as many as 14 ran in, but three were the rule in winter.

The Ardee and Cookstown branches were short, and both ended at market towns. Though Cookstown was the larger, Ardee enjoyed the better service

Tramcar No. 10 waits to leave for Warrenpoint, with the Rostrevor Hotel in the distance.
Charles Friel Collection

until the aftermath of the 1933 strike ended passenger workings. Cookstown got its best weekday service, seven per day, during World War II, and it was then that a couple of Sunday trains began to run.

Since the Antrim branch, running from Knockmore Junction to Antrim town, provided a connection between the Great Northern's system and the coast towns of the north of Antrim, through running was possible, but this was not exploited until 50 years after the branch was opened. Previously the train service was the usual three or four daily runs of the country branches, with nothing on a Sunday. In fact the branch was purely local, being worked from Lisburn, and not, as later became the practice, from Belfast.

After about 1910, as a means of stimulating the expanding summer holiday traffic, arrangements were made between the two companies concerned for the running of through coaches between Dublin and Portrush. In the down direction the coaches were slipped from the 9 am between Knockmore and Lisburn and were worked from Lisburn to Antrim and attached there to an NCC train which had come from Belfast (York Road). In the up direction, the Great Northern received the Portrush coaches from the NCC at Antrim, ran them to Lisburn, and attached them there to the 2.45 pm Belfast-Dublin. This working remained in force up to the start of World War II; it was in fact the last Great Northern slip working. On some Saturdays in the summer of 1939 the excursions had become so popular that a relief left Dublin at 9.20 am, with through coaches for Portrush, Newcastle via Banbridge, and Bangor via the Belfast Central. A buffet car from this train went as far as Antrim, where it became part of the up train leaving there at 1.20 pm. The return coaches were brought to Belfast, where they were marshalled to form the 2.55 pm to Dublin.

'AL' class 0-6-0 No. 55 leaves Drogheda with a cattle train for Dublin North Wall.   *F.R. Hebron*

An 'SG2' class 0-6-0 departs Clones with a cattle train, probably the 'Enniskillen Shipper' bound for Belfast Maysfields via Armagh and Portadown, on 7th June, 1957.

On other days, Portrush coaches went north on the 9 am from Amiens Street, were detached at Lisburn, and worked down to Antrim. Returning they were taken to Belfast, and then up on the 2.45 pm express.

The local service to Antrim at the outbreak of war in 1939 consisted of four daily trains each way, with two more on Saturdays, two on Saturdays only from Belfast to Aldergrove, and two on Sundays.

During the war, heavy traffic resulted from the expansion of Aldergrove aerodrome and the creation of a large aircraft assembly and repair establishment at Gortnagallon. The latter merited the construction of a 2¼ mile siding opened in May 1942, which diverged one mile north of Crumlin and ended in a station and sidings. There was no terminal loop, and trains had to be propelled in one direction.

The peak period of wartime activity over the Antrim branch came in 1943-4. There were then four workmen's trains running seven days per week into Gortnagallon from the city; one leaving Belfast at 12.15 am, calling at Lisburn, Ballinderry, and the Siding junction. It left the junction at 1 am and terminated at 1.15 am. These workmen's trains also gave rise to some propelling movements as far as Crumlin and light-engine running on the branch. On the branch as a whole, there were 24 daily passenger trains in each direction, compared to eight in 1938. During June 1944, traffic rose to an all-time high, with 52 special passenger and 88 special goods on to the branch. Troop movements accounted for much of this.

The use of mixed trains as a characteristic of the minor branch lines has already been mentioned. On the secondary and main lines, there was an extensive goods train service, much of it timed to run during the night or early morning so as not to interfere with passenger trains on the single lines. Belfast in the busy months of summer 1944 may be quoted as an example: the Gortnagallon workmen's train was followed at 12.45 am by the Banbridge goods; five minutes later Maysfields dispatched the Portadown goods; the Newry goods left at 1.35 am; Antrim goods at 2 am; Armagh goods at 4 am; and Lisburn goods at 5.35 am. A goods train ran to Lurgan and Portadown at 9.55 am. The next booked goods movement was the Maysfields to Omagh, which left at 7.50 pm. The Enniskillen and Antrim goods trains followed at 9 and 9.15 pm. The first Londonderry goods was away at 9.50 pm and a second at 11 pm, arriving in Londonderry at 5.30 and 6.30 am. Finally a Portadown goods left at 11.55 pm.

Livestock traffic formed an important part of the freight workings. Much of it was contributed from the west of the province, often coming from the SLNC Railway into Enniskillen.

In connection with the periodic fairs that were held at various places, special livestock trains were run to each centre monthly, or in some cases fortnightly. In the area served by the Great Northern system there were about 50 such fairs held in the course of a month. Animals were generally walked in by their owners to the fairground in the early morning; after sale they were driven to the railway station for loading and dispatch by a train which had come in empty earlier in the day. In some cases one station's traffic was contributed by several neighbouring fairs; thus Carrickmacross derived traffic not only from its own

An 'AL' class 0-6-0 shunts cattle wagons at Drogheda onto the back of a Dublin train.

fair, held on the second Thursday of each month, but from Bailieborough (first Monday of each month) and Shercock (second Tuesday of each month) as well. Kells drew in stock from the fairs at Athboy, Delvin, and Mullagh, and held its own fair on the second Friday of 10 months of this year, the last Tuesday of five months, and the third Tuesday of December. The complexity of fair movements is obvious, and it was enhanced by the need to get the trains of stock on their way to catch cross-channel steamers. Not only had sufficient covered wagons to be provided to remove the estimated number of cattle, but in some cases additional accommodation had to be made available for the drovers. Thus in the 1939 Appendix:

> COOTEHILL FAIR. Third Friday of every month. Stock to be forwarded by 1.20 pm. Mixed Train. Clones to attach a Small Third Class Carriage to 11.10 am. ex Derry for Dealers returning from the Fair.

A schedule of permissible axle loads classified the engines into six groups, ranging from the heaviest class of the five class 'V' compounds, with a maximum of 21 tons, down to the 13.5 tons class which included the DN&G saddle-tanks. Nothing above 15.2 tons was allowed on the Scarva-Banbridge, Bundoran, Cootehill, and Maysfields-South Quays sections, or on the Newry-Greenore part of the DN&G. The Dundalk-Greenore line, which had two long viaducts, had 13.5 tons imposed as its limit.

Chapter Eighteen

Accidents

The history of accidents, not on the GNR(I) alone but in Britain, is overshadowed by the Armagh disaster of 1889. The results were tragic in themselves, and this accident was the cause of urgent Parliamentary legislation which made compulsory the use of the automatic vacuum brake and of the block telegraph system on all lines.

On 12th June, 1889 a heavily-laden passenger special was scheduled to run from Armagh to Warrenpoint, carrying a Sunday School excursion to the seaside. The train had left Dundalk at 6.40 am, as empty carriage stock. As marshalled at Armagh, it consisted of a 2-4-0 tender engine, a brake van, 13 carriages, and a brake carriage. All the coaching stock had six wheels and was fitted with the Smith non-automatic vacuum brake. The engine was No. 86, an 1880 Beyer, Peacock engine of class 'H', with Thomas McGrath as driver and Henry Parkinson as fireman. Acting guard William Moorehead travelled in the front van, and Guard Thomas Henry in the rear vehicle. To safeguard the capacity load of 940 passengers, many of them children, the carriage doors were locked before the train left Armagh. In charge of the train and travelling on the footplate was James Elliott, chief clerk at Armagh.

Two carriages had been added to the train at Armagh to take an unexpected number of passengers. As a result, McGrath regarded his train, 15 vehicles totalling 185 tons loaded, as beyond the capacity of his four-coupled engine. His protests were dismissed by John Foster, station master at Armagh, who was doubtless keen to see the excursionists on their way. Offered the banking assistance of the regular passenger train, due to follow them, McGrath indignantly refused and insisted on proceeding unaided.

The line, via Markethill and Newry, was worked on the usual train staff and ticket system, with Markethill the first staff station. The time interval for one passenger train to follow another was 20 minutes, for passenger following goods 20 minutes, and for goods following passenger five minutes. The train, due to leave at 10 am, was delayed and did not leave until 10.15 am.

Just over ¼ mile from the station, the train met a gradient of 1 in 82. After two-thirds of a mile, this steepened to 1 in 75 and rose at this for 2½ miles. Two hundred yards short of the summit, called Dobbin's Bridge, the engine stalled. The time was 10.33 am. Largely on Elliott's responsibility, it was decided to divide the train and to bring the first part on to the loop at Hamiltonsbawn, two miles ahead. This was done in preference to protecting the train in the rear, awaiting the arrival of the regular passenger train, and being pushed by it over the summit. The available space in the loop decided where the division would be done, and couplings and vacuum bags were separated between the fifth and sixth vehicles from the front. This immediately left the rear 10 vehicles entirely dependent on the handbrake in the last vehicle. Henry, the guard, who should have been in his compartment, was by the lineside under Elliott's orders, attempting to scotch the wheels with stones. He left in his compartment 14 or 15 unauthorised passengers, including two children. By this time the regular 10.35 am passenger train from Armagh to Newry had left and was climbing the bank towards the halted special.

As a result of impact when the train engine set back, and probably because some of the occupants of the rear brake carriage had unwittingly unscrewed the handbrake, the rear portion of the special train began to move backwards down the grade towards Armagh. Henry and Elliott leapt back into the crowded vehicle, but their efforts to apply the brake were useless. Further frantic efforts to recouple, and to scotch the wheels with more ballast, were in vain. With their load of mystified, and then terrified, passengers, unable to open their carriage doors and escape, the 10 carriages swept down the bank towards the oncoming train. This was headed by No. 9, an 1858 vintage 0-4-2 that had been No. 20 on the Dublin & Drogheda Railway. Patrick Murphy was driving and William Herd firing. Behind it came a horsebox, brake van, three carriages and a third brake. With a good head of steam, the train was taking the climb at about 30 mph and was 1½ miles out of Armagh when Herd glimpsed the appalling sight of the excursion coaches, tearing towards him and obviously out of control. Murphy immediately shut off steam and braked, getting his speed down to an estimated 5 mph before the impact. Against his engine, at perhaps 10 times that speed, plunged the runaway. Already the occupants of the rear brake compartment had jumped for their lives; so had the fireman of No. 9.

The collision occurred in Killoney townland, on a 47 ft high embankment. The force of the impact completely destroyed the rear three vehicles of the excursion train. Murphy's engine was tossed from the rails and finished on the slope of the embankment, its wheels in the air and surrounded by the awful debris of the shattered carriages.

Murphy himself was thrown on to the coal-plate of his tender, which broke away from its engine. The regular train was thus rendered temporarily brakeless, and as the coupling between the horsebox and the five following vehicles snapped it broke into two parts. So the divided parts of the regular train in their turn began to run away towards Armagh. Murphy, shocked and dazed, managed to screw down his tender brake and to halt tender and horsebox three carriage lengths away from the remainder of the train. Daniel Graham, the guard, had applied his handbrake and pulled his portion up after a run of a quarter of a mile. Eighty excursionists died, 22 of them children. The father, mother, and two children forming one Armagh family were all killed. The injured totalled 260. Compensation paid to the dependants, and medical and legal expenses, cost the company around £145,000.

A complete description of the other accidents is beyond the scope of this volume, but Appendix Three contains a reasonably complete list. Quite a high proportion of the early accidents were derailments, reflecting the light weight of the track and the comparatively low standard of permanent way maintenance. The lines of the Irish North seem to have been especially prone to such mishaps. However, the most serious was on the old Belfast Junction main line, three years before the Armagh disaster.

On 30th June, 1886, a day of hot sun, the 1.30 pm Belfast-Dublin passenger train left Portadown at 2.31 pm, one minute late. Behind the engine were five six-wheeled carriages and a brake van. A short way south of Irwin's Crossing, 2½ miles from Portadown, the greater part of the train ran off the line. The engine was No. 37, an 1866 Beyer, Peacock 2-4-0 of the former D&BJR, driven by Thomas Tiernan. Both Tiernan and his fireman, Robert Hughes, survived the accident, which threw the engine on its side and spread the rails. Behind, two first and second composites were telescoped and thrown clear of the road. Three passengers were killed on the spot, three died later, and 29 were injured. General Hutchinson, reporting to the Board of Trade, listed three contributory factors: the speed of the train was unduly high, the permanent way work had been poorly done and the ballasting was incomplete, and the heat had probably expanded and displaced the rails. A contemporary photograph confirms the second of these.

Among the earliest accidents was that which occurred near Trillick. On 15th September, 1854, about 8 pm, an excursion train of 19 carriages was returning from Londonderry to Enniskillen, with about 700 members of a Protestant organisation on board. The train was double-headed by Nos. 11 and 12, 2-2-0WT engines built by Robert Stephenson. Contemporary reports say that the leading engine gave three jumps before running down an embankment. The second engine and the leading carriage followed it, and it was fortunate that only one of the firemen was killed. The derailment was produced by the malicious placing of three large stones from a bridge parapet on the line.

The poor state of the old L&E permanent way contributed to the Mountjoy derailment on 11th April, 1871. A double-headed mixed train came off the road where the old iron rails joined new replacement 75 lb. flange rails laid on transverse wooden sleepers. Another serious derailment, blamed on excessive speed, took place nearby in the following November.

The Square Crossing at Dundalk was the scene of several accidents. One of them, on 3rd October, 1896, fortunately verged on the ludicrous. A Ballybay to Barrack Street goods, in charge of driver and fireman who had spent their time unwisely in a Castleblayney public house *en route*, went through signals and at the crossing hit a light engine on its way to the shed. Little serious damage can have resulted to either party, for the goods later carried on towards Barrack Street yard. On the way there, the engine and tender became detached from the train, but the crew failed to notice this until their arrival at the terminus. They reversed to bring in their train, and hastening to cover up their own succession of faults they failed to stop in time and hit their own wagons with some force. The official report does not detail subsequent events.

The lightweight engines of the L&E made a poor enough job of working trains. In addition, the ease with which they derailed resulted in a fireman's death on the up Mail from Derry on the night of 9th October, 1857. Four miles from the terminus the driver caught a momentary glimpse of something white, but he had no time to slow his train before he was off the road, with his tender and a second class carriage after him. The fireman was thrown from the footplate and run over by the tender. The obstacle turned out to have been a wandering cow.

Broken drawbars caused two accidents in 1878 due to the division of moving trains, the lack of the automatic vacuum brake resulting in a collision. In July, two passengers in a mixed train between Beragh and Omagh were injured; in the

'S2' class 4-4-0 No. 190 at Dromiskin in 1933. This incident claimed the lives of two railwaymen.
Duffner

The aftermath of the accident at Gortavoy, near Pomeroy on 6th September, 1946 when a goods train derailed and tumbled down an embankment when a culvert collapsed. The fireman lost his life. *Charles Friel Collection*

following month the engine and tender parted from the train between Skerries and Balbriggan and five passengers were injured in the resulting impact.

The East Wall Junction collision early on Christmas Day 1886 was due to carelessness on the part of the crew of the up Mail. Ignoring a succession of signals at danger, and running 91 minutes late, they hit an empty passenger train on its way from Amiens Street to North Wall. For slow-moving trains the results were spectacular; the engine of the Mail ran off to the left and into the signal cabin. The ground floor of the cabin happened to be a dwelling house which supported the cabin proper. It was fortunate for the occupants that they were away at early Mass, for the impact completely demolished the house and threw the signal cabin and the signalman into the street below.

Malicious action by irresponsibles during the 1933 rail strike caused two serious derailments. The first of these was at milepost 49, near Dromiskin; removal of a length of rail on the down main threw the whole of a six-coach passenger train off the road. Locomotive 190 of class 'S2' finished up on its side, and the two leading vehicles were telescoped. Two railway officials were killed, though the engine crew escaped. Proof of the reason for this accident was found when the adjacent up road was seen also to have a rail missing.

In March 1933 a Dungannon-Derry mixed trained headed by class 'Q' No. 122 found the points at the Omagh Market Branch Junction half across. The engine and two carriages took to the branch, couplings parted, and the engine ran on ahead until it stopped. The carriages were violently derailed close to the junction, one being overturned. The rest of the train kept to the main line but left the rails and tore up the track.

The peat bogs south of Lough Neagh were the setting for the sudden termination at Annaghmore of the evening train from Portadown to Dungannon on 9th September, 1858. The cause was an unusual one. An elopement had been arranged between Miss Telford, who with her sister ran a public house close to Annaghmore station, and John Hardstaff, the driver of the train. The girl's father objected violently to the match and stormed the station. He succeeded in dividing the four members of the station staff into opposing factions. The girl's supporters, who included Robert McConner, the station master, saw her luggage safely into the van and hoisted her into the train on the side away from the platform. Their gallant efforts were frustrated by one of the porters, Reilly, who was a close acquaintance of the family. Apparently at the instigation of her father, Reilly had set the points so that the train ran into a blind siding. In his pardonable excitement, Hardstaff failed to realise where he was heading, demolished the chock block, and ran his engine into the bog beyond. The report by Capt. Ross, RE, to the Board of Trade relates that 'Miss Telford . . . in the alarm of the moment, jumped out of the carriage she was in into a pond contiguous to the siding. It is said that the driver and she afterwards consoled each other for their misadventures before a good fire in the station . . .'

Into quite a different category fall the acts of sabotage suffered by the railway, in common with other Irish lines, in the early 1920s. Civil disturbances attendant on the political division of the country resulted in several derailments, and in two cases goods trains were stopped in remote localities and set on fire. The most serious of these accidents was the mining of the troop train at Adavoyle in June 1921.

Chapter Nineteen

The Great Northern Railway Board, 1953-1958

The events which led up to the formation of the GNRB as a nationalised railway undertaking have been described earlier. Out of its five nominees, each government appointed a senior member, A.P. Reynolds from the Republic and G.B. Howden from Northern Ireland; chairmanship and vice-chairmanship alternated annually between these two.

The Board was required by the terms of the two Acts to undertake the running of the old GNR(I) undertaking and 'so to conduct its undertaking as to secure, as soon as may be, that taking one year with another the revenue of the board should be not less than sufficient to meet the charges properly chargeable to revenue'. Furthermore, the Board was required to comply with directions given jointly on policy matters by both Ministers and with directions given by either Minister on matters of policy relating exclusively to the conduct of the undertaking in his area. All of which might have been excellent if the two governments had acted in unison and been both disposed to treat the Board's undertaking as something other than a sickly antique.

Consideration of the history of the Great Northern from the mid-1920s made it clear at the time of formation of the GNRB that its duties could not be fulfilled by merely continuing the practice of its predecessor. All things considered, the policy of the GNR(I) had been remarkably progressive, but it had been necessarily limited by the limitations of the economic resources at its disposal. Under the new regime, it was evident that both rapid and drastic modernisation would be necessary if the concern were to survive at all.

Apart from the diesel-engined vehicles, the bulk of the rolling stock which the Board inherited on 1st September, 1953 was worn out and obsolete. The urgent need for replacement may be gauged from the fact that the average age of the 194 steam locomotives was 37 years, and 33 of them were over 55 years old. The coaching stock, totalling 329 carriages, had only 14 new vehicles added to it during the previous 10 years, and 127 coaches had outlasted their estimated economic life of 45 years. Nearly half of the wagon stock of 5,570 vehicles was over 35 years old. Apart from its age and uneconomic operation, public sympathy would be further lost by its continued use. It was decided that no further renewals of steam locomotives would be undertaken, and that diesel haulage would replace steam as soon as possible.

It is perhaps appropriate here to consider the position of the Board's southern neighbour, Coras Iompair Eireann which had been formed on 1st January, 1945. Financially this concern faced much the same problems as the GN did; at the time of its nationalisation in 1950 its rail motive power consisted of 405 steam locomotives with an average age of 51 years, while passengers were conveyed in 680 coaches with an average age of 48 years. Also a nationalised concern, CIE required government approval before embarking on major expenditure; but as it lay entirely within the Republic, approval was not a bipartite matter. With three years' start on the GNRB, a vigorous campaign of imaginative renewal was already begun: in 1952 60 diesel multiple-unit railcars were ordered, and in 1953 113 diesel locomotives of varying sizes. Appropriate carriage and freight stock renewal was also provided for.

The GNRB's first step in modernisation was the decision to increase the diesel multiple-unit railcar stock from 20 vehicles to 44, at an estimated cost of £528,000. It took nine months to get the necessary go-ahead from both governments, whereupon the orders were placed with the manufacturers.

With CIE experience doubtless providing a yardstick, the next stage in the GNRB's plan was the introduction of diesel locomotives, the replacement of all obsolete carriages and wagons, and the modernisation of goods stores, stations, and the Dundalk works. Proposals covering these were submitted for government approval during the first year of the Board's career, and at first there were high hopes that sanction would be forthcoming. The months and then the years dragged out, and in spite of continued pressure by the Board for an early decision it was becoming obvious that the dual ownership was not going to yield the same effective treatment that CIE had received. In consequence of the delay, abnormally high operating costs continued to be incurred, and much money and ingenuity were expended in keeping worn-out engines, coaches, and wagons on the move. Successive reports of the Board, published annually, reflect the growing sense of frustration that this treatment produced among all levels of the staff.

Amongst the Board's earliest proposals was the closure of some uneconomic stretches of line. Accordingly, all train services ended after 1st May, 1955 on the Scarva-Banbridge section, between Banbridge and Castlewellan (thus ending workings over the isolated remnant of the old Belfast & Co. Down line into Newcastle), and between Goraghwood and Markethill (surviving fragment of' the old Newry & Armagh company's line). On the Cookstown branch, passenger services ended on 16th January, 1956. Banbridge was finally without rail services when on 30th April, 1956 all traffic ended from Knockmore Junction.

Radical differences in the viewpoints of the two governments exhibited by the Ministers, hitherto latent, became apparent when during 1956 proposals of widespread closure were made public. These emanated from the Northern Minister of Commerce, who proposed to close the Omagh-Newtownbutler, Portadown-Tynan, and Bundoran Junction-Belleek sections, a total of 115 miles. While these proposals were unilateral in that they were not supported by the Minister's Southern counterpart, in their potential effect they were certainly not so. For, if carried out, rail access to the Monaghan-Cavan-Clones section would be only by way of the remnant of the old Irish North Western road. County Fermanagh would be completely deprived of railways, with the Sligo, Leitrim & Northern Counties strangled by the removal of its Enniskillen connections. Most absurd of all, the Bundoran branch would be reduced to an eight mile scrap, isolated from other railway contacts and patently unworkable. The Dundalk-Clones section of the Irish North, and its feeders from Cavan and Monaghan, would be largely paralysed and forced by circumstances dictated by the Northern Government to close sooner than later.

Following the statutory procedure laid down in the 1953 GNRB Acts, the respective Ministers of Commerce referred these drastic proposals to the chairmen of the Transport Tribunals in Belfast and in Dublin. At the subsequent public inquiry, it was noteworthy that the Northern Minister of Commerce was not represented, nor was any evidence presented on his behalf, though he had proposed the closures.

Evidence at the inquiry was confined, therefore, to material submitted by the GNR Board, the UTA, and organisations such as urban and county councils, chambers of commerce, and business organisations, and the trades unions. These were unanimously opposed to closure. Mr J.F. McCormick, General Manager of the GNRB, described the receipts and expenditure on the sections which it was proposed to close, and he showed that the net saving to the Board would amount to only £14,000 a year, while if diesel traction were used exclusively the net result of closure would be a loss of £68,000 a year. Mr McCormick further stated that the considered opinion of the Board was that no main or secondary lines should be closed without a trial being given to the dieselisation proposals already submitted to both governments.

The results of the public inquiry and its findings were contained in a report issued in September 1956. In Northern Ireland, the Tribunal chairman rejected the GNR Board's evidence and recommended that the lines be closed. In direct contrast, the chairman of the Tribunal for the Republic gave a reasoned argument against the closure proposals and advised accordingly. But so far as the Northern Government was concerned, the matter was *fait accompli*, and in due course the Northern Ireland Minister of Commerce announced his intention to proceed with closure. The Board was informed on 5th June, 1957 that all services on the lines were to end at the end of September 1957.

There was thus enacted a scene probably unique in the history of transport, in which almost a quarter of a railway system was closed, not by the decision or by the request of its operators, but by the over-riding decision of the Government. This action was taken against the advice of the persons publicly regarded as competent to manage the railway undertaking, and in spite of evidence which showed that any economies would be more than negatived by widespread consequential losses. It demonstrated more clearly than at any time previously that the policy of the Government of Northern Ireland was to sacrifice their national asset of the railways in an attempt to satisfy the demands of the road organisation which they had set up in 1935.

In the Republic, the Minister for Industry and Commerce had therefore no choice but to legislate for the trimming of the amputated ruin of the Great Northern railway system. The GNRB, as caretaker for the two governments, had to make the best of the situation with which they had been saddled. Since it was obviously useless to try to perpetuate passenger traffic on the contiguous lines in the Republic, they made application to end passenger services on the affected sections: Dundalk-Castleblayney-Clones, Cavan-Clones-Monaghan-Glaslough, and the Belturbet and Carrickmacross branches, in all 84 miles. The inevitable public inquiry was held on 20th September, 1957, and although the outcome was that the Board should be permitted to do as they had proposed, it was not possible to introduce the necessary legislation before the end of the month. Therefore the bizarre situation existed, from 1st to 13th October, that the GNRB operated passenger services on what they officially termed the 'stump' lines, up to the station nearest to the inter-state border. This was done from Dundalk to Clones, and from Clones to Cavan and to Glaslough. Road omnibus services of the UTA and the Erne Co. took passengers from the railheads to their destinations. Foreseeing this strange situation, the Public Timetables 'From 1st October 1957' were page-numbered to allow a loose and bulky supplement to be inserted before issue. The anomaly lasted until formal authority was given to withdraw passenger workings; thereafter the lines remained open solely for goods traffic.

These disturbing events apart, the Board had its full share of misfortunes to contend with. On the night of 8th/9th December, 1954, torrential rain caused widespread flooding, and the River Tolka, entering the sea half a mile north of Amiens Street station, became a torrent which tore away one of the piers of bridge No. 3. This bridge, carrying the twin tracks of the main line, collapsed and effectively isolated the Dublin passenger and goods termini and the locomotive depot from the rest of the Great Northern system. The construction of a temporary single line Bailey bridge was at once entrusted to contractors, and it was completed and under test by the end of December. Normal working into Amiens Street was resumed on 4th January, 1955. A permanent concrete structure was built during 1955 and went into use on 12th January, 1956.

While the Tolka bridge was down, emergency traffic arrangements had to be improvised. First of all, stock trapped in Amiens Street was released over CIE lines, through Clonsilla Junction and up the Meath road to Navan Junction, whence it was taken down the Oldcastle branch to Drogheda. For a few days goods trains from the north worked to and from Sutton, a procedure simplified by the fact that the usual Howth branch services were replaced by buses. A regular timetable was instituted for Great Northern goods trains via Navan, and from 13th December to 1st January seven goods trains a day were worked over this route, three of them from Amiens Street. Great Northern engines of classes 'SG3', 'SG', 'LQG' and 'UG' formed the motive power, with CIE conductors and CIE banking engines out to Ashtown.

During December 1954, Clontarf became the Dublin passenger terminus with bus connections to and from Amiens Street. At Clontarf the advertised Amiens Street departure times were adhered to, and the buses left Amiens Street 15 minutes earlier. Since the most southerly turntable on the main line was at Drogheda, engines could not be turned at Dublin, and as far as possible tank engines handled the traffic between Clontarf and Drogheda. GNRB 4-4-2T and UTA 2-6-4T engines were employed on this, the latter coming down from their usual shed at Adelaide for the purpose.

During 1955-6, three stations were closed. Dromin Junction had lost much of its value since the Ardee branch had ceased to have passenger services, and it was closed at the end of January 1955. On 1st August, 1956, Stewartstown was closed to goods traffic and on 3rd September Clontarf. In compensation, Derriaghy was reopened on 30th April, 1956, after a three year closure, and a new halt was opened at Harmonstown on 7th January, 1957 to serve a Dublin housing estate.

Then on 7th September, 1955 Dundalk works suffered trial by fire, when a severe outbreak completely destroyed the road motor shop and its contents. Nearby the timber seasoning store was also burnt out, and the total damage was estimated to cost £70,000.

CIE Metro-Vick diesel No. A26 waits to depart Cavan with a goods train for Mullingar on 7th June, 1957. In the distance is GNR 'PP' class 4-4-0 No. 75.

'U' class 4-4-0 No. 201 *Meath* at Monaghan Road with the 10.30 am from Dundalk on the last day of passenger services between Dundalk and Clones, 12th October, 1957.   *A. Donaldson*

Out to the west, the Bundoran branch became unworkable when an embankment subsided at Ross Harbour, alongside Lough Erne, between Pettigo and Castlecaldwell stations. Temporary road services from Pettigo to Bundoran replaced rail workings until repairs were completed and the line was reopened on 18th October, 1956.

Passenger traffic on the long branch to Oldcastle had been very light for some years; it had been largely worked by railbuses, while certain services only ran as far as Navan. Passenger services were ended completely after 12th April, 1958. Further station closures became effective after the end of May 1958, on lines from which passenger services had already been withdrawn; these were at Duleek, Beauparc, Ballybeg, and Virginia Road on the Oldcastle road, and Culloville, Monaghan Road, Redhills, Smithborough, and Glaslough on the lines converging on Clones. With Glaslough closed close to the border, the daily goods operating on the stump of the amputated Ulster line went no further than Monaghan.

Further trials came to the operating department between February and June 1957, when political troubles caused a succession of cases of malicious damage, recalling the troubles of 1919-23. On 17th February, explosions damaged an underbridge and an overbridge between Pomeroy and Carrickmore, and the single line was closed for four days.

Detonators and red lamps, correctly used, brought the 9.30 pm Enniskillen-Londonderry goods to a hurried stop at Porthall in the early hours of 2nd March. Out of the darkness came three armed men, who ordered the train crew to abandon their train and to set off walking up the track towards Strabane. The raiders boarded the engine (No. 13, class 'SG3') and turned off the injectors which had been thoughtfully put on by the fireman. They restarted and set off towards Londonderry. At St Johnstown they slowed to exchange staffs, but the signalman noticed the absence of the regular crew, and his suspicions were aroused. Some way beyond St Johnstown they abandoned the train with the regulator open, and let it run out of control towards the terminus. Meanwhile, the St Johnstown signalman had rung through to his opposite number at Londonderry and warned him what he might expect, and the runaway was diverted into the arrival platform of the empty station. Surprisingly little damage was done to the engine, though seven wagons were wrecked. Up at the Londonderry goods yard the same night the offices were maliciously set on fire.

Damage to the permanent way occurred twice in April. On the 18th, the main line was cut near Adavoyle when a small underbridge was blown up. Single-line working came into force on the next day and continued for a week. Then on the 26th, another explosion damaged the line between Portadown and Lurgan. Finally, on 11th June, the signal cabin at Coalisland was blown to pieces.

The final act in the relations between the governments and the Board began in June 1957, when the Northern Minister of Commerce announced his intention of ending the agreement made under the Act of 1953 for the joint operation of the railway through the GNRB. At the same time he stated that the line between Portadown and Londonderry had no long-term future, and that it was proposed to channel rail transport between Belfast and Londonderry via Ballymena. Similar notice was given by the Minister for Industry and

Commerce in the Republic, and it was agreed between the two governments that the undertaking would be divided between the two nationalised railway concerns already in existence in the two states, namely the Ulster Transport Authority and Coras Iompair Eireann. The staff would be similarly transferred.

Legislation to carry the division into effect was passed and resulted in the Transport Act (NI) 1958, dated 29th July 1958, and the GNR Act 1958, dated 16th July, 1958. From midnight on 30th September/1st October, 1958, the Great Northern Railway Board ceased to exist and the railway's assets became vested in CIE and UTA. Special consideration was given to the Dundalk works, since under the new regime its geographical position near the frontier meant that it was anything but centrally placed in relation to CIE's rail system. Furthermore, CIE already had two railway workshops capable of tackling heavy repairs, at Inchicore and Limerick, and with a shrinking rail mileage it would not require the addition of Dundalk. Serious redundancy and unemployment would have resulted if the works at Dundalk had been shut down, and to avoid this it was decided to form a company, The Dundalk Engineering Works Ltd, to take over and operate the establishment. This action became effective on 10th January, 1958.

The new Dundalk company continued to do rail and road maintenance for the GNRB and its successors, but at the same time it looked outside for contracts in general engineering work. So far as the Great Northern was concerned, the new company completed work on the diesel railcar programme, and it continued railway maintenance. After the undertaking had been divided between CIE and UTA, rolling stock maintenance was gradually transferred to CIE's Inchicore works and UTA's York Road and Duncrue Street works.

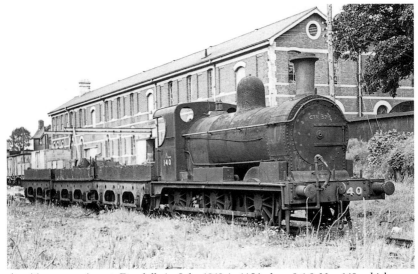

Awaiting scrapping at Dundalk in July 1960 is 'AL' class 0-6-0 No. 140 which was originally built in 1894, and rebuilt in 1919. It gave more than 60 years service to the GNR before being withdrawn in 1957.   *Author*

Chapter Twenty

Conclusion

The component parts of the Great Northern Railway of Ireland took four decades to gather. Once assembled, it was the second largest and the most prosperous of the Irish railway systems, and almost unchanged it lasted over 80 years. In linking Dublin and Belfast, the two largest cities in Ireland, its main line was assured of success. Its secondary lines and its branches were less fortunate, for the larger towns that they served never achieved the phenomenal growth-rate of Belfast, and their agricultural hinterland suffered from the general trend of depopulation. But the couple of dozen stations through which commuter traffic passed to and from the terminal stations were always busy.

The political division of Ireland in 1921 presented the company with problems experienced by no other major railway in these islands. It is difficult to separate the effect which this had from that of the gradual loss to the roads of its monopoly of long distance transport, which became apparent in the mid-1920s. Under able management, the GNR (I) withstood the assaults remarkably well; energy coupled with imagination together replied to the challenge in the form of pioneer railbuses and railcars. The substitution of these probably kept the minor lines open to traffic for an additional 20 years.

Falling receipts after World War II and a rapid increase in private motoring forced the company to admit with reluctance that it could no longer carry on its business, and forced the two governments to purchase it and maintain essential public transport. A five year interim followed, with the GNRB under the joint direction of the governments of the Republic and of Northern Ireland. Between the two, marked contrasts in policy and in treatment became apparent. Much of the system in Northern Ireland was declared to be uneconomic and was closed in favour of road transport. Efforts to modernise the rolling stock were frustrated, and eventually what was left of the old Great Northern Railway of Ireland was divided between Coras Iompair Eireann and the Ulster Transport Authority. Thereafter the Great Northern became merely a name in Irish railway history.

Creaghanroe station closed in 1923 and later suffered the ultimate indignity - conversion to a petrol station. This view dates from 1960.   *Author*

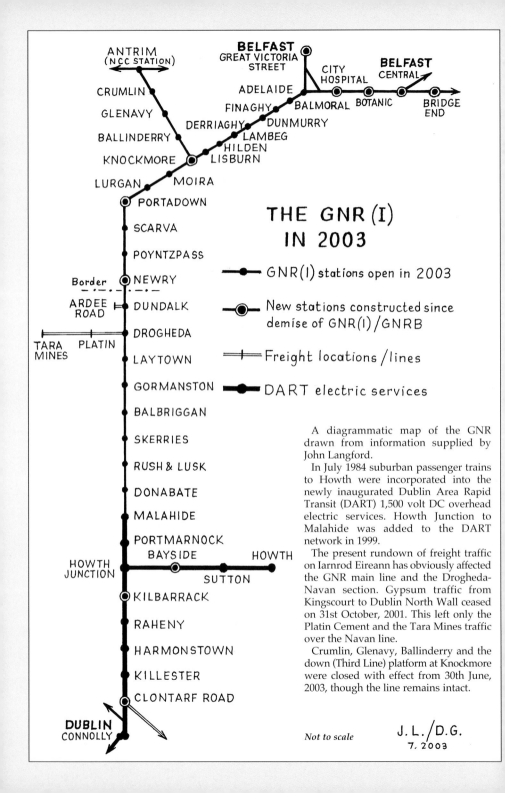

ANTRIM
(NCC STATION)

BELFAST
GREAT VICTORIA
STREET

CITY
HOSPITAL

BELFAST
CENTRAL

CRUMLIN

ADELAIDE

GLENAVY

FINAGHY

BALMORAL

BOTANIC

BRIDGE
END

DERRIAGHY

DUNMURRY

BALLINDERRY

LAMBEG
HILDEN

KNOCKMORE

LISBURN

LURGAN

MOIRA

PORTADOWN

THE GNR (I)
IN 2003

SCARVA

POYNTZPASS

●━━━● GNR(I) stations open in 2003

Border

NEWRY

ARDEE
ROAD

DUNDALK

◉━━━◉ New stations constructed since
demise of GNR(I)/GNRB

DROGHEDA

TARA
MINES

PLATIN

LAYTOWN

╪━━╪ Freight locations/lines

GORMANSTON

●━━━● DART electric services

BALBRIGGAN

SKERRIES

A diagrammatic map of the GNR
drawn from information supplied by
John Langford.

RUSH & LUSK

In July 1984 suburban passenger trains
to Howth were incorporated into the
newly inaugurated Dublin Area Rapid
Transit (DART) 1,500 volt DC overhead
electric services. Howth Junction to
Malahide was added to the DART
network in 1999.

DONABATE

MALAHIDE

PORTMARNOCK

BAYSIDE

HOWTH

HOWTH
JUNCTION

SUTTON

The present rundown of freight traffic
on Iarnrod Eireann has obviously affected
the GNR main line and the Drogheda-
Navan section. Gypsum traffic from
Kingscourt to Dublin North Wall ceased
on 31st October, 2001. This left only the
Platin Cement and the Tara Mines traffic
over the Navan line.

KILBARRACK

RAHENY

HARMONSTOWN

Crumlin, Glenavy, Ballinderry and the
down (Third Line) platform at Knockmore
were closed with effect from 30th June,
2003, though the line remains intact.

KILLESTER

CLONTARF ROAD

DUBLIN
CONNOLLY

Not to scale

J.L./D.G.
7. 2003

Appendix One

List of Stations and Halts

*Main Line**   *Miles*

Belfast (Great Victoria St)	0	The original station closed in 1976. A new station (4 platforms) opened on 30th September, 1995 along with Westlink Junction to City Junction curve. Belfast-Dublin services used Central station from 1976-1995 (see Belfast Central Railway section, page 222).
Adelaide	1½	Opened 1897.
Balmoral	2¼	Opened *c.*1858.
Finaghy	3	Opened 1907.
Dunmurry	4	
Derriaghy	5	Open 1907-1953. Reopened 1956.
Lambeg	6	Opened 1877.
Hilden	6½	Opened 1907.
Lisburn	7½	
Knockmore Junction Halt		Open 1932-1934 and *c.*1945/1946.
Knockmore	8½	Knockmore station opened 1974 (up platform on main line, down platform on Third Line: the latter closed 30th June, 2003).
Maze	10	Open 1895-1974.
Broomhedge	11	Open 1935-1953.
Damhead	12½	Open 1935-1973.
Moira	14½	
Pritchard's Bridge	17	Open 1841-44.
Lurgan	20	
Goodyear	21	Open 1970-1983. Served tyre factory.
Seagoe	24¼	Open 1841-42 as terminus.
Portadown	25	Open 1842-48. Rebuilt on adjacent site 1863. Closed 1970.
Portadown	25½	Open 1848-1863. A new station on almost the same site opened in 1970.
Tanderagee	30½	Open 1852-1965.
Scarva	33	Closed 1965, reopened 1984.
Poyntzpass	35½	Closed 1965, reopened 1984.
Goraghwood	40¾	Open 1854-1965.
Newry (Armagh Road)	41¾	Named Mullaghglass 1852-55. Closed 1856.
Bessbrook	43	Open 1855. Originally Newry (Main Line), then Newry Monaghan Road). Closed *c.*1942. Reopened as 'Newry' 1984.
Adavoyle	50	Opened 1892. Closed to passengers 1933.
Mount Pleasant	55	Named Plaster 1850-51, Mount Pleasant & Jonesborough 1851-55, reopened but closed by 1887.
Dundalk	58¼	New 'Junction' station opened 1894.
Dundalk	58½	DBJR station. Open 1849-1894.
Castlebellingham	65¼	Open 1851-1976.
Dromin Junction	69	Open 1896-1955.

* These tables are presented in the form chosen by Dr Patterson in the 1962 edition of this book, but updated to include subsequent developments. In the case of the main line, note that the down direction is *from* Dublin, so the mileages given are not those shown on the mileposts.

Main Line (cont.)	Miles	
Dunleer	70¾	Open 1851-1976 and 1979-1984.
Newfoundwell	80	DBJR terminus 1849-1855.
Drogheda	80¾	
Bettystown	84	Open 1844-47.
Laytown	85½	Named Laytown and Bettystown from 1913 to the 1920s.
Butlin's (Mosney)	86¾	Opened 1948; timetabled station from 1958. Latterly named 'Mosney'. Closed 2001.
Gormanston	88½	
Balbriggan	90¾	
Skerries	94½	
Skerries Golf Links Halt	95	Open 1927-1967.
Baldungan	96¼	Open 1845-1847.
Rush and Lusk	98½	
Donabate	101	
Malahide	103½	
Portmarnock	105¾	
Baldoyle	107¼	Open 1844-46.
Howth Junction	107¾	
Kilbarrack	108	Opened 1969.
Raheny	108¾	
Harmonstown	109½	Opened 1957.
Killester	110¼	Opened 1923.
Clontarf	110¾	Open 1844-1956.
Clontarf Road	111¼	Opened 1997.
Dublin, Amiens Street	112½	

Belfast Central Railway

Ulster Junction (exchange platform only)	0	All opened for passenger service 5th August, 1878, closed 30th November, 1885.
Windsor (or Botanic Road)	½	
Ormeau	1	
Belfast Queen's Bridge	2	

The whole section, including the link to Ballymacarrett Junction (BCDR) closed to goods traffic, and passenger excursions to and from Bangor, in 1965. The line lay dormant from then until 1976. After a gap of more than 90 years the route was reopened to passengers. Belfast Central station opened on 12th April, 1976 for Bangor line trains and on 26th April, 1976 for GNR line trains.

Central Junction	0	
City Hospital	¼	Opened 1986.
Botanic	½	Opened 1976.
Belfast Central	1½	

It might also be noted that the present Bridge End station (just short of the former Ballymacarrett Junction with the BCDR) is actually on former GNR territory. It was opened on 9th May, 1977 and replaced Ballymacarrett Halt (BCDR).

Irish North Western Main Line

Dundalk	0	Dundalk-Clones closed to passengers 1957 and to goods in 1959.
Kellybridge	4	Opened about 1924.
Inniskeen	7¼	

Irish North Western Main Line (cont.)

	Miles	
Blackstaff	9½	Opened 15th August, 1927 ('Halt' shown on nameboard).
Culloville	12	
Castleblayney	18	
Ballybay	24¾	
Monaghan Road	29½	
Newbliss	35	
Clones	39½	Clones-Omagh closed to all traffic 1st October, 1957.
Newtownbutler	44½	
Lisnaskea	51¼	
Maguiresbridge	53¾	Opened 1859.
Lisbellaw	57	
Enniskillen	62	
Gortaloughan Halt	64½	
Drumcullion Halt	66	Opened early 1940s for seaplane base on Lough Erne.
Ballinamallard	67½	
Bundoran Junction	70	Named Lowtherstown Road 1854-1861, Irvinestown 1861-63, Irvinestown Road 1863-66.
Trillick	71½	Closed for a time by INWR.
Dromore Road	75¼	
Fintona Junction	81	Opened to Fintona (81¾ m.), 1853.
Omagh	87¾	Omagh to Newtownstewart double in 1853. Singled in 1869. Omagh-Londonderry (Foyle Road) closed 1965.
Mountjoy	91¼	Open 1852-59, 1870-78, 1928-35.
Newtownstewart	97¼	
Victoria Bridge	101¾	
Sion Mills	103½	
Strabane	106¾	
Porthall	109¾	
Carrickmore	111½	Open 1847-53.
St Johnstown	114	
Carrigans	115¾	
Londonderry	120¾	Cow market terminus 1847-50.
Londonderry, Foyle Road	121½	

Portadown	0	Portadown to Omagh closed in 1965.
Annaghmore	6¾	
Vernersbridge	9¼	Named Verner at first. Closed 1954.
Trew and Moy	10¾	
Dungannon	14½	Terminus before tunnel built, open 1858-61.
Dungannon	15	Opened 1861.
Donaghmore	17¾	Closed 1965.
Pomeroy	24	
Carrickmore	29	Closed 1959.
Sixmilecross	32¾	
Beragh	34¼	
Omagh	41¾	

Portadown	0	Portadown to Glaslough closed in 1957, but first mile retained to Brownstown siding until 1965.
Richhill	6¼	
Retreat Halt	7½	Opened 1936. No platform.

	Miles	
Armagh	10¾	
Killylea	15¼	
Tynan	17¾	Named Tynan, Caledon and Middletown 1858-80.
Glaslough	21¾	Glaslough-Monaghan closed in 1958.
Monaghan	27½	Monaghan-Cavan section closed 1959.
Smithborough	33¼	Opened 1863.
Clones	39¼	
Redhills	46¼	
Ballyhaise	48¼	Formerly Belturbet Junction.
Loreto College	52¾	Opened in 1930. 'Loreto Halt' on latter-day tickets.
Cavan	54¾	MGWR station.

Ballyhaise	0	
Belturbet	4¼	Branch open 1885-1959. Closed to passengers in 1957, but Belturbet station remained for CIE (C&L) trains until 1959.

Dungannon	0	Dungannon to Cookstown closed to passengers 1956. Dungannon to Coalisland worked as siding 1959-1965.
Coalisland	5½	
Stewartstown	8½	
Killymoon Golf Halt	?	Opened *c.*1945.
Cookstown	14½	Branch open 1879-1959.

Bundoran Junction	0	(See INW section for original naming.)
Irvinestown	3½	
Kesh	9¾	
Pettigo	15	
Castlecaldwell	22¾	First station 1867-1870 ½ mile east of 1870 station.
Belleek	27½	
Ballyshannon	31½	
Bundoran	35¼	Branch open 1866-1957.

Fintona Junction		
Fintona	0¾	Open 1853-1957.

Armagh	0	Armagh-Keady open 1909-1957. Closed to passengers 1932.
Armagh, Irish Street	1	
Milford	2½	
Ballyards	3¾	
Tassagh	6½	Opened 1911.
Keady	8	Keady-Castleblayney open 1910-23.
Carnagh	12	Opened 1911.
Creaghanroe	14¼	
Castleblayney	18¼	

Dromin Junction	0	
Ardee	5	Branch open for passengers 1896-1934, closed for goods in 1975.

Drogheda	0	Drogheda-Oldcastle closed to passengers 1958.

	Miles	
Duleek	4¾	
Lougher Halt	8¼	Opened c.1940.
Beauparc	11¾	
Navan	16½	Original D&DR terminus east of viaduct 1850-1864.
Navan	17	Navan-Oldcastle open 1864-1961, section to Tara
		Mines (18 m.) reopened 1977.
Navan Junction	17¼	Open as a passenger station for GNR trains 1869-1947.
Ballybeg	23	Opened 1855.
Kells	26¾	
Virginia Road	33¼	
Oldcastle	39½	

Inniskeen	0	
Essexford	3½	Closed 1922-25.
Carrickmacross	6½	Branch open 1886-1959, but closed to passengers in 1947.

Shantonagh Junction	0	No platform at Junction.
Rockcorry	3½	
Cootehill	7½	Branch open 1860-1955, but closed to passengers in 1947.

Knockmore Junction	0	
Newport Halt	1¾	Opened 1942.
Hillsborough	2¾	
Ballygowan	4¾	Opened 1930.
Magherabeg	6¾	Opened 1929.
Dromore	8¼	
Ashfield	10¼	Opened 1930.
Mullafernaghan	11½	Closed to Banbridge 1956.
Banbridge	15	Closed beyond Banbridge 1955.
Corbet	18¼	Opened 1882.
Poland's Bridge	20	Opened 1932, no platform.
Katesbridge	22	
Ballyroney	24	
Drumadonald	26	Opened 1933, no platform.
Ballyward	27¾	
Leitrim	29¼	
Savage's Bridge	30¾	Opened 1932.
Castlewellan	33¼	Joint with BCDR.
Newcastle	37¼	BCDR station.

Scarva	0	Branch opened 1859 (with Laurencetown the only
		stopping point). Closed 1933 (strike). Reopened 1934
		with five new rail-level halts. Service operated by
		railbus/railcar. Closed 1955 to all traffic.
Martin's Bridge	1¼	Opened 1937/1938.
Kernan Cross		Opened 1953 (shown as Kernon Cross on tickets).
Drumhork Cross	3½	Opened 1934.
Laurencetown	4	
Chapel Row Cross	4¼	Opened 1934, closed c.1940.
Hazelbank Cross	4½	Opened 1934.
Lenaderg	5	Open January-June 1904, reopened July 1912.
Millmount Cross	6¼	Opened 1934.
Banbridge	6¾	

	Miles	
Armagh	0	Armagh-Goraghwood closed to passengers 1933. Armagh-Markethill closed to goods 1933.
Armagh	1	Temporary terminus at Drummondmore Bridge 1864/1865.
Hamiltonsbawn	4¾	
Markethill	8¾	Markethill-Goraghwood closed 1955.
Glen Anne	11½	Named Loughgilly 1897-1924.
Loughgilly	12	First station 1864-1897.
Ballydougherty Halt	13½	Open 1912-1933.
Goraghwood	17¼	Goraghwood-Warrenpoint closed 1965.
Newry, Edward Street	20¾	
Newry, Dublin Bridge	21½	Dublin Bridge-Warrenpoint NW&R Section open 1849.
Narrow-Water	26¼	Closed 1850-1855. Finally closed c.1958.
Warrenpoint	27½	

Knockmore Junction	0	Branch closed to passengers 1960, reopened 1974 with three stations only, plus a new platform on 'Third Line' named 'Knockmore'. Line closed to regular traffic on 30th June, 2003, but remains intact.
Brookmount	1¾	
Brookhill	3	Opened 1933.
Meeting House Halt	4¼	Opened 1939, no platform.
Ballinderry	5¼	Station reopened 1974.
Legatiriff	6½	Opened 1936.
Glenavy	8½	Station reopened 1974.
Crumlin	11	Station reopened 1974. Siding to Gortnagallon at 12 miles.
Aldergrove	13¼	
Millar's Bridge	15¾	Opened 1938, no platform.
Antrim	18½	

Siding Junction	0	Branch open 1942-1945 and lifted c.1950, served aircraft factory.
Gortnagallon	2¼	

Howth Junction	0	Named Junction until 1912.
Bayside	1	Open 1973, island platform.
Sutton and Baldoyle	1¾	
Howth	3½	Temporary terminus at 2¾ miles from 1846-47.

Hill of Howth Tramway

Sutton	0	Terminus beside railway station. Hill of Howth Tramway closed in 1959.
Sutton Cross		
Strand Road		
Howth Demesne		
St Fintan's		
Barren Hill		
Baily Post Office		
Stella Maris		
Hill of Howth		407 ft above sea level. Summit of tramway.
Dungriffen Road		
Balglass		Used during holiday peak periods.
Howth	5¼	Terminus beside railway station.

Appendix Two

Officers of the Railways

Northern Railway 1875-76
Chairman: J.W. Murland. *Secretary:* Joseph P. Culverwell. *Engineers:* Marcus Harty (Southern Section), William M'Cartan (Northern Section). *Locomotive Superintendent:* W. Curry. *Carriage Superintendent:* Thos. Callaghan.

Great Northern Railway 1876-1952
Chairmen: Jas. W. Murland, 1876-90; James Gray, 1890-1903; Sir William Q.Ewart, 1903-05; L.O. Hutton, 1905-09; Fane Vernon, 1909-23; William P. Cairnes, 1923-25; Sir George S. Clark, 1925-34; Sir Lingard Goulding, 1934-36; W.B. Carson, 1936-38; Lord Glenavy, 1938-52.
Secretaries: J.P. Culverwell, 1876-90; Henry Plews, 1890-96; Thomas Morrison, 1896-1919; J.B. Stephens, 1919-26; F.C. Wallace, 1926-52.
Civil Engineers: Marcus Harty, C.R. Atkinson, W. M'Cartan, W. Greenhill, J. Glenny, 1876-77; William H. Mills, 1877-1909; F.A. Campion, 1909-29; George B. Howden, 1929-39; C.H. Slater, 1939-52.
Locomotive Engineers: John Eaton, Thos. Callaghan, William Curry, Charles Clifford, 1876-80; J.C. Park and John Eaton, 1880-85; J.C. Park. 1885-95; Charles Clifford, 1895-1912; George T. Glover, 1912-33; G.B. Howden, 1933-39; H. McIntosh, 1939-50; R.W. Meredith, 1950-52.
Traffic Managers: Thos Shaw (Belfast), Henry Plews (Enniskillen), Thos Cowan (Dundalk), 1876-90; Thos Shaw (Belfast), Henry Plews (Enniskillen), 1890.
General Managers: Thomas Robertson, 1890-96; Henry Plews, 1896-1911; John Bagwell, 1911-26; J.B. Stephens, 1926-39; G.B. Howden, 1939-52.

Great Northern Railway Board 1952-58
Chairmen: George B. Howden and A.P. Reynolds (joint).
Secretary: P. K. M. Carey.
Civil Engineers: C.H. Slater, 1952-54; H.C. Stone, 1954-58.
Locomotive Engineers: R.W. Meredith, 1952-57; H.E. Wilson, 1957-58.

Locomotive Superintendents of the Constituent Companies
Ulster Railway: Thos Firth, ?1844-51; Jas. Firth, 1851-57; John Eaton, 1857-76.
Dublin & Drogheda Railway: Sylvester Lees, 1844-49; Patrick Connor, 1849-?; William Dundas, 1861-63; William Curry, 1863-75.
Dublin & Belfast Junction Railway: (Dargan's Contract, 1849-52); R. Ogilvie, 1852-54; H. Harden, 1854-72; Thomas Armitage, 1872-75.
Dundalk & Enniskillen Railway (later Irish North Western Railway): (Dargan's Contract, 1848-50); T.C. Bell, 1850-52; John Blue, 1852; R. Needham, 1852-58; Fredk Pemberton, 1858-69; T.N. Haigh, 1870-71; Charles Clifford, 1871-75.
Londonderry & Enniskillen Railway: William Webster, 1846-47; James Firth, 2/1847-6/1847; John S. Domville, 6/1847-10/1848; Robert Dods, 10/1848-9/1853; James W. Smith, 9/1853-11/1854; M. Forde, 11/1854-2/1855; James Barber, 2/1855-4/1857; John Duncan, 5/1857-1861; thereafter under the supervision of INWR.
Newry & Enniskillen Railway (later Newry & Armagh Railway): R. Hassard, ?1854-61; --- Swan, 1862; Edward Leigh, 1864-68; J.L.D. Meares, 1868-73; Denis Byrne, 1873-75; J.L.D. Meares, 1875-79.
Newry, Warrenpoint & Rostrevor Railway: J.T. Taylor, 1849-50; (Dargan's Contract, 1850-56); William Maddison, 1855-58; John Dodds, 1858-66; Peter Roe, 2/1866-5/1873; T. Smith, 5/1873-? 1886.
Belfast Central Railway: apparently under the supervision of the Manager, J. Bucknall Cooper.

In some cases, the individuals held other posts as well, either as 'Engineer' or as 'Superintendent'.

Appendix Three

Accidents and Incidents

23rd May, 1844	Location not recorded (D&DR) - *1 person killed*. Man repeatedly put his leg out of carriage.
14th May, 1845	Portadown (UR) - *1 person injured*. Engine hit horse and cart led by farmer, at level crossing.
7th August, 1845	Location not recorded (UR) - *1 person killed*. Engine hit workman digging clay in cutting.
10th September, 1853	Gormanston (D&DR). Derailment.
30th March, 1854	St Johnstown (L&ER) - *4 persons injured*. Collision, mail train and light engine.
18th September, 1854	Trillick (L&ER.) - *1 person killed, 2 injured*. Malicious derailment.
19th February, 1855	Drogheda (D&DR) - *7 persons injured*. Collision between goods and passenger, goods crew asleep.
6th August, 1856	Near Newry Main Line station (DBJR) - *1 person killed, 3 injured*. Collision, ballast and goods trains.
31st October, 1856	Ballybay (D&ER) - *1 person injured*. Collision, mail train and wagons.
9th October, 1857	Carrigans (L&ER) - *1 person killed*. Mail train hit white cow, derailed.
30th July, 1858	Glaslough (UR) - *4 people injured*. Up mail derailed, rails spread.
11th September, 1858	Lisnaskea (D&ER) - *2 people injured*. Collision.
30th July, 1859	Richhill (UR) - *6 people injured*. Two trains collided, lack of signals.
8th January, 1862	2 m. east of Annaghmore (UR.) - *1 person killed, 7 injured*. Collision, passenger train and halted goods train.
5th September, 1862	Newry Edward Street (N&AR) - *2 people injured*. Slight collision
17th December, 1862	Newgate, near Navan (D&DR) - *2 people injured*. D&MR passenger train ran through level crossing gates.
10th October, 1863	Between Fintona and Dromore Road (INWR) - *8 people injured*. Derailment, defective cast iron chair.
26th August, 1864	3 m. from Ballybay (INWR) - *3 people injured*. Derailment
8th November, 1864	Londonderry station (INWR) - *5 people injured*. Collision, Canadian mail and train.
22nd November, 1864	Between Beragh and Omagh (UR) - *1 person injured*. Collision, two parts of divided goods.
12th May, 1865	Enniskillen (INWR) - *2 people killed*. Derailment.
16th March, 1867	Castleblayney (INWR) - *1 person killed, 2 injured*. Derailment, probably malicious.
8th January, 1869	3 m. from Londonderry (INWR) - *1 person killed, 1 injured*. Derailment.
14th February, 1870	1¼ m. west of Loughgilly (N&AR) - *8 people injured*. Collision, passenger train and Directors' special.
11th April, 1871	Mountjoy (INWR) - *1 person killed, 2 injured*. Derailment, double-headed mixed train, bad permanent way.
13th May, 1871	Goraghwood (DBJR) - *1 person killed, 7 injured*. Collision, mail train and following goods, at 4 am.
16th November, 1871	Mountjoy (INWR) - *1 person killed, 8 injured*. Derailment, excessive speed.
14th May, 1872	Fintona (INWR) - *1 person injured*. Collision, horse tram and engine.
21st December, 1872	Portadown (UR) - *8 people injured*. Collision, three trains in station.
26th September, 1874	Dundalk Square Crossing (DBJR) - *1 person killed, 28 injured*. Collision with INWR train.

6th July, 1875	Dromore (UR) - *1 person killed, 2 injured*. Derailment, mixed train, defective permanent way.
12th August, 1875	Newbliss (INWR) - *2 people injured*. Collision, mixed train and goods.
28th August, 1875	Lisburn (UR) - *1 person killed*. Fire of whisky in wagon, fireman suffocated while stealing it.
1st August, 1877	3½ m. south of Fintona Junction - *5 people injured*. Derailment, mixed train, broken axle.
21st July, 1878	Between Beragh and Omagh - *2 people injured*. Collision between two parts of divided train.
27th August, 1878	Between Skerries and Balbriggan - *5 people injured*. Collision between passenger train and its engine, broken drawbar.
11th October, 1878	Navan Station - *2 people injured*. Collision, express and wagons.
6th November, 1879	Portadown - *2 people injured*. Collision, passenger and goods trains.
12th November, 1879	Belturbet Junction - *1 person killed*. Collision, between mixed and special cattle trains.
27th June, 1881	Howth - *3 people injured*. Buffer collision
18th September, 1882	Ballyshannon station - *75 people injured*. Collision, passenger and goods in crowded station
16th November, 1882	Bessbrook - *1 person injured*. Collision between passenger and cattle train.
16th December, 1882	Bundoran Junction - *3 people injured*. Derailment, mixed train.
16th April, 1883	3 m. north of Drogheda - *4 people injured*. Collision, passenger train hit disabled goods.
30th June, 1886	Brackagh Moss, 2½ m. south of Portadown - *6 people killed, 29 injured*. Derailment, express passenger, defective permanent way.
25th December, 1886	East Wall Junction, Dublin - *6 people injured*. Collision, up mail and empty passenger train.
12th June, 1889	Killuney, 1¼ m. east of Armagh - *88 people killed, 400 injured*. Collision, divided train ran back into passenger train.
17th August, 1896	North Wall, Dublin - *4 people injured*. Buffer collision.
26th December, 1899	Portadown station - *8 people injured*. Collision, locomotive and rear of passenger.
6th August, 1910	Dundalk, between Central and West Cabins - *2 people killed*. Collision, DN&G passenger train and goods wagons.
2nd May, 1911	Adelaide Yard - *3 people injured*. Collision, light engine and ballast train.
6th August, 1919	Malicious derailment of 3.30 am goods in Beauparc/Navan section.
16th December, 1919	Damage to 11.20 am ex-Derry, Monaghan Road/Shantonagh section.
July 1920	Armed robbery of Belfast Pay Office by two men. £1,000 stolen.
17th July, 1920	Night Belfast-Derry goods held up at Donaghmore by 40 armed men. Official and police mail stolen.
9th August, 1920	Driver and fireman of 10 pm train at Newry stripped and tarred by rebels. Driver Bruce pilloried (tarred and tied to a lamp-post) in Dublin because he drove a munitions train.
28th August, 1920	Bundoran branch closed beyond Irvinestown due to civil unrest. Certain men refused to work trains containing military traffic.
2nd November, 1920	Dundalk to Enniskillen line and branches closed. Belturbet branch closed.
14th November, 1920	Removal of four rail lengths from up and down lines between Smithborough and Clones. Engineer's train derailed.
23rd April, 1921	Line blocked at McCavanagh's Crossing, between Glaslough and Monaghan. Down 11.30 pm goods ambushed. Large crowd set fire to entire train after looting it. Forty-one wagons lost and engine damaged.

29th April, 1921	Main line blocked in Wellington Cutting, between Bessbrook and Adavoyle, by large rocks prised from sides. 9.30 pm goods Belfast-Dublin held up.
9th May, 1921	Wagons burned at Balbriggan.
16th June, 1921	Rail removed, Drogheda-Dunleer section. Goods derailed and two wagons set on fire.
24th June, 1921	Bomb thrown at 9.55 am ex-Howth, at Killester. Troop train conveying 10th Hussars from Belfast to Curragh mined at Adavoyle. Guard and five soldiers killed, and train wrecked and horses killed.
11th February, 1922	Attack by IRA on 'Special' police, Clones station.
April 1922	Trains from Northern Ireland being searched and passengers interrogated by armed men at Dundalk.
12th May, 1922	Light engine held up by ambush on line near Adelaide and Windsor. Pay clerk on board. £10,000 pay for shed men stolen. Down goods stopped at St Johnston by armed men. Bacon, butter and other foodstuffs stolen from vans.
3rd June, 1922	British military order closure of NI portion of Bundoran branch. Re-opened between Bundoran Junction and Belleek from 13th June. Staff on Belleek-Bundoran section given notice.
1st July, 1922	Laytown viaduct blown up. Mutineers in possession of Drogheda station.
20th July, 1922	Malicious derailment of 6.00 am Dublin-Belfast goods between Clontarf and Killester.
26th July, 1922	Malacious derailment of down goods at Howth Junction.
3rd November, 1922	Derailment of empty cattle special between Castlebellingham and Dromin.
29th December, 1922	Malacious burning of three coaches of Limited Mail near Castlebellingham.
6th January, 1923	Collision of 7.15 ex-Howth with engine maliciously derailed at Killester.
9th January, 1923	Malacious derailment of 6.30 passenger at Mountpleasant.
30th January, 1923	John Bagwell, Senator, General Manager of the company, kidnapped by a party of armed men as he was walking home from Sutton station.
26th April, 1923	Rebels destroyed Amiens Street signal box. On 1st May a DSER train working by flag signals ran through the turntable, off the end of the siding and fell into the GPO Telegraph Office, injuring two clerks.
28th April, 1923	An explosion occurred at Amiens Street station. Troops who were protecting the station were heavily fired on from concealed positions as they rushed to the spot. A departing train was riddled with bullets and a number of passengers were injured.
1st February, 1933	Dromiskin - *2 people killed.* Malicious derailment, passenger.
21st March, 1933	Omagh Market Junction. Malicious derailment, mixed.
26th April, 1944	Dundalk Square Crossing - *1 person injured.* Collision, railbus and DN&G passenger train.
17th November, 1944	Lambeg - *10 people injured.* Train ran into fallen tree.
14th December, 1945	Donabate - *2 people killed, 1 injured.* Locomotive firebox perforated by broken connecting rod.
6th September, 1946	Gortavoy, near Pomeroy - *1 person killed.* Derailment, locomotive of goods train; culvert collapsed.
25th January, 1947	Cavan - *2 people injured.* Gas explosion in kitchen car.

Locomotive and Tender Liveries

Original Green Livery of GNR(I) Engine and Tender

Engine
Boiler: green with 2 in. black straps edged with white both sides.
Dome: green.
Safety valves: green (later vermilion), with polished brass tops.
Smokebox: front and sides black, with polished door hinges and handles.
Chimney: black.
Cab: sides and front green, panelled with 1¼ in. black lines edged with white both sides.
Interior green.
Trailing splasher: green, edged with ½ in. black, with white line inside.
Driving splasher: large, green with 1½ in. double brass mouldings, polished, around side; between these mouldings lake edged with vermilion lines, 8 in. coat of arms in centre.
Main frame: green, outside, vermilion inside.
Outside platform: lake edged with fine black line top and bottom, with vermilion lines inside.
Wheels: green, with white lines on boss, ends of axles black. Later entirely green.
Buffer plank: vermilion edged with ½ in. black with white line inside.
Buffers: casings lake, heads polished.
Bogie splasher and side steps: lake edged with black and vermilion lines.
Connecting rods: polished.
Engine nameplate on boiler: Jupiter, rectangular brass plate painted vermilion, raised polished letters.
Engine number plate on buffer plank and side of cab: '75' 6 in. gold numbers shaded with black.
Handrails: boiler and cab, polished.

On six-coupled goods engines, the maker's plate was on the leading splasher, and a GNRI monogram on the driving splasher.

Tender
Body: green, panelled similarly to engine cab.
Main frame: lake edged with black and fine vermilion line inside.
Axleboxes: lake.
Wheels: green.
Lettering: GNR 6 in. gold letters shaded with black.

During the earlier years of this livery, a deeper shade of green was used on the tenders outside of the black lining. The official name of the main colour was Brunswick green. The deeper green has been referred to as 'dark sage green'.

Black Livery of GNR(I) Engine and Tender

Engine
Boiler: black, with vermilion lines to edges of straps, and at back of smokebox.
Dome: black.
Safety valves: black casing, valves polished brass.
Smokebox: front and sides black, with polished door hinges and handles.
Chimney: black.
Cab: sides and front black, panelled with vermilion lines. Interior black 1912-20, thereafter light brown.

Small splashers: unlined black.
Large splashers: black, with vermilion lines.
Main Frame: black outside, vermilion inside.
Outside platform: black, with vermilion lines top and bottom.
Wheels: black, vermilion line around wheel boss. Ends of axles black edged with vermilion line.
Buffer plank: vermilion with black around.
Buffers: casings black, heads polished.
Side steps: black, panelled with vermilion lines.
Connecting rods: polished.
Engine number on buffer plank and sides of cab: 6 in. gold numbers, shaded with black.
Handrails: boiler and cab, polished.

Tender
Body: black, panelled similarly to engine cab.
Main frame: black, with vermilion lines.
Axleboxes: black.
Wheels: black.
Lettering: GNR 6 in. gold letters, shaded with black, standard practice on tenders and on the sides of tank engines.

Note: Towards the latter years of the GNR(I), the vermilion lining on black engines was deleted and the only relief was the number on the cab, the 'G.N.R.' on the tender or tank, and the front and back vermilion buffer planks, with the number only on the engine plank. In many cases even 'G.N.R.' was omitted.

Blue Livery of GNR(I) Engine and Tender

Engine
Boiler: blue with 2 in. black straps edged with white both sides.
Safety valves: blue casing, valves polished brass.
Smokebox: front and sides black, with polished door hinges and handles.
Chimney: black.
Cab: sides and front blue, panelled with 1¼ in. black lines edged with white both sides. Interior light brown.
Small splashers: as for cab.
Large splashers: as for cab. Brass nameplate at top with 8 in. coat of arms in centre.
Main Frame: above platform blue, below platform black. Vermilion inside.
Outside platform: vermilion with ½ in. black line at bottom edged with white top side.
Wheels: blue. Ends of axles black edged with white. Tyres black.
Buffer plank: vermilion with black around, edged with white inside.
Buffers: casings, vermilion, heads polished.
Side steps: black.
Connecting rods: polished.
Engine nameplate on large splasher: radiused brass plate, polished, sunk letters painted black.
Engine number on buffer plank and sides of cab: 6 in. gold numbers shaded with black.
Handrails: boiler and cab, polished.

Tender
Body: blue, panelled front and back similarly to engine cab.
Main frame: vermilion, with black line edged with white.
Axleboxes: black.
Wheels: blue, tyres black.
Lettering: 'G.N.' 12 in. gold letters shaded with black and fine white line. Large 18 in. coat of arms between letters.

Note: The blue was 'azure' similar to the shade used on the former Caledonian Railway, and as distinct from the darker 'Oxford blue' used on the carriages and omnibuses.

Appendix Five

List of Locomotives built at Dundalk Works

Works No.	Date Complete	Class	Wheels	Running Nos.	Name	Remarks
1	6/1887	BT	4-4-0T	100/1/119		Rebuilt to 0-6-0T in 1920. Scrapped 1935.
2	12/1887	BT	4-4-0T	2		Withdrawn 1921
3	7/1888	BT	4-4-0T	3		Withdrawn 1921
4	1/1888	BT	4-4-0T	4		Withdrawn 1921
5	6/1889	BT	4-4-0T	5		Withdrawn 1921
6	12/1889	BT	4-4-0T	6		Withdrawn 1920
7	10/1890	A	0-6-0	60		
8	2/1891	A	0-6-0	33		
9	6/1891	BT	4-4-0T	7	*Ardee* (1896)	Withdrawn 1920
10	6/1893	BT	4-4-0T	8		Withdrawn 1921
11	8/1893	BT	4-4-0T	91/13		Withdrawn 1921
12	11/1893	BT	4-4-0T	92/14		Withdrawn 1921
13	11/1894	AL	0-6-0	32	*Drogheda*	To UTA 1958, renumbered 32X 1959, withdrawn 1960
14	2/1895	AL	0-6-0	29	*Enniskillen*	
15	11/1895	AL	0-6-0	55	*Portadown*	
16	8/1895	JT	2-4-2T	93	*Sutton*	To Belfast Museum, 1955
17	2/1896	JT	2-4-2T	94	*Howth*	Withdrawn 1956
18	12/1896	AL	0-6-0	56	*Omagh*	To UTA 1958, renumbered 56X 1959, withdrawn 1960
19	1/1898	JT	2-4-2T	90	*Aster*	Withdrawn 1957
20	7/1898	JT	2-4-2T	95	*Crocus*	Withdrawn 1955
21	12/1899	PG	0-6-0	78/151	*Strabane*	
22	6/1900	PG	0-6-0	100	*Clones*	To UTA 1958, renumbered 100X 1959
23	1/1902	JT	2-4-2T	13/91	*Tulip*	
24	8/1902	JT	2-4-2T	14/92	*Viola*	Withdrawn 1956
25	9/1903	PG	0-6-0	11	*Dromore*	To UTA 1958, renumbered 11X 1959, withdrawn 1960
26	3/1904	PG	0-6-0	10	*Bessbrook*	To UTA 1958, renumbered 10X 1959
27	1905	P 5'6"	4-4-0	88	*Victoria*	Withdrawn 1956
28	1905	P 5'6"	4-4-0	89	*Albert*	Withdrawn 1956
29	1906	P 5'6"	4-4-0	104	*Ovoca*	Withdrawn 1956
30	1906	P 5'6"	4-4-0	105	*Foyle*	
31	1908	LQG	0-6-0	78/119	*Pettigo*	
32	1908	LQG	0-6-0	108	*Pomeroy*	To UTA 1958, scrapped 1959
33	4/1911	PP	4-4-0	25	*Liffey*	
34	211911	PP	4-4-0	43	*Lagan*	To UTA, 1958, renumbered 43X 1959, withdrawn 1960
35	1937	UG	0-6-0	78		To UTA 1958, renumbered 45
36	1937	UG	0-6-0	79		To UTA 1958, renumbered 46
37	1937	UG	0-6-0	80		
38	1937	UG	0-6-0	81		
39	1937	UG	0-6-0	82		To UTA 1958, renumbered 47
40	5/1938	S	4-4-0	173	*Galteemore*	To UTA 1958, renumbered 61
41	6/1938	S2	4-4-0	192	*Slievenamon*	To UTA 1958, renumbered 63
42	9/1939	S	4-4-0	171	*Slieve Gullion*	
43	10/1938	S	4-4-0	172	*Slieve Donard*	To UTA 1958, renumbered 60
44	1/1939	S2	4-4-0	191	*Croagh Patrick*	
45	6/1939	S	4-4-0	170	*Errigal*	
46	7/1938	S2	4-4-0	190	*Lugnaquilla*	To UTA 1958, renumbered 62
47	10/1939	S	4-4-0	174	*Carrantuohill*	

Appendix Six

Allocation of Motive Power to CIE and UTA 1958, and UTA renumbering 1959

Steam

Class	CIE	UTA
4-4-0		
VS	206, 207, 209	208, 210 (renumbered .58, 59)
V	84,85	83, 86, 87
S	170, 171, 174	172, 173 (renumbered 60, 61)
S2	191	190, 192 (renumbered 62, 63)
QLs	-	127, 156, 157
Qs	123, 130, 131, 132, 136	121, 122, 125, 135
Ps 6 ft 6 in.	27, 72, 73	-
PPs	12, 44, 71, 75, 106	42, 43, 46, 50, 74, 76, 107
U	197, 198, 199, 203, 204	196, 200, 201, 202, 205 (renumbered 64-68)
Ps 5 ft 6 in.	105	-
0-6-0		
SG3	8, 14, 47, 48, 96, 117, 118	6, 7, 13, 20, 40, 41, 49, 97 (renumbered 30-37)
SG2	15,19, 180, 181, 184	16, 17, 18, 182, 183 (renumbered 38-42)
SG	177, 178, 179	175, 176 (renumbered 43, 44)
LQGs	110, 158, 159, 161, 163, 164	108, 111, 119, 160, 162
LQGNs	-	9, 39, 109, 165
NQGs	38, 112	-
QGs	152, 153, 154, 155	-
UG	80, 81, 145, 147, 148	78, 79, 82, 146, 149 (renumbered 45-49)
PGs		10, 11, 100, 101, 102, 103, 151
AL	29, 35, 55, 57, 58, 59	32, 56
A	33, 60, 150	-
4-4-2T		
T1	188	185, 186, 187, 189
T2	1, 3, 62, 63, 65, 67, 115, 116, 139, 143, 144	2, 4, 5, 21, 30, 64, 66, 69, 142
2-4-2T		
JT	91	-
0-6-4T		
RT	-	22, 23, 166, 167
0-6-2T		
QGTs	99	-

	Diesel	
Class	CIE	UTA
AEC	600, 601, 604, 605, 608, 609, 612, 613, 616, 617	602, 603, 606, 607, 610, 611, 614, 615, 618, 619 (renumbered 111-120)
BUT	700, 704, 706, 708, 710, 712, 714	701, 702, 703, 705, 707, 709, 711, 713, 715 (renumbered 121-129)
BUT	900, 904, 906	901, 902, 903, 905, 907 (renumbered 131-135)
MAK	800	-
Various	C.1, C.2, E, G	A, C.3, D, F (renumbered 101-104)

Bibliography

Half-Yearly Reports of the GNR(I) and of the constituent companies.

Annual Reports of the GNR(I) , 1913-1952.

Annual Reports of the GNRB, 1953-1958.

Minute Books of the GNR(I) and constituent companies.

Public and Working Timetables of the GNR(I) and GNRB.

Appendix to the GNR(I) Working Timetable, 1930.

Supplementary Appendices to GNR(I) Working Timetables, 1932 and 1939.

GNR(I) Rule Books, 1901, 1914 and 1949 editions.

Regulations for Train Signalling on Double and Single Lines of Railways, GNR(I), 1927.

Working of L.M. & S.R. (D.N. & G. Railway) from 1-7-1933, GNR(I) 1933.

House of Commons: Minutes of evidence taken before the Committee on the Dublin & Drogheda Railway. London, 1836.

F. Whishaw, *The Railways of Great Britain & Ireland*, London, 1840.

The Handbook to the Dublin & Drogheda Railway, Dublin, 1844.

John D'Alton, *History of Drogheda*, Dublin, 1844 - introductory memoir of the Dublin & Drogheda Railway, Vol. I, pp. xvii-cxxxiv.

A letter written by Thomas Brodigan, &c., respecting his claims against the D&D Railway Company. (Pamphlet) Dublin, 1847.

The Ulster Railway Handbook and Traveller's Companion of the Way, Belfast, 1848.

J.G.V. Porter, *Mistakes of the Dundalk & Enniskillen Railway Company's Directors and their consequences to the Shareholders, to the Co. Fermanagh and to the Province of Ulster.* (Pamphlet) Dublin, 1859.

Board of Trade: Reports of Railway Accidents.

Bigg's General Railway Acts, 1830-1898, London, 1898.

Bradshaw's Railway Manual, Shareholders' Guide and Directory (various editions).

Cmd. 10 (1922), Cmd. 160 (1934), Cmd. 198 (1939), Cmd. 232 (1946), Cmd. 310 0952), HMSO, Belfast.

J.C. Conroy, *A History of Railways in Ireland*, London, 1928.

Kevin Murray, *The Great Northern Railway (Ireland) - Past, Present and Future*, Dublin, 1944.

Planning Proposals for the Belfast Area. HMSO, Belfast, 1945.

W.S. Marshall, *LMS-NCC. The Operating Department in Wartime*, Belfast, 1945.

J. Tatlow, 'Fifty Years of Railway Life', *Railway Gazette*, London, 1920.

Report on Transport in Ireland (Milne Report), SO, Dublin, 1948.

Report of the Committee of Inquiry into Internal Transport, SO, Dublin, 1957.

Great Northern Railway Act, SO, Dublin, 1953.

W. R.Hutchinson, *Tyrone Precinct*, Belfast, 1951.

E.L. Ahrons, *Locomotive and Train Working in the latter part of the19th Century*, Vol. 6, pp. 65-77, Cambridge, 1954.

D.S.M. Barrie, *The Dundalk, Newry & Greenore Railway*, Oakwood Press, 1957.

UTA, *Aspects of Relations between the Public and the Authority*, Belfast, 1959.

S. Johnson, *Johnson's Atlas & Gazetteer of the Railways of Ireland*, Midland Publishing Co., 1997.

N. Johnston, *Locomotives of the GNRI*, Colourpoint Books, 1999.

The Railway Magazine:

1898   D.T. Timmins, 'Great Northern of Ireland Railway', **2**, 17.

1899   'Illustrated Interviews: Mr Henry Plews' **5**, 385.

1901   'Illustrated Interviews - Mr Charles Clifford', **9**, 385.

1903   'Royal Trains of the Irish Railways', **13**, 224.

1910   'The Dublin-Belfast Trains of the GNR(I)', **27**, 518.

1911   'The GNR(I) - its history and progress', **29**, 94.

1912   Dublin Transfer Facilities, **31**, 383.

1913   'New locomotives and improved train services on the GNR(I), **33**,225.

1914   Ambulance Trains on British Railways, **35**, 389.

1914   H. Fayle, 'The Castleblayney, Keady & Armagh Railway', **35**, 148.

1917   J.F. Gairns, 'Dundalk Works', **40**, 159.

The Railway Magazine (continued):
1917   W.H.F. Patterson, 'An up-to-date Irish Train: a fine run from Dublin to Belfast', **41**, 265.
1922   Enginemen's Instruction Cars, **50**, 91.
1932   'Mercury', 'New Compound Locomotives on the GNR (I)', **67**, 35.
1932   C.J. Allen, 'British Locomotive Practice and Performance', **67**, 39.
1936   H.C.B. Rodgers, 'The Bundoran Branch of the GNR(I), **78**, 319.
1937   The Irish International Main Line, **80**, 353.
1939   B. Reed, 'Railcars on the GNR (I)', **82**, 354.
1947   J.M. Robbins, 'The Lisburn & Antrim Branch', **93**, 67.
1950   Diesel Train Services for the GNR (I), **96**, 490.
1950   New Restaurant and Buffet Cars for the GNR (I), **96**, 415.
1950   W.A. Ryan, 'An early Irish Cross-Channel Excursion', **96**, 338.
1953   G.R. Mahon, 'Irish Railways in 1853', **99**, 625.
1954   H. Fayle, 'Dublin Suburban Services', **100**, 297.
1956   C.J. Allen, 'British Locomotive Practice and Performance', **102**, 835.
1956   N. Crump, 'West Road signal box, Dublin', **102**, 842.
1957   E. Treby, 'The Hill of Howth Tramway', **103**, 351.
1958   Diesel Railcars for Ireland, **104**, 351.
1958   C.E. Lee, 'The 6 ft 2 in. Gauge in Ireland', **104**, 502.
1959   E.M. Patterson, 'The Great Northern Railway (Ireland)', **105**, 297.

Journal of the Irish Railway Record Society:
1947   J.M. Robbins, 'Locomotive Performance on the GNR', **1**, 32.
1948   J.M. Robbins, 'Travelling Post Offices', **1**, 81.
1948   'The Enterprise Express, GNR', **1**, 39.
1949   K.A. Murray, 'The Boyne Viaduct', **1**, 141.
1949   J.P. O'Dea, 'Some Features of Irish Railway Signalling', **2**, 48.
1950   K.A. Murray, 'William Dargan', **2**, 94.
1954   G.R. Mahon, 'Irish Railways in 1853', **3**, 200.
1955   G.R. Mahon, 'Irish Railways in 1854', **4**, 53.
1956   R.N. Clements, 'The Londonderry & Coleraine Railway', **4**, 103.
1956   C.D. Seymour, 'The Dundalk, Newry & Greenore Railway', **4**, 148.
1956   G.R. Mahon, 'Irish Railways in 1855', **4**, 156.
1956   E. Kelly, 'From Road to Rail', **4**, 119.
1957   J. O'Meara, 'The Meath Road', **4**, 2 18.
1957   G.R. Mahon, 'Irish Railways in 1856', **4**, 26 1.
1957   (R. N. Clements), 'Progress - the GNR Closures', **4**, 300.
1958   GNR Derry Service, **5**, 39.
1958   G.R. Mahon, 'Irish Railways in 1857', **5**, 15, 48.
1959   R.N. Clements, 'GNR Locomotive Development', **5**, 97.
1959   L.H. Liddle, 'GNR Restaurant Cars and Services', **5**, 107, 135.
1959   J. Poole, 'Dundalk and the GNR in 1906', **5**, 143.
1960   'GN Locomotive Performance', **5**, 266.
1960   G.R. Mahon, 'Irish Railways in 1858', **5**, 184 and 279.
1961   N.J. McAdams, 'Coaching Stock of the GNR', **6**, 1.
1961   G.R. Mahon, 'Irish Railways in 1859', **6**, 33 and 57.
Various references in 'Recent Developments' sections in Vols. 1-5.

Trains Illustrated:
1958   J.N. Faulkner, 'The end of the GNR (I), **11**, 96.

Railway World:
1960   E.M. Patterson, 'The career of the Irish North', **21**, 120.

Railway Gazette:
1923   Converting Locomotives for superheated steam. Experience on the GNR (I), **38**, 490.
1934   Pneumatic tyred Railbus, **60**, 704.
Many references to current developments throughout.

Acknowledgements

Throughout the preparation of this book I have been fortunate in having had the encouragement and help of many of the officers and staff of the former Great Northern Company, and to them I am greatly indebted. I have had the privilege of stimulating discussions with Mr G.B. Howden which have helped me in planning the book. My particular thanks are due to Mr W.A. Ryan, whose personal interest in Great Northern history has been of immense value, and to Mr H.E. Wilson, whose wide knowledge of rolling stock development at Dundalk has been unfailingly available. Messrs W.A. Latimer and T.A. Carson have also given assistance in tracing documents and maps. Mr B.A. McGirr of Omagh and Mr A. Lawlor, formerly of Portadown, went to considerable trouble in unearthing old timetables for me, and similar help came from the staff at many of the stations. I have valued the company and good fellowship of many footplate crews during travel on the system.

Among the present Ulster Transport Authority officers, Messrs J.H. Houston, the Curator of Historical Relics, Mr W.S. Marshall, and Mr H.C.A. Beaumont have rendered help in a variety of ways.

Much of the interest and value of a book such as this lies in the story of the motive power, and at an early stage in the preparation of this book I found that a vast amount of painstaking research work on the history of the steam locomotive had been done by Mr R.N. Clements, of Celbridge, Co. Kildare. Not only has Mr Clements generously allowed me to make use of as much of this largely unpublished information as space permitted, but he has also advised and assisted me in the preparation of certain other sections.

Certain facts on the history of Portadown and the bulk of the information on Great Northern passenger coaching stock have come from Mr N.J. McAdams of Clontarf. Mr K.A. Murray of Dun Laoghaire kindly allowed me to abstract information from his book on the railway which was published by the company in 1944 and is now long out of print.

The personal recollections of Major-General Sir Cecil Smith of Weybridge and his collection of excellent photographs have together been of the greatest assistance. Advice in the compilation of the list of stations came from Mr J.G. Spence of Caterham. Mr A. Fulton of Saltcoats helped me in preparing material for block-making.

I am grateful to Mr R.M. Hogg and his staff in the British Transport Historical Records Office in Edinburgh, where I received unfailing help in literature searches. Mr David L. Smith of Ayr has also assisted in this connection. My wife has encouraged and helped me and has accompanied me along many Great Northern railway byways during the writing of this book.

Index